Alternative Medicine

Edzard Ernst

Alternative Medicine

A Critical Assessment of 150 Modalities

 Springer

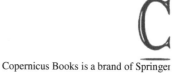

Copernicus Books is a brand of Springer

Edzard Ernst
Cambridge, UK

ISBN 978-3-030-12600-1   ISBN 978-3-030-12601-8 (eBook)
https://doi.org/10.1007/978-3-030-12601-8

This Copernicus imprint is published by the registered company Springer Nature Switzerland AG.
The registered company address is: Gewerbestrasse 11, 6330 Cham, Switzerland

To Danielle

Preface

In their famous editorial of 1998, Angell and Kassirer concluded that "It is time for the scientific community to stop giving alternative medicine a free ride. There cannot be two kinds of medicine—conventional and alternative. There is only medicine that has been adequately tested and medicine that has not, medicine that works and medicine that may or may not work. Once a treatment has been tested rigorously, it no longer matters whether it was considered alternative at the outset. If it is found to be reasonably safe and effective, it will be accepted. But assertions, speculation, and testimonials do not substitute for evidence. Alternative treatments should be subjected to scientific testing no less rigorous than that required for conventional treatments."[1]

Twenty years later, alternative medicine remains popular, and assertions, speculation, and testimonials still substitute for evidence. We are still being inundated with misleading advice, biased opinions, uncritical evaluations, commercially driven promotion and often even fraudulently wrong conclusions. Consequently, consumers find it hard to access reliable data. As a result, they often make misguided, sometimes even dangerously wrong decisions.

I have researched alternative medicine for more than 25 years. Through this work, I have gathered a wealth of knowledge, facts, and experience. In this book, I have summarised the essentials into an easily accessible text. My book offers an introduction into the most important issues around alternative medicine as well as a concise, evidence-based analysis of 150 alternative therapies and diagnostic techniques.

Such information is surely a good thing, but it should nevertheless come with a warning: it may not please everybody! If you are a believer in alternative medicine who does not care about the facts, or an enthusiast for whom alternative medicine has become some sort of a religion, or a person who thinks that science is less important than anecdote, you better return this book to its shelve; reading it will only disquiet you.

---

[1] http://www.kitsrus.com/pdf/nejm_998.pdf.

If, however, you are looking for the facts about alternative medicine, trust in science, prefer critical assessment to commercial promotion, it might well be a book for you.

I hope that you belong to the latter group and trust this book will help you making the right therapeutic decisions for yourself and your family.

Cambridge, UK   Edzard Ernst
November 2018

Contents

Chapter 1
Introduction

1.1 Introduction

Thank you for your interest in my book. In most countries, alternative medicine is popular (Fig. 1.1), and there are hundreds, if not thousands of books on the subject. I have not read them all, of course, but those two or three hundred that I did study were full of uncritical promotion of bogus, potentially harmful treatments. In case you suspect that this might be an exaggeration, I should tell you that my team once studied 7 bestselling books on alternative medicine in detail. We found 35 conditions for which more than 50 different alternative treatments were recommended by their authors; the worst was cancer for which 133 different therapies were recommended. Needless to say that only very few of these treatments were supported by good evidence.[1] In my view, this level of misinformation intolerable: it misleads consumers into making wrong therapeutic decisions, wasting their money, and—in extreme cases—putting their life in danger.

I cannot guarantee that you will like my book, but I can assure you that it will be evidence-based, critical and honest.

1.2 The Aim of The Book

Alternative medicine is a vast and confusing subject. It includes well over 100 different therapies and many diagnostic methods. Even though they all fall under the umbrella of alternative medicine, they have little in common. They all have a different history, make different assumptions, and are supported by different evidence of different quality. Any judgement on, or evaluation of alternative medicine as one single entity is therefore quite simply impossible.

---

[1]https://www.amazon.co.uk/Desktop-Guide-Complementary-Alternative-Medicine/dp/0723433836/ref=sr_1_1?ie=UTF8&qid=1543598976&sr=8-1&keywords=desktop+guide+to+complementary.

© Springer Nature Switzerland AG 2019
E. Ernst, *Alternative Medicine*,
https://doi.org/10.1007/978-3-030-12601-8_1

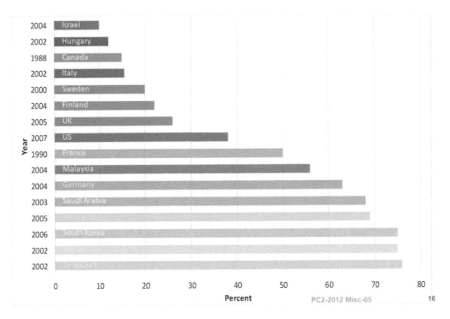

Fig. 1.1 One-year prevalence of alternative medicine in different countries according to surveys on representative samples of the general population; the numbers refer to the years of publication

Therefore, we must assess every modality on its own merits. And, to be reliable, our assessments must be based on a critical evaluation of the best available evidence. If there is contradictory evidence—as there often is—we must assess the totality of the reliable studies. This is by no means a small task. To the best of my knowledge, no book has so far provided a concise yet comprehensive, critical yet fair summary of the evidence that is easily accessible to a lay-person. My aim is to fill this gap.

1.3   About The Author

Am I up to such an enormous task? Can you trust my judgements? These are justified questions; let me try to answer them by giving you my professional background and by explaining my previous involvement in alternative medicine.

I grew up in Germany where alternative medicine is nothing unusual. Our family doctor was a prominent homeopath, and alternative medicine was an entirely normal form of healthcare for me. It was only when I studied medicine that I began to understand some of the differences between conventional and alternative healthcare.

My first job as a junior doctor happened to be in a homeopathic hospital and, early on in my professional career, I learnt how to practice a range of alternative techniques. Later, I became a conventional doctor, immersed myself for several years into basic research, did a PhD, returned to clinical medicine, became professor of rehabilitation medicine first in Hanover, Germany, and then in Vienna, Austria. During all these years, I kept an interest in alternative medicine and when, in 1993, the opportunity presented itself, I took the Chair in Complementary Medicine at the University of Exeter. In this capacity, I built up a multidisciplinary team of about 20 researchers conducting research into all sorts of alternative modalities. After 19 years, I retired and now I am an emeritus professor at the University of Exeter. This means that I have:

- experienced alternative medicine as a patient,
- practised alternative medicine as a clinician,
- researched alternative medicine as a scientist.

I should perhaps also mention that I have published more peer-reviewed articles on the subject than anyone on the planet (sounds pompous, but it's true), and that, contrary to many authors of books on alternative medicine, I have no conflicts of interest (sounds unlikely, but it's also true).

Yet, this does not mean that I have not been accused of being biased; and to some extent, I probably am. I trust in science, want to see sound evidence, hope to improve healthcare, insist that patients deserve the best treatments available, and feel that ethics are of paramount importance in any type of healthcare. If I am brutally honest, I also do not like charlatans, liars or entrepreneurs selling false hope. If that makes me biased, so be it!

1.4   About The Book

When writing a book that covers 150 modalities (I use this term to capture both alternative therapies and alternative diagnostic methods), one is very much in danger of creating a colossal volume that few consumers would ever want to look at. I therefore decided to restrict myself to the bare minimum.

In part 1 of the book, you find 6 introductory chapters that will be helpful for understanding some of the issues around alternative medicine. Part 2 of the book the offers 150 short chapters each focussed on one specific modality. This section is divided into 4 alphabetically-ordered chapters according to the nature of the modality. Below the title of each of the short chapters, there is a list of related modalities which are discussed in separate chapters.

The choice of subjects included in part 2 was guided mainly by popularity. My aim was to cover as many modalities known to the public as possible, plus a few therapies that are quite exotic and thus interesting. To keep the short chapters as concise as possible, I summarised each modality by making just seven short points. They differ from modality to modality and are meant to tell you what matters most in relation to each of them. My ambition was not to provide exhaustive information on each modality, but to give a flavour and offer enough evidence for making informed decisions and perhaps encourage further reading.

As I wanted this book to be as evidence-based as possible, I needed to supply references to the most relevant research articles. Here too, I decided to restrict myself to the bare maximum. This restriction frequently meant omitting important references, focussing occasionally on my own research, and merely citing the most reliable, most recent reviews.

To make things as clear as possible, I concluded each of the short chapters with this standard table.

PLAUSIBILITY
EFFICACY
SAFETY*
COST
RISK/BENEFIT BALANCE

These five criteria included in the table require some explanation:

- PLAUSIBILITY addresses the question whether the basic assumptions on which the modality is based are in line with the laws of nature and our current knowledge of the human body. For instance, the notion of reflexologists that specific areas on the soles of our feet correspond to specific organ systems cannot be called plausible, because it contradicts the basic facts from anatomy and physiology. By contrast, the notion that a herbal remedy is effective is plausible, because plants contain lots of chemicals which might have pharmacological activity.
- EFFICACY deals with the question whether, according to the published evidence, a modality works or not. In the case of a therapy, the question usually is, does it work better than a placebo? As a treatment might be efficacious for one condition but not for others, the decision is not always straight forward. When evaluating the published evidence, it is, of course, important to consider the quality of the published studies. This is not always an easy task, but many years of experience have enabled me to reliably spot poor research and pseudoscience. In the case of a diagnostic method, the issue is whether it is useful for identifying a disease. It is important to remember that a modality which is not supported by reliable evidence can only be characterised as being not of proven efficacy. In the tables, they must therefore be rated as 'negative'.
- SAFETY addresses the question whether the modality per se can do any harm. In the short chapters, I usually omit all indirect risks of alternative medicine. Yet, such indirect risks can be significant, for instance, if an alternative therapy is promoted as an alternative treatment in a case of serious disease. To avoid tedious repetitions, these indirect risks are discussed in some detail in part 1 of this book.

- COST provides a rough judgement on the expense associated with the modality. In making these judgements, I also considerd whether a therapy usually requires more than one session which would, of course, increase the total expense.
- RISK/BENEFIT BALANCE combines the issues of efficacy and safety by asking whether the modality in question generates more good than harm. When considering such verdicts, it is crucial to remember two things. Firstly, the risk/benefit balance cannot be positive, even for a totally harmless therapy, if that therapy has not been documented to be efficacious. Secondly, in routine healthcare, it is generally wise to only employ treatments which have a clearly positive risk/benefit balance.

With these tables, I attempt to offer my assessments by using just three very simple grades:

- positive

- debatable

- negative

On the one hand, such simplicity is desirable for accessibility and easy reading. On the other hand, it does not allow much subtlety and nuance. When making these judgement calls, I often had to rely on more evidence than I was able to cite in the text. Therefore, they represent my overall assessments based on the collective evidence from 25 years of research.

The tables are meant to complement the text; together they are designed to give you a quick and reliable idea whether the modality in question might be of any value for you. As mentioned, all my assessments are based on critical evaluation of the existing evidence. Some readers might feel that I judged their favourite therapy too harshly. Others will no doubt get the impression that I was too lenient. My aim was to be consistently critical but not dismissive.

It is nevertheless important to realise that my guidance cannot be absolute. I am only able inform you about what the evidence tells me. I do not know your precise circumstances nor your preferences. My book is therefore not meant as medical advice on specific conditions and treatments.

1.5 How to Make The Best Use of This Book

I recommend you take your time to familiarise yourself with the concept of this book. Even though the chapters are written such that they can stand alone, it might be best to first read part 1 in its entirety. This should enable you to develop a good understanding of alternative medicine and the sometimes-confusing issues that are involved. Subsequently, you might look up the therapies and diagnostic methods that you have used, are tempted to employ or simply have an interest in. I tried my best not to use technical jargon, yet occasionally I had to employ some terms that might not be familiar. For this reason, I included an extensive glossary where you will find useful explanations for terms that might be unfamiliar.

I stress again that my evaluations are deliberately critical and never promotional. I feel that consumers are already exposed to such an abundance of uncritical promotion of useless and even dangerous treatments, that a critical stance is badly needed. I am convinced that this approach is the best way to assist you in finding your way through the disorientating maze of misinformation that all too often characterises the realm of alternative medicine.

Chapter 2
Why Evidence?

In Chap. 1, I have been banging on about 'evidence'. But what is evidence? And why is it important? These are some of the questions I will address in this chapter.

2.1 Experience Is Good, but It's not Evidence

Clinicians often feel quite strongly that their daily experience tells them about the efficacy of their interventions. If their patients get better, they assume this to be the result of their treatment. I do sympathise with this notion, not least because it prevents practitioners from losing faith in their own work. But is the assumption really correct?

The short answer is NO. Two events [the treatment administered by the clinician and the improvement experienced by the patient] that follow each other in time are not necessarily causally related. The crowing of the cock is not the cause of the sun rising in the morning. We all know that, of course. So, we ought to consider alternative explanations for a patient's improvement after therapy.

Even the most superficial glance at the possibilities discloses several options:

- the natural history of the condition (most conditions get better, even if they are not treated at all),
- regression towards the mean (outliers tend to return to the mean when we re-check them),
- the placebo-effect (expectation and conditioning affect how we feel),

This chapter is a revised and extended version of a chapter in my book HOMEOPATHY, THE UNDILUTED FACTS, Springer 2016 (https://www.hive.co.uk/Product/Professor-Edzard-Ernst/Homeopathy—The-Undiluted-Facts–Including-a-Comprehensive-A-Z-Lexicon/19719982).

- concomitant treatments (people often take more than one treatment when ill),
- social desirability (patients tend to claim they are better simply to please their therapist).

These and other phenomena (Fig. 2.1) can determine any clinical outcome in such a way that inefficacious treatments appear to be efficacious. For instance, an ineffective treatment given for a cold that has run its course could give the impression that a useless therapy taken at this stage had been effective.

It follows that the prescribed treatment is only one of many factors affecting the clinical outcome. Thus, even the most impressive clinical experience of the perceived effectiveness of a treatment can be totally misleading. In fact, experience might just reflect the fact that we tend to repeat the same mistakes. Put in a nutshell: the plural of anecdote is anecdotes, not evidence.

Some clinicians get upset when someone tries to explain to them how multifactorial the situation really is, and how little their experience tells us about the efficacy of the treatment they selected. Here are seven arguments (together with the counter-arguments) they often produce:

(1) The improvement was so prompt that it was obviously caused by my treatment [this notion is unconvincing, since placebo-effects can be just as prompt and direct].
(2) I have seen it so many times that it cannot be a coincidence [some clinicians are very charismatic; they will thus regularly generate powerful placebo-responses].

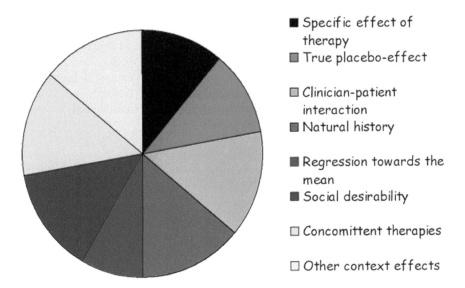

■ Specific effect of therapy
■ True placebo-effect

□ Clinician-patient interaction
■ Natural history

■ Regression towards the mean
■ Social desirability

□ Concomittent therapies

□ Other context effects

Fig. 2.1 Various phenomena that can contribute to the perceived therapeutic effect of a treatment. *Source* E Ernst

(3) A study with several thousand patients shows that 71% of them improved after receiving that treatment [such response rates are not uncommon, even for ineffective treatments, if patient-expectation was high].

(4) Surely chronic conditions don't suddenly get better; my treatment therefore cannot be a placebo [this is incorrect, most chronic conditions eventually improve, if only temporarily].

(5) I had a patient with a serious condition (e.g. cancer) who received my treatment and was cured [if one investigates such claims, one often finds that the patient also took a conventional treatment; also, in rare instances, even cancer-patients show spontaneous remissions].

(6) I have tried the treatment myself and had a positive result [clinicians are not immune to the multifactorial nature of the perceived clinical response outlined above].

(7) Even children and animals respond to my treatment; surely, they are not prone to placebo-effects [animals can be conditioned to respond; and then there is, of course, the natural history of the disease, as mentioned above].

Does this mean that clinical experience is useless? Clearly not! But when it comes to defining therapeutic effectiveness, clinical experience can be no replacement for evidence. It is invaluable for a lot of other things, but, at best, it provides us with a suggestion that the therapy in question might be effective.

2.2 What Is Evidence?

As the clinical outcomes after treatments have many causes, we need a different approach for verifying therapeutic effectiveness. Essentially, we need to know what would have happened, if our patients had <u>not</u> received the treatment in question.

The multifactorial nature of a clinical response requires accounting for all the factors that might determine the outcome other than the treatment per se. Ideally, we would need to create an experiment where two groups of patients are exposed to the full range of factors, and the only difference is that one group does receive the treatment, while the other one does not. This is precisely the model of a controlled clinical trial.

Controlled clinical trials are designed to minimise all possible sources of uncertainty about what might have been the cause of the observed effect. They have, as the name says, a control group which means that we can, at the end of the treatment period, compare the effects of the treatment in question with those of another intervention, a placebo or no treatment at all.

Many different variations of the controlled trial have been developed so that a study can be adapted to the requirements of the treatment under scrutiny and the specific research question at hand. The over-riding principle is, however, always the same: we want to make sure that we can reliably determine whether the treatment was the cause of the clinical outcome.

Causality is the key in all of this; and here lies the crucial difference between clinical experience and scientific evidence. What clinician witness in their routine practice can have a myriad of causes; what scientists observe in a well-designed trial is most likely caused by the treatment. The latter is evidence, while the former isn't.

But clinical trials are rarely perfect. They can have many flaws and have rightly been criticised for a plethora of inherent limitations. Yet, despite all their short-comings, they are far superior than any other method for determining the efficacy of medical interventions; they are, so to speak, the worst kind of evidence, except for all other options.

To be extra sure that a finding is reliable, we should not rely on the findings of one single study. Independent replications are usually required before we can be reasonably sure. Unfortunately, the findings of these replications do not always confirm the results of the previous study. Whenever we are faced with conflicting results, it is tempting to cherry-pick those studies which seem to confirm our prior belief—tempting but very wrong indeed! To arrive at the most reliable conclusion about the effectiveness of any treatment, we need to consider the totality of the reliable evidence. This goal is best achieved by conducting what experts call a 'systematic review'.

In a systematic review, we assess the quality and quantity of the available evidence, try to synthesise the findings and arrive at an overall verdict about the effectiveness of the treatment in question. Systematic reviews and meta-analyses [these are systematic reviews where the data of individual studies is pooled mathematically] constitute the best, i.e. most trustworthy, evidence for or against the effectiveness of any treatment. In this book, I will, whenever possible, depend on this type of evidence and provide links to the original articles.

2.3   Why Is Evidence Important?

In a way, this question has already been answered: only with reliable evidence can we tell with any degree of certainty that it was the treatment per se—and not any of the other factors mentioned above—that caused the clinical outcome we observe on ourselves or on others. Only if we have such evidence can we be certain about cause and effect. And only then can we make sure that patients receive the best possible treatments currently available.

But there are those who say that causality does not matter all that much. What is important, they claim, is to help the patient. If it was a placebo-effect that did the trick, who cares?

While this argument sounds empathetic, there are many reasons why this attitude is deeply misguided. To mention just one: we all agree that the placebo-effect can benefit many patients, yet it would be wrong to assume that we need a placebo treatment to generate a placebo-response. If a clinician administers an efficacious therapy [one that generates benefit beyond placebo] with compassion, time, empathy and understanding, she will generate a placebo-response **plus** a response to the therapy administered. In this case, the patient benefits from two elements:

- from the placebo-effect,
- and from the specific effect of the prescribed therapy.

It follows that, merely administering a placebo is less than optimal; in fact, it usually means cheating the patient of the effect of an efficacious therapy.

Yet, some say that there are many patients who are ill without an exact diagnosis and who therefore cannot receive a specific treatment. This may be true, but even those patients' symptoms can be alleviated with effective symptomatic therapy. The administration of an ineffective treatment is surely not preferable to using an effective symptomatic therapy.

2.4   When Do We Have Enough Evidence?

Most research papers end with a sentence stating that more research is needed. In many cases, this is true. But there are exceptions. When is the existing evidence enough for making reasonable therapeutic decisions? This is a question that is relevant to much of alternative medicine. Take homeopathy, for instance; how much more negative data do we need to concede that highly diluted homeopathic remedies do not work beyond placebo?

This systematic review[1] assessed the effectiveness and safety of oral homeopathic medicinal products compared with placebo or conventional therapy to prevent and treat acute respiratory tract infections in children. Eight studies of 1562 children receiving oral homeopathic medicinal products or a control treatment (placebo or conventional treatment) for upper respiratory tract infections were included. All studies assessed as at low risk of bias showed no benefit from oral homeopathic medicinal products; trials at uncertain or high risk of bias reported beneficial effects. The authors concluded that "pooling of two prevention and two treatment studies did not show any benefit of homeopathic medicinal products compared to placebo on recurrence of ARTI or cure rates in children. We found no evidence to support the efficacy of homeopathic medicinal products for ARTIs in children. Adverse events were poorly reported, so conclusions about safety could not be drawn."[2]

In their paper, the authors stated that "there are no established explanatory models for how highly diluted homeopathic medicinal products might work. For this reason, homeopathy remains highly controversial because the key concepts governing this form of medicine are not consistent with the established laws of conventional therapeutics." In other words, there is no reason why highly diluted

---

[1]Hawke et al. (2018).
[2]Hawke et al. (2018).

homeopathic remedies should work. Yet, remarkably, when asked what conditions responds best to homeopathy, most homeopaths would probably include acute respiratory tract infections of children. The authors of the review also pointed out that "the results of this review are consistent with all previous systematic reviews on homeopathy. Funders and study investigators contemplating any further research in this area need to consider whether further research will advance our knowledge, given the uncertain mechanism of action and debate about how the lack of a measurable dose can make them effective."

I would be more outspoken regarding the need of further research. In my view, it would be a foolish, wasteful and therefore unethical activity to fund, plan or conduct further research in areas where there is no or just minimal chance of rigorous investigations finding a positive result. In alternative medicine, this is frequently the case.

2.5   Conclusions

Helping the patient is the most important task of any clinician. This goal is best achieved by maximising the non-specific effects [e.g. placebo], while making sure that, at the same time, the patient benefits from the specific effects of what medicine has to offer. If that is our aim in clinical practice, we need reliable evidence and experience. Evidence without experience is just knowledge. With my book, I cannot hope to transmit experience, but I hope to inform you regarding the evidence. Whichever way you want to look at it, evidence is an essential precondition for making sound decisions. This book is an attempt to outline the evidence as it applies to alternative medicine.

Reference

Hawke K, van Driel ML, Buffington BJ, McGuire TM, King D (2018) Homeopathic medicinal products for preventing and treating acute respiratory tract infections in children. Cochrane Database Syst Rev (4):CD005974

Chapter 3
The Attractiveness of Alternative Medicine

Alternative medicine is attractive to many customers; the amount we currently spend on it provides ample proof. By 2025, we are predicted to spend just short of US$ 200 billion worldwide on alternative medicine, and most of this sum comes directly out of the consumer's pocket.[1] Such a figure begs the question as to the reason for this extraordinary attractiveness. In this chapter, I will analyse some of them and try to assess their validity.

3.1 Alternative Medicine Is Effective

The most obvious attraction of any therapy would be its effectiveness. Patients use a medical treatment because they are ill and hope for a cure. So, is alternative medicine effective? As we are dealing with a plethora of different modalities, the answer will differ for each of them. Therefore, I will not attempt to address it here, but refer you to part 2 of this book where it will be evaluated for each treatment separately based on the most reliable evidence available to date.

At this point, it seems important to note that the attractiveness of alternative medicine can instantly turn into the opposite when the hope invested in it is betrayed. Once we realise that a frequently-made claim is untrue, our attraction is likely to change into the opposite. If, for instance, we find that therapeutic claims made for an alternative medicine are unfounded, false or fraudulent, we are no longer attracted but put off by it. This remarkable reversal of attractiveness into unattractiveness is a phenomenon that will a constant companion in this chapter.

---

[1]https://www.prnewswire.com/news-releases/alternative–complementary-medicine-market-worth-19687-billion-by-2025-grand-view-research-inc-619591673.html.

© Springer Nature Switzerland AG 2019
E. Ernst, *Alternative Medicine*,
https://doi.org/10.1007/978-3-030-12601-8_3

3.2   Alternative Medicine Is Risk-Free

The belief that alternative medicine is risk-free is commonly held and attracts many consumers. Anyone who goes on the Internet or reads a book about alternative medicine will be bombarded with this message. "Alternative medicine is gentle and harmless, pleasant and holistic, agreeable and relaxing. Contrary to conventional medicine, it has an unblemished safety record. Adverse effects belong to synthetic drugs and not to alternative medicine." These are just some of the notions we hear regularly. They are well suited to boost the alternative medicine businesses, I am sure. Yet, they have one crucial disadvantage: they are not true!

In part 2 of this book, we will see that many alternative therapies can cause direct adverse effects. To mention just a few:

- Acupuncture might cause infections and organ injuries.
- Alternative diets can cause malnutrition.
- Aromatherapy could cause allergic reactions.
- Chiropractic and osteopathic spinal manipulations can cause a stroke.
- Colonic irrigation may cause a perforation of the colon.
- Herbal remedies might cause liver damage or interact with prescription drugs.

In conventional medicine, stringent mechanisms are in place to monitor adverse effects of drugs, so that action can be taken, once serious problems emerge (it is because of such safe-guards that drugs are withdrawn from the market with some regularity). Remarkably, nothing remotely similar exists in the realm of alternative medicine. This is why we currently have only scant data on problems caused by alternative medicine; and the few reports that do get published depict almost certainly only the tip of a much bigger ice-berg.

Because the specifics of **direct** risks depend entirely on the treatment in question, they will be mentioned in the short chapters of part 2 dedicated to specific modalities. Here I intend to focus on the **indirect** risks of alternative medicine. Indirect risks are not caused by the treatment per se but arise in the context in which therapy is given. If, for instance, a completely harmless but ineffective alternative treatment replaces a vital conventional one, the harmless therapy becomes life-threatening. Proponents of alternative medicine tend to claim that this situation hardly ever arises. Sadly, this claim is not true.

To explain this more clearly, I invite you conduct a little thought experiment with me: imagine 10 groups each of 100 patients suffering from the following conditions:

- cancer
- AIDS
- Ebola
- sepsis
- tuberculosis
- multiple sclerosis
- coronary heart disease

- stroke
- diabetes
- peripheral vascular disease.

Now imagine that all of these patients receive an alternative treatment in the form of homeopathy (or energy healing, or any other alternative therapy) and ask yourself in how many of these patients this approach would hasten death (i.e. contribute to a fatal outcome earlier than necessary). Surely, the figures would be not far from 100% (and surely with conventional medicine, they would be close to 0%).

As homeopaths and other alternative practitioners regularly claim to be able to treat those conditions (go on the Internet, if you doubt this assertion), my little thought experiment is not as theoretical as it may seem. In fact, it is frightfully realistic. A homeopathic remedy might well be harmless, however, the same does not necessarily apply to the homeopath.

To explain this point better, let me recount the story of a patient seeking care from a range of clinicians. The story is fictional but based on many real experiences of a similar nature.

Tom is in his mid-50s, happily married, mildly over-weight and under plenty of stress. In addition to his demanding job, he has recently moved home and, because of lots of heavy lifting, his body aches everywhere, particularly in his back. Having experienced episodes of back trouble before, Tom re-starts the exercises a physiotherapist once taught him. A few days later, the back-pain has improved, and most other pains have subsided as well; only a dull and nagging pain around his left shoulder and arm persists.

He is tempted to see his GP, but his wife is fiercely alternative. She was also the one who, years ago, dissuaded Tom from taking Statins for his high cholesterol and put him on Garlic pills instead. Now she gives Tom a bottle of her Rescue Remedy and tells him that this will do the trick. Yet, after a week of taking it, Tom's condition is unchanged. His wife therefore persuades him to consult alternative practitioners for his 'shoulder problem' which she assumes to be due to too much heavy lifting during the recent move. Thus, Tom sees a succession of five of her favourite therapists.

1. THE CHIROPRACTOR examines Tom's spine and diagnoses subluxations to be the root cause of his problem. Tom thus receives a series of spinal manipulations and feels a little improved each time. But he is disappointed that the pain in the left shoulder and arm returns. His wife therefore makes another appointment for him.
2. THE SPIRITUAL HEALER diagnoses a problem with Tom's vital energy as the root cause of his persistent pain. Tom thus receives a series of healing sessions and feels a little improved each time. But he is disappointed that the pain in the left shoulder and arm returns. His wife therefore makes another appointment for him.

3. THE REFLEXOLOGIST examines Tom's foot and diagnoses knots on the sole of his foot to cause energy blockages which are the root cause of his problem. Tom thus receives a series of most agreeable foot massages and feels a little improved each time. But he is disappointed that the pain in the left shoulder and arm returns. His wife therefore makes another appointment for him.

4. THE ACUPUNCTURIST examines Tom's pulse and tongue and diagnoses a chi deficiency to be the root cause of his problem. Tom thus receives a series of acupuncture treatments and feels a little improved each time. But he is disappointed that the pain in the left shoulder and arm returns. His wife therefore makes another appointment for him.

5. THE NATUROPATH examines Tom and diagnoses some form of auto-intoxication as the root cause of his problem. Tom thus receives a full program of detox and subsequently feels a little improved. But he is disappointed that the pain in the left shoulder and arm returns. His wife therefore wants to make another appointment for him.

But this time, Tom had enough. His shoulder pain has not really improved, and he is not feeling well. At the risk of a marital dispute, he consults his GP. The doctor looks up Tom's history, asks a few questions, conducts a brief physical examination, and arranges for Tom to see a specialist. A cardiologist diagnoses Tom to suffer from coronary heart disease due to a stenosis in one of his coronary arteries. She explains that Tom's dull pain in the left shoulder and arm is a rather typical symptom of this condition. Tom is put on a six-week long waiting list for a stent to be put into the affected coronary artery. One week before his appointment, Tom dies of a massive heart attack.

There is no question that the **indirect** risks of alternative medicine are considerably more important than the often just minor **direct** risks.[2,3] They may take a range of forms:

- An infective alternative therapy replaces an effective conventional treatment.
- Alternative practitioners advise parents against immunising their child.
- Alternative practitioners recommend stopping a prescribed medication.
- A patient feels that her self-medication of a serious condition will cure it.

None of these concerns are just theoretical. On the contrary, there are far too many instances where lives have been lost in this way.[4] It follows that the notion of alternative medicine being risk-free is dangerously mistaken.

The solution surely is an open and frank approach to discussing the indirect risks of alternative medicine. Such a discussion should make several points abundantly clear and transparent:

---

[2]Ernst (2001a).

[3]Ernst (2001b).

[4]http://www.ebm-first.com/.

- Alternative practitioners are usually not trained to advise patients responsibly, particularly in cases serious disease.
- Alternative practitioners often do not know their limits and over-estimate what their therapy can reasonably achieve.
- They rarely refer their patients to conventional healthcare practitioners.
- The patients of alternative practitioners are often either desperate or gullible and thus likely to fall for bogus claims.
- Alternative practitioners have a significant conflict of interest—to make a living, they need to treat as many patients as possible; they are therefore rarely motivated to refer patients to more suitable care.
- Alternative practitioners are frequently in denial when it comes to the risks of their treatments.
- Alternative practitioners are not educated such that they understand the full complexities of most diseases.
- As a result, alternative practitioners far too often misguide their patients to make wrong choices thus putting their health at risk.

In most countries, the regulators turn a blind eye to these problems. Yet, they are by no means trivial. They relate to our ethical duty of keeping patients and consumers as safe as reasonably possible. It has been estimated that, in oncology alone, up to 5% of deaths are due to patients opting to have alternative instead of conventional treatments. This amounts to an unbearably high absolute number of patients dying prematurely due to the indirect risks of alternative medicine.

3.3 Alternative Medicine Is Natural

Alternative medicine is attractive not least because it is natural medicine—so much so that an entire branch of alternative medicine, naturopathy, has its name based on this assumption. Alternative practitioners use natural products, employ natural forces as treatments, and are devoted to treating their patients naturally.

These assumptions are so deeply engrained in our minds that few people ever question them. Once we think about them rationally, however, considerable doubts might emerge:

- What is natural about sticking needles into a patient's body, as acupuncturists do?
- What is natural about forcing spinal joints out of their physiological range of motion, as chiropractors regularly and osteopaths occasionally do?
- What is natural about endlessly diluting substances until no molecule is left of them in a remedy, as homeopaths do?
- What is natural about pushing a tube up a patient's back-passage and filling her colon with water, as colon therapists do?

- What is natural about injecting a local anaesthetic into the body, as practitioners of neural therapy do?
- What is natural about saturating a sample of blood with ozone, as practitioners of ozone therapy do?

The answer is simple: nothing!

Some alternative therapy may well be natural in the sense that they employ the means supplied by nature, but many others are clearly not natural at all and employ this label mainly because it is good for business. Once we rationalise the advertising gimmick, this attraction of alternative medicine being natural turns out to be a mere distraction.

3.4   Alternative Medicine Is Holistic

Alternative practitioners tend to stress that, contrary to conventional healthcare, alternative medicine is holistic. To most consumers, that sounds most attractive. On closer inspection, however, we must realise that few concepts in medicine are more often abused than that of holism.

Holism means considering a patients as whole human beings with a mind body and soul. The holistic approach to healthcare is most certainly positive. But holism is not the monopoly of alternative medicine. It does not belong to any type of health care, it is an essential characteristic of any form of good medicine. Without it, health care is quite simply defective.

In 1803, Percival stated: "The feeling and emotions of the patients require to be known and to be attended to, no less than the symptoms of their diseases." More recently, John Macleod in his 1964 book 'Clinical Examination' commented that "we should aim to be holistic in our care." The seminal work by Michael Balint, 'The Doctor, the Patient and his Illness', first published in 1957, is yet a further reminder that the patient must be understood as a whole rather than as an isolated pathology. A holistic approach is good practice and has been strongly advocated by conventional medicine's professional bodies for many years.

Proponents of alternative medicine, however, tend to see this differently. They have jumped on the 'holistic band-wagon' and frequently claim that they now own it: they pretend to be the only clinicians who practice holistically. The implication, of course, is that conventional medicine is not holistic. Practitioners of alternative medicine have managed to do a thorough job:

- they hijacked holism,
- they claimed they have a monopoly on it,
- they used it to create a straw man misleading the public,
- and they perverted holism into a tool for attracting the often all too gullible public.

3.5 Alternative Medicine Has Stood the Test of Time

We all tend to trust time-tested methods more than new developments. The idea is that, if something has survived for many decades, it must be fine—otherwise it would have been discarded long ago. To some degree, the concept makes sense. And because it seems rational and attractive, proponents of alternative medicine like to apply it to their trade. Thus, the term 'traditional medicine' is often used by practitioners pointing that:

- Acupuncture has a history of 2000 years.
- Faith healing was already mentioned in the Bible.
- Herbal medicine has been used in all ancient cultures.
- Homeopathy has already survived more than 200 years.
- Chiropractic and osteopathy are more than 120 years old.
- Naturopathy has ancient roots.
- Etc., etc.

There is, of course nothing wrong with naming the age and explaining the history of a treatment. A problem, however, arises when it is implied that a long history is a proof for the notion that the treatment is effective and safe. And, because having passed the test of time appeals to consumers, this is precisely what happens in alternative medicine.

The notion that a long history can substitute scientific evidence is not just false, it can also be dangerous. There are many historical examples to demonstrate this. For instance, blood letting was used in many cultures for hundreds of years. Today we know that it did not only not cure the sick, it also hastened the death of millions.

A recent study might serve as a fitting example for showing that tradition is no replacement for evidence.[5] This trial tested the efficacy of *Rhodiola crenulata (R. crenulata)*, a remedy which has been used for ages in Tibet to prevent acute mountain sickness. Healthy adult volunteers were randomized to two treatment sequences, receiving either 800 mg *R. crenulata* extract or placebo daily for 7 days before ascent and two days during mountaineering. After a three-month wash-out period, they were crossed over to the other treatment. On each occasion, the participants ascended rapidly from 250 to 3421 m. The primary outcome measure was the incidence of acute mountain sickness with headache and at least one of the symptoms of nausea or vomiting, fatigue, dizziness, or difficulty sleeping. One hundred and two participants completed the trial. No significant differences in the incidence of acute mountain sickness were found between *R. crenulata* extract and placebo groups. If anything, the incidence of severe acute mountain sickness with the herbal extract was slightly higher compared to the one with placebo: 35.3% versus 29.4%.

Similar examples could be found by the dozen; think of blood-letting, mercury cures, trepanation, etc. They demonstrate that out trust in the 'test of time' is

---

[5]Chiu et al. (2013).

erroneous: a treatment which has a long history of usage is not necessarily effective (or safe)—not only that, it might be dangerous. The true value of a therapy cannot be judged by experience, to be sure, we need rigorous clinical trials. Acute mountain sickness is a potentially life-threatening condition for which there are reasonably effective treatments. If we replace science with 'ancient wisdom', we might find ourselves paying a high price indeed.

3.6   Alternative Medicine Tackles the Root Causes of an Illness

Alternative practitioners are adamant that they—and only they—treat the root causes of a disease. The claim is regularly pronounced with such deep conviction that there can be little doubt that they fully and wholeheartedly believe it. The implication usually is that, in conventional medicine, clinicians only treat the symptoms of our patients; they put sticky plasters on broken bones, so to speak. The effect on consumers is twofold: they feel attracted to alternative medicine and put off by conventional healthcare.

The notion that alternative practitioners treat the root causes is based on the practitioners' understanding of aetiology.

- If a traditional acupuncturist is convinced that all disease is the expression of an imbalance of life-forces, and that needling acupuncture points will re-balance these forces thus restoring health, he must automatically assume that he is treating the root causes of any condition.
- If a chiropractor believes that all diseases are due to 'subluxations' of the spine, it must seem logical to him that spinal 'adjustment' is synonymous with treating the root cause of whatever complaint his patient is suffering from.
- If a homeopath thinks that the condition of his patient is due to a deficit in vital energy, he will assume that strengthening it by his treatment tackles the root cause of the disease.

There is an obvious problem with the assumption that alternative practitioners treat the root cause of a condition. Think of a condition like migraine, for instance; if the acupuncturist, the chiropractor, the homeopaths, etc. all assume to treat the root cause, yet this root cause differs between these approaches, they cannot possibly be all correct. There can only be one root cause, but in alternative medicine, there are usually as many different root causes as there are alternative therapies.

But let us disregard this problem and assume for a minute that all these practitioners are correct in believing that their interventions are directed against the root cause of a disease. Successful treatment of the cause can only mean that the therapy in question completely heals the problem at hand. If we abolish the cause of a disease, we would expect the disease to disappear for good.

But are there any alternative treatments that completely cure a disease? I have contemplated this question frequently and discussed it often with alternative practitioners but, so far, I have not identified a single one. Even those alternative therapies which might be effective are not causal but symptomatic by nature. The herbal remedy, St John's wort, for instance, is effective for mild to moderate depression; but even this well-supported alternative therapy is not a causal treatment.[6]

It follows that the notion that alternative medicine tackles the root causes of an illness is a myth. It does attract consumers, but it is a falsehood that is spread widely, not least because it attracts customers, but it has no basis in fact.

3.7 Alternative Medicine Is Inexpensive

Compared to many conventional therapies, most of alternative medicine is indeed cheap, and there can be no doubt, a low price is attractive to consumers. But what does a low-price tag really mean?

Take homeopathy as an example; the typical homeopathic remedy is not expensive. But the real costs of homeopathy are, of course, much higher. They include, for instance, the time for the clinicians. As homeopathic consultations can be longer than one hour, this inevitably amounts to a tidy sum. To these costs, we must add the costs for educating and training the homeopaths, the expense for the support staff, the costs for the premises where homeopathy is practised, etc. Therefore, homeopathy is not nearly as inexpensive as some people claim.

In any case, looking at the absolute costs for anything is of limited value. A car that you have bought cheaply, but that does not work and is beyond repair, was probably not truly cheap. In other words, we need to consider not just the costs of a therapy, but also its effectiveness. In part 2 of this book, we shall see that, for many alternative medicines, there is reasonable doubt in this respect.

Our review of studies addressing the costs of alternative therapies concluded cautiously: "Spinal manipulative therapy for back pain may offer cost savings to society, but it does not save money for the purchaser. There is a paucity of rigorous studies that could provide conclusive evidence of differences in costs and outcomes between other complementary therapies and orthodox medicine. The evidence from methodologically flawed studies is contradicted by more rigorous studies, and there is a need for high quality investigations of the costs and benefits of complementary medicine."[7] The important message here is that the costs of alternative medicine may well be low; however, this does not necessarily mean that alternative medicine is value for money.

---

[6]Ernst (2009).
[7]White and Ernst (2000).

3.8 Alternative Medicine Is a Small, Innocent Cottage Industry

Alternative medicine has the image of a small cottage industry. Many consumers find this attractive, not least because they hear so much about the unattractive machinations of Big Pharma. Proponents of alternative medicine are united in their intense dislike for Big Pharma. Essentially, they see this sector as:

- Driven by profit
- Employing unethical means to maximise profit
- Not caring for the needs of patients
- Attacking alternative medicine for fear of losing profit.

And, of course, they claim that alternative medicine is fundamentally different from the pharmaceutical industry. I have no intention to defend the ways of this sector. It is usually responsible to its share-holders, a constellation that can lead to excesses which are counter-productive to our needs. What I will question, however, is the notion that alternative medicine is fundamentally different from Big Pharma.

We all have to make a living; to some extend we are therefore driven by our need to earn money. In alternative medicine, there are certainly not as many mega-enterprises as in the pharmaceutical industry, but nobody can deny that many sizable firms exist which make a tidy profit selling alternative remedies of one type or another. In 2016, the German turn-over of homeopathic products amounted to Euro 622 million, for instance, and Boiron, the world's largest manufacturer of homeopathics proudly announced its 2016 sales figure amounting to 614,489,000 Euro.

Similarly, alternative therapists are also not exempt from the need to make a living. Sure, this is on a different scale from Big Pharma, but it nevertheless constitutes an undeniable need for profit. If we multiply the relatively small sums involved by the vast number of therapists, the grand total might even approach similar orders of magnitude.

And would the alternative sector employ unethical means for securing or maximising profits? My 25 years of experience of this sector have let me witness several incidents which I would not hesitate to call unethical. One of the least pleasant, from my point of view, was the discovery that several German homeopathic manufacturers were supporting a 'journalist' with sizable amounts of cash for systematically defaming me.[8]

Alternative practitioners and their organisations make a plethora of therapeutic claims which are not substantiated. One of our own investigations into this, for instance, concluded that "the majority of chiropractors and their associations in the English-speaking world seem to make therapeutic claims that are not supported by sound evidence, whilst only 28% of chiropractor websites promote lower back pain,

---

[8]http://www.quackometer.net/blog/2012/07/german-homeopathy-companies-pay-journalist-who-smears-uk-academic.html.

which is supported by some evidence. We suggest the ubiquity of the unsubstantiated claims constitutes an ethical and public health issue."[9] Who would deny that misleading patients into making wrong health care decisions is not the opposite from 'caring'?

What seems even worse, in my view, is the behaviour that often follows the exposure of such misdemeanour. If someone is courageous enough to disclose the irresponsibility of bogus claims, he might be attacked or even taken to court by those who should do their utmost to get their house in order.[10]

Finally, we have the notion of Big Pharma is trying to suppress the innocent little cottage industry of alternative medicine. I see absolutely no evidence for this assumption. Even those who articulate it can, when challenged, not produce any. The opposite is often the case: big pharmaceutical firms buy into the alternative medicine market as soon as they see a commercially viable opportunity.

Thus, the notion of alternative medicine being a small cottage industry might be attractive to consumers, however, it is largely a myth. A recent survey evaluated dietary supplements (DS) usage by US adults and concluded that "the use of DSs among older adults continues to be high in the United States, with 29% of users regularly taking ≥ 4 DSs, and there is a high concurrent usage of them with prescription medications."[11] Such data are impressive and contradict the assumption that alternative medicine is a small cottage industry. The truth is that it is an industry like most others.

3.9 Alternative Practitioners Are More Human

Many people experience conventional medicine as too technical, impersonal or even heartless; similarly, they feel that many conventional doctors are lacking in compassion and empathy. Alternative practitioners, on the other hand, are more human, dedicated and compassionate. The notion that alternative medicine is more human understandably attracts many consumers.

A normal consultation with a general practitioner often lasts less than 10 min. This lack of time deeply frustrates patients, as it rarely offers enough opportunity for a warm and constructive therapeutic relationship to develop. What is more, during such short consultations, many physicians seem to pay more attention to their computer than to the individual in front of them. At the end, many patients feel palmed off with a prescription before they were able to express all their problems, concerns and worries.

The situation is often different when they consult an alternative therapist. Here, a session can last one hour or more and there is plenty of time to talk about whatever

---

[9]Ernst and Gilbey (2010).

[10]https://en.wikipedia.org/wiki/British_Chiropractic_Association_v_Singh.

[11]White and Ernst (2000).

issue might be important to the patient. The therapists listen patiently, show understanding and empathy, offer seemingly plausible explanations for the symptoms, and discuss their therapeutic approach in much detail with their patients. As a result, patients feel as empowered partners in their own health and cared for as unique individuals.

It is thus not in the least surprising that patients rate the quality of the therapeutic relationship with their alternative practitioner significantly higher than that with their conventional doctor. Patients usually treasure the human aspects of alternative medicine very much. For many of them, the treatment per se is of secondary importance, while the time, understanding and emotional support that alternative therapists manage to offer is what they need to cope with their illness.

3.10 Conventional Medicine Does not Live up to Its Promises

Not only the practitioners of conventional medicine but also their treatments can be disappointing. In the past, many hugely exaggerated promises have been made about the future of conventional medicine. For many consumers, they seemed to raise the hope that we might soon be approaching an age of universal good health. Sadly, the reality turned out to be very different. Disappointed by such developments, many people feel attracted to alternative medicine.

The suffering of too many patients continued unabated. Their quality of life remained impaired, their hope for a cure got harshly disappointed, and the conventional treatments were burdened with significant side-effects which often seemed to make matters even worse. In some cases, modern medicine turned apparently healthy individuals into patients with symptoms; for instance, a perfectly symptom-free patient might consult his doctor who diagnosed hypercholesterolemia and prescribed statins; because of taking this medication, the patient might suffer from all sorts of symptoms and even develop muscle pain or liver problems.

Understandably, patients perceive this as a broken promise of conventional medicine. Consequently, they look for other, more attractive solutions to their health problems and find them in the form of alternative medicine. If they hear about considerable doubts regarding the effectiveness of alternative therapies, they might respond that modern medicine has helped them little; alternative medicine offers at least the compassion they crave. Even if the alternative treatment per se has little or no effects, compassion alone might suffice for easing their suffering and improving their well-being.

3.11 Conclusion

At first glance, there are numerous reasons why consumers find alternative medicine attractive. When we analyse them more closely, we realise that some of them are fallacious. Others are due to the many undoubted deficits of modern medicine. Overall a sense emerges that the current popularity of alternative medicine is to some degree a sharp criticism of the failures of today's conventional healthcare.

References

Chiu TF, Chen LL, Su DH, Lo HY, Chen CH, Wang SH1, Chen WL (2013) Rhodiola crenulata extract for prevention of acute mountain sickness: a randomized, double-blind, placebo-controlled, crossover trial. BMC Complement Altern Med 13:298

Ernst E (2001a) Complementary medicine: its hidden risks. Diab Care 24(8):1486–1488

Ernst E (2001b) Intangible risks of complementary and alternative medicine. J Clin Oncol 19 (8):2365–2366

Ernst E (2009) St John's wort superior to placebo and similar to antidepressants for major depression but with fewer side effects. Evid Based Ment Health 12(3):78

Ernst E, Gilbey A (2010) Chiropractic claims in the English-speaking world. N Z Med J 123 (1312):36–44

White AR, Ernst E (2000) Economic analysis of complementary medicine: a systematic review. Complement Ther Med 8(2):111–118

Chapter 4
The Unattractiveness of Alternative Medicine

The previous chapter, we discussed the reasons that attract consumers to alternative medicine. As we have seen, these attractions often turn into the opposite, once we realise that they are unfounded. Attractions can thus turn out to be indirect distractions. In this chapter I will outline several direct reasons for people to be disenchanted with alternative medicine.

4.1 It Is not Plausible

As even the most superficial glance at the multiple tables in part 2 of this book reveals, most of the underlying assumptions of alternative medicine lack plausibility. There is, for instance, little or no scientific basis for believing that:

- the vital force that many alternative therapies postulate exists,
- connections exist between the iris and our organs, as iridologists assume,
- there are connections between the outer ear and our organs, as auriculo-therapists would have it,
- remedies which are devoid of a single molecule of active substance have an effect, as homeopaths believe,
- subluxations of spinal joints are the cause of most diseases, as many chiropractors would tell us,
- healing 'energy' sent by a healer can cure diseases,
- integrating bogus treatments into routine care will improve healthcare, as proponents of integrative medicine proclaim,
- etc., etc.

© Springer Nature Switzerland AG 2019
E. Ernst, *Alternative Medicine*,
https://doi.org/10.1007/978-3-030-12601-8_4

The prior probability of a research hypothesis relates to its scientific plausibility. This means that statistics which do not account for this probability, are unsuitable for such studies.[1] Any statistical significance achieved in clinical trials of alternative medicine should therefore be considered with great caution and may be better applied to more plausible hypotheses (like placebo effect) than the specific efficacy of an implausible alternative therapy. Unfortunately, this rule is almost never followed by researchers of alternative medicine. In this context, experts have made the following important points:[2]

- "It is often forgotten that frequentist statistics, commonly used in clinical trials, provides only indirect evidence in support of the hypothesis examined."
- "The p-value inherently tends to exaggerate the support for the hypothesis tested, especially if the scientific plausibility of the hypothesis is low."
- "When the rationale for a clinical intervention is disconnected from the basic principles of science, as in case of complementary alternative medicines, any positive result obtained in clinical studies is more reasonably ascribable to hypotheses (generally to placebo effect) other than the hypothesis on trial, which commonly is the specific efficacy of the intervention."
- "Since meaningful statistical significance as a rule is an essential step to validation of a medical intervention, complementary alternative medicine cannot be considered evidence-based."

Positive results from clinical trials of implausible forms of alternative medicine are thus likely to be due to either chance, bias the placebo effect.

Proponents of alternative medicine tend to reject this line of thought. They usually insist on what we might call a 'level playing field' and fail to see why their assumptions require a higher level of evidence and a plausible scientific hypothesis. In doing so, they forget, however, that the playing field is not level to start with: the implausibility of their modalities has already tilted it.

4.2   There Is no Evidence

A medical field that has not been sufficiently investigated, must seem less attractive that one that has been fully researched. Opponents of alternative medicine often claim that there is no evidence in this area. This assumption is clearly not true. As of August 2018, the largest data-bank for scientific articles, Medline, listed for instance:

- 37,994 papers for herbal medicine,
- 28,627 papers for acupuncture,
- 7517 papers for chiropractic,

---

[1]Pandolfi and Carreras (2014).
[2]Pandolfi and Carreras (2014).

- 5669 papers for homeopathy.

What is true, however, is that these figures are small compared to those of conventional medicine and that the existing papers are deficient in many ways:

- Most of these articles are not research papers but comments, view-points, essays, editorials, etc.
- Those that are original research articles are often of poor methodological quality and their findings are thus less than reliable.
- Of those articles that are of high quality, the majority fail to demonstrate that the treatment in question is effective.

These are, of course, rather sweeping statements; more details to back them up will be provided in part 2 of this book.

While the sceptics' assumption that 'there is no evidence' is wrong, we must still ask what this evidence can tell us. The answer is very little!

4.3 The 'Promised Land' for Charlatans

Charlatans are people who profess to have knowledge or expertise that they do not have. Charlatans exist in all walks of life, of course, but in alternative medicine they seem to accumulate and significantly contribute to its unattractiveness.

A Canadian study, for instance, demonstrated how many chiropractors, naturopaths, homeopaths and acupuncturists might be charlatans.[3] The authors studied 392 chiropractic, naturopathic, homeopathic and acupuncture clinic websites. The main outcome measures were: mention of allergy, sensitivity or asthma, claim of ability to diagnose allergy, sensitivity or asthma, claim of ability to treat allergy, sensitivity or asthma, and claim of allergy, sensitivity or asthma treatment efficacy. The results showed that naturopath clinic websites had the highest rates of advertising at least one of diagnosis, treatment or efficacy for allergy or sensitivity (85%) and asthma (64%), followed by acupuncturists (68 and 53%, respectively), homeopaths (60 and 54%) and chiropractors (33 and 38%). Of the interventions advertised, few were scientifically supported; the majority lacked evidence of efficacy, and some were potentially harmful. The authors concluded that "the majority of alternative healthcare clinics studied advertised interventions for allergy and asthma. Many offerings are unproven. A policy response may be warranted in order to safeguard the public interest.[4] The authors also stated that these claims raise ethical issues, because evidence in support of many of the tests and treatments identified on the websites studied is lacking. For example, food-specific IgG testing was commonly advertised, despite the fact that the Canadian Society of Allergy and Clinical Immunology has recommended not to use this test due to the absence of a

---

[3]Murdoch et al. (2016).
[4]Ernst (2004).

body of research supporting it. Live blood analysis, vega/electrodiagnostic testing, intravenous vitamin C, probiotics, homeopathic allergy remedies and several other tests and treatments offered all lack substantial scientific evidence of efficacy. Some of the proposed treatments are so absurd that they lack even the most basic scientific plausibility, such as ionic foot bath detoxification…Perhaps most concerning is the fact that several proposed treatments for allergy, sensitivity or asthma are potentially harmful. These include intravenous hydrogen peroxide, spinal manipulation and possibly others. Furthermore, a negative effect of the use of invalid and inaccurate allergy testing is the likelihood that such testing will lead to alterations and exclusions in diets, which can subsequently result in malnutrition and other physiological problems…"

Cancer quackery is wide-spread in Germany. Dozens of private clinics have sprung up that seem to specialise in treating rich cancer patients for eye-watering amounts of money. One often-mentioned clinic may serve as an example; it offers amongst other treatments the following (the descriptions below are quotes from the clinic's website):[5]

- "Orthomolecular medicine aims to restore the   ideal and beneficial environment of the body by correcting molecular imbalances, and this approach is used in cancer, infections, depression and atherosclerosis, among others."
- "…every patient receives a well-balanced supportive infusion program consisting of anti-inflammatory, potent anti-oxidant and detoxifying substances, which help you recover from previous treatments, minimize side effects from current treatments and strengthen your immune system to enhance treatment effects. Substances used are for example vitamin C, selenium, zinc, L-ornithine aspartate, glutathione, alpha lipoic acid, among many others."
- "Vitamin C, also known as ascorbic acid, is an essential vitamin. It is a potent antioxidant which helps to protect against free radical damage to our proteins, fats, carbohydrates, DNA and RNA. Vitamin C is used to boost the immune system."
- "Ozone is a powerful oxidizing agent. While high concentrations can be toxic, small ozone doses may increase naturally occurring antioxidants in the body. Antioxidants help to eliminate malignant cells and are needed to keep the body healthy. Ozone used for treatment is known for its bactericidal, fungicidal and virostatic properties. It also stimulates circulation and immune functions, and revitalizes the body."
- "Hyperbaric oxygen therapy is used to treat several medical conditions. It is a well-established treatment for decompression sickness, a hazard of scuba diving. Other conditions treated with hyperbaric oxygen therapy include serious infections, skin lesions or radiation injury. Wounds for example need oxygen to heal properly, and exposing a wound to 100% oxygen can improve and speed the healing process. This has been shown in a number of studies. The goal of this treatment is to increase the amount of oxygen your blood can carry in order

---

[5]https://www.hallwang-clinic.com/.

to restore normal levels of blood gases and tissue function to promote healing and cure infection."

- "Whole body hyperthermia can be applied in a number of different diseases, including malignant, immunological, viral and other diseases. The aim of WBH is the destruction of malignant cells by induction of apoptosis via hyperthermia along with elimination of malignant cells that have become resistant to chemotherapy. With the help pf WBH, effects of other treatments, including chemotherapy and immunotherapy, can be enhanced."

None of these treatments have been shown to cure cancer. David Gorski, a prominent US oncologist has commented that this clinic "uses very experimental treatments in a 'blunderbuss' fashion, basically throwing everything but the kitchen sink together with no sophistication. We can't even know if these doctors know what the hell they are doing. Patients are treated, and, as far as we can tell, no systematic record of how well these patients do and how long they survive is kept, or, if such records are kept, they are kept secret."[6]

4.4 Pseudo-Science

The dominance of unattractive pseudo-science strikes us even as we try to make sense of the terminology used by alternative practitioners. Many well-defined medical terms are being re-defined and abused—think, for instance, of terms like subluxation, energy, potency, detox, essential oil. The effect is confusion and the end-result is that alternative medicine acquires respectability where it does not deserve any.

The language used by researchers of alternative medicine equally reflects the abundance of pseudo-science in this area. In a paper analysing this issue in detail I concluded that "… pseudo-scientific language … can be seen as an attempt to present nonsense as science…this misleads patients and can thus endanger their health…"[7] To provide a little flavour, here are just three examples of pseudo-scientific language from that paper:

Quote No. 1

The biophysical control processes are superordinate to the biochemical processes. In the same way as the atomic processes result in chemical compounds the ultrafine biocommunication results in the biochemical processes. Control signals have an electromagnetic quality. Disturbing signals or 'disturbing energies' also have an electromagnetic quality. This is the reason why they can, for example, be conducted through cables and transformed into therapy signals by means of sophisticated electronic devices. The purpose is to clear the pathological part of the signals.

---

[6]https://respectfulinsolence.com/2016/11/08/the-deadly-false-hope-of-german-cancer-clinics/.
[7]Ernst (2004).

Here the author uses highly technical language which sounds very complicated and scientific. However, after a minimum of scrutiny, one is bound to discover that the words hide more than they reveal. In particular, the scientific tone distracts from the lack of logic in the argument. The basic message, once the pseudoscientific veneer is stripped away, seems to be the following. Living systems display electromagnetic phenomena. The electromagnetic energies that they rely upon can make us ill. The energies can also be transferred into an electronic instrument where they can be changed so that they don't cause any more harm.

Quote No. 2

> The question how causative the Bioresonanz-Therapy can be must be answered in a differentiated way. The BR is in the first place effective on the informative level, which means on the ultrafine biokybernetical regulation level of the organism. This also includes the time factor and with that the functional aspect, and thus it influences the material-biochemical area of the body. The BRT is in comparison to other therapy procedures very high on the scale of causativeness, but it still remains in the physical level, and does not reach into the spiritual area. The freeing of the patient from his diseases can self evidently also lead to a change and improvement of conduct and attitudes and to a general wellbeing of the patient.

If my reading is correct, the author essentially wants to tell us that BR interferes with the flow of information within organisms. The process is time-dependent and therefore affects function, physical and biochemical properties. Compared to other treatments, BR is more causative without affecting our spiritual sphere. As BR cures a disease, it can also change behaviour, attitudes and wellbeing.

Quote No. 3

> MORA therapy is an auto-iso-therapy using the patient's own vibrations in a wide range of the electromagnetic spectrum. Strictly speaking, we have hyperwaves in a six-dimensional cosmos with two hidden parameters (as predicted by Albert Einstein and others). Besides the physical plane there are six other planes of existence and the MORA therapy works in the biological plane, a region called the M-field, according to Sheldrake and Burkhard Heim.

Here we are told that the MORA therapy is a self-treatment using the body's own resources, namely a broad range of electromagnetic waves. These waves are hyperwaves in 6 dimensions and their existence has already been predicted by Einstein. Six (or 7?) planes of existence seem to have been discovered and the MORA therapy is operative in one of them.

The unattractiveness of pseudo-scientific language in health care is obvious: it misleads us into believing that nonsense is credible; to express it more bluntly: it is a method of cheating the unsuspecting public. Thus, it leads to wrong therapeutic decisions and endangers the health of those who fall for it.

The dominance of pseudo-science in alternative medicine becomes even more obvious, if we try to understand the published studies in this field. There are thousands of examples for this; in fact, it is more difficult to locate a trial of alternative medicine that is based on good science than to find one that is steeped in pseudo-science. Here, just three examples will have to suffice.

The first is a 2018 paper exploring the prevalence with which Australian herbalists treat menstrual problems and their related treatment, experiences, perceptions, and inter-referral practices with other health practitioners. Members of the Practitioner Research and Collaboration Initiative practice-based research network identifying as Western Herbalists (WHs) completed an online questionnaire. The analyses showed that WHs regularly treat menstrual problems, perceiving high, though differential, levels of effectiveness. For menstrual problems, WHs predominantly prescribe individualised formulas including core herbs, such as Vitex agnus-castus (VAC), and problem-specific herbs. Estimated clients' weekly cost (median = $25.00) and treatment duration (median = 4–6 months) covering this Western herbal medicine treatment appears relatively low. Only 19% of WHs indicated direct contact by conventional medical practitioners regarding treatment of clients' menstrual problems despite 42% indicating clients' conventional practitioners recommended consultation with WH. The authors concluded that "Western herbal medicine may be active treatment option amongst women with menstrual problems. A detailed examination of the behaviour of women with menstrual problems who seek and use Western herbal medicine warrants attention to ensure this healthcare option is safe, effective, and appropriately co-ordinated within women's wider healthcare use."[8]

The researchers could not possibly draw conclusions about the cost-effectiveness of Western herbalism, because it had not been assessed in this study. There is also no reason to assume that individualised herbalism is effective and several reasons to fear that it might cause harm (the larger the amount of herbal ingredients in one prescription, the higher the chances for toxicity and interactions). The only systematic review on the subject concluded that "there is a sparsity of evidence regarding the effectiveness of individualised herbal medicine and no convincing evidence to support the use of individualised herbal medicine in any indication."[9] All that this survey really suggests is that the practice of Western herbalists is not evidence-based, potentially harmful and costly.

My second example is a trial of Shiatsu aimed at evaluating its effects on mood, cognition, and functional independence in patients undergoing physical activity. Alzheimer disease (AD) patients with depression were randomly assigned to the "active group" (Shiatsu + physical activity) or the "control group" (physical activity alone). Shiatsu was performed by the same therapist once a week for ten months. Global cognitive functioning (Mini Mental State Examination—MMSE), depressive symptoms (Geriatric Depression Scale—GDS), and functional status (Activity of Daily Living—ADL, Instrumental ADL—IADL) were assessed before and after the intervention. The researchers found a within-group improvement of MMSE, ADL, and GDS in the Shiatsu group. However, the analysis of differences before and after the interventions showed a statistically significant decrease of GDS score only in the Shiatsu group. The authors concluded that "the combination of

---

[8]Fisher et al. (2018).

[9]Guo et al. (2007).

Shiatsu and physical activity improved depression in AD patients compared to physical activity alone. The pathomechanism might involve neuroendocrine-mediated effects of Shiatsu on neural circuits implicated in mood and affect regulation."[10]

The study is called a 'pilot'; as such it cannot draw conclusions about the effectiveness of Shiatsu. The study does not account for the placebo effect; therefore, it is impossible to attribute the observed outcome to Shiatsu. The point about the mode of action is pure speculation, and not borne out of the data presented.

My third example is a German study of osteopathic intra-vaginal manipulation to ease back pain in pregnant women. It showed no effect of this treatment compared to the control group. Yet, the authors concluded that "in this sample a series of osteopathic treatments showed significant effects in reducing pain and increasing the lumbar range of motion in pregnant women with low back pain. Both groups attained clinically significant improvement in functional disability, activity and quality of life. Furthermore, no benefit of additional intravaginal treatment was observed."[11]

How can it be ethical for osteopaths (in Germany, they have no relevant training to speak of) to manipulate women intra-vaginally? The scientific validity of this study is also questionable: the hypothesis which this trial claims to be testing is but a very odd idea. The control-intervention is inadequate in that it cannot control for the (probably large) placebo effects of intra-vaginal manipulations. The observed outcomes are based on within-group comparisons and are therefore most likely unrelated to the treatments applied, but due to a placebo response.

Pseudo-science is a poor imitation of science and not merely unattractive but also harmful. In my memoir, I expressed it as follows: "When science is abused, hijacked or distorted in order to serve political or ideological belief systems, ethical standards will inevitably slip. The resulting pseudo-science is a deceit perpetrated on the weak and the vulnerable. We owe it to ourselves, and to those who come after us, to stand up for the truth, no matter how much trouble this might bring."[12]

4.5 Conclusions

We frequently hear that alternative medicine attracts many consumers; yet we rarely note that many rational thinkers find it deeply unattractive. There are many reasons why people might be put off by alternative medicine, and I have outlined merely those which I felt to be particularly important in the context of this book. Most of them relate to the myriad of ethical problems with alternative medicine. They are the subject of the next chapter.

---

[10]Lanza et al. (2018).

[11]Wiesner (2017).

[12]https://www.amazon.co.uk/Scientist-Wonderland-Searching-Finding-Trouble/dp/1845407776.

References

Ernst E (2004) Bioresonance, a study of pseudo-scientific language. Forsch Komplementarmed Klass Naturheilkd. 11(3):171–173

Fisher C, Adams J, Frawley J, Hickman L, Sibbritt D (2018) Western herbal medicine consultations for common menstrual problems; practitioner experiences and perceptions of treatment. Phytother Res 32(3):531–541

Guo R, Canter PH, Ernst E (2007) A systematic review of randomised clinical trials of individualised herbal medicine in any indication. Postgrad Med J 83(984):633–637

Lanza G, Centonze SS, Destro G, Vella V, Bellomo M, Pennisi M, Bella R, Ciavardelli D (2018) Shiatsu as an adjuvant therapy for depression in patients with Alzheimer's disease: a pilot study. Complement Ther Med 38:74–78

Murdoch B, Carr S, Caulfield T (2016) Selling falsehoods? A cross-sectional study of Canadian naturopathy, homeopathy, chiropractic and acupuncture clinic website claims relating to allergy and asthma. BMJ Open 6:e014028

Pandolfi M, Carreras G (2014) The faulty statistics of complementary alternative medicine (CAM). Eur J Intern Med 25(7):607–609

Wiesner A (2017) Osteopathic intravaginal treatment in pregnant women with low back pain. IUGA Academy

Chapter 5
Ethical Problems in Alternative Medicine

Medical ethics are rules that inform us what actions in healthcare are morally right and which might be problematic. They apply to all areas of medicine, including of course alternative medicine. In this chapter, I will focus on those ethical issues which arguably are the most important ones in the context of this book; a full debate of medical ethics in alternative medicine can be found elsewhere.[1]

5.1 First Do No Harm

When we think of medical ethics, we almost automatically think of the sentence 'first do no harm'. It is often thought to originate from the Hippocratic oath which allegedly all doctors must take when finishing medical school. This assumption is wrong on two accounts: doctors don't usually take this oath, and the famous sentence does not appear in Hippocrates' oath.

Yet, doctors are obliged to 'first do no harm'. Wrong again! If it were true, doctors would have to stop almost completely practicing medicine—because we do harm all the time. Our injections hurt, our diagnostic procedures can be unpleasant and sometimes painful, our medications cause adverse effects, our surgical interventions are full of risks, etc., etc.

The ethical imperative is not "first do no harm", but "do more good than harm". Of course, clinicians must be allowed to do even quite serious harm, as long as the risk/benefit balance of their actions is positive. And this means that:

- if the known risks of a treatment are greater than the expected benefits, we cannot ethically prescribe it;
- if the benefits outweigh the risks, we can consider it as a reasonable option.

---

[1]https://www.amazon.co.uk/More-Harm-than-Good-Complementary-ebook/dp/B078ZQXQNP/.

© Springer Nature Switzerland AG 2019
E. Ernst, *Alternative Medicine*,
https://doi.org/10.1007/978-3-030-12601-8_5

Obviously, these rules can only be applied to treatments where both the risks and the benefits are well-understood. What about the many alternative treatments where uncertainty often exists over both these factors?

This question is impossible to answer in the abstract. The ethical solution is to look at the best evidence as it applies to each specific case and, together with the patient, try to make an informed judgement. Take homeopathy as an example:

- highly diluted remedies are not effective beyond placebo;
- highly diluted remedies contain nothing and are therefore harmless.

One might argue that, in this case, the balance of risk versus benefit might be positive. But this would ignore an important issue: harm can be done not just by the remedy itself (see above). The harm caused by applying an ineffective treatment for conditions that are otherwise effectively treatable (usually referred to as neglect, see below) can be considerable, even fatal. So, for homeopathy the situation is as follows:

- no benefit beyond placebo;
- high risk of neglect.

And this, of course, results in a negative risk/benefit balance. In turn, this means that the practice of homeopathy does not generate more benefit than harm and is strictly speaking not ethical.

5.2 Informed Consent

Informed consent is an essential precondition for any type of healthcare, and this includes alternative medicine. Informed consent requires the practitioner to give the patient full information about the situation. Amongst other things, the following information may be needed:

- the nature of the condition,
- the prognosis of the condition,
- the evidence regarding the efficacy of the proposed treatment,
- the risks of the proposed treatment,
- the evidence regarding alternative options.

Depending on the precise circumstances, a patient's consent can be given either in writing or verbally. Not obtaining any informed consent is not just unethical, but it is also unlawful. Yet, in alternative medicine, informed consent is being woefully neglected. The reasons for this deplorable fact are threefold:

1. alternative practitioners are usually not adequately trained in medical ethics,
2. there often is no adequate regulation and control of alternative practitioners,
3. practitioners frequently have conflicts of interest and might view informed consent as a commercial threat.

To explain this more fully, let me outline three scenarios from the realm of chiropractic (I have chosen chiropractic merely as an example—the issues also apply to most other forms of alternative medicine). Imagine an asthma patient consulting a chiropractor for help.

Scenario A

Our patient has experienced breathing problems and has heard from a friend that chiropractors are able to help this kind of condition. He consults a 'straight' chiropractor (one who adheres the gospel of subluxation). She explains to the patient that chiropractors use a holistic approach. By adjusting subluxations in the spine, she stimulates healing which will naturally ease the patient's breathing problems without having to use any dangerous drugs. No conventional diagnosis is discussed, nor is there any mention of the prognosis, likelihood of benefit, risks of treatment or alternative therapeutic options.

Scenario B

Our patient consults a chiropractor who does not fully adhere to the subluxation theory of chiropractic. She conducts a thorough examination of our patient's spine and diagnoses several spinal segments that are blocked. She tells our patient that he might be suffering from asthma and that spinal manipulation might remove the blockages and thus increase the mobility of the spine which, in turn, would alleviate his breathing problems. She does not mention risks of the proposed interventions nor other therapeutic options.

Scenario C

Our patient visits a chiropractor who considers herself a back-pain specialist. She takes a medical history and conducts a physical examination. Subsequently she informs the patient that his breathing problems could be due to asthma and that she is neither qualified nor equipped to ascertain this diagnosis. She tells him that chiropractic is not an effective treatment for asthma, but that his GP would be able to make a proper diagnosis and prescribe an effective treatment for his condition. She writes a short note summarizing her thoughts and hands it to the patient to give it to his GP.

These scenarios cover a realistic spectrum of what a patient consulting a chiropractor might encounter in real life. It seems clear, that the chiropractor in scenario A and B failed regarding informed consent. In other words, only scenario C describes a behaviour that is ethically (and legally) acceptable. Scenario C is, however, a rare turn of events. Even if well-versed in both medical ethics and scientific evidence, most chiropractors might think twice about providing all the information required for informed consent—because, as scenario C demonstrates, fully informed consent in chiropractic would often prevent a patient from agreeing to be treated. In other words, chiropractors and most other alternative practitioners have a powerful conflict of interest which keeps them from adhering to the rules of informed consent and medical eithics.

A study of chiropractic from Canada demonstrated that these concerns are not just theoretical. It highlights the conclusions from Canadian courts: "informed consent is an ongoing process that cannot be entirely delegated to office person-nel..."[2] A further <u>study</u> from the UK[3] showed that valid consent procedures are either poorly understood or only selectively implemented by chiropractors.

5.3 Neglect

Neglect often occurs when a patient is not given an effective therapy for a serious condition. This means that much of alternative medicine is suspect of constituting medical neglect. Cases of neglect are not usually reported in the medical literature but may, like this one,[4] appear in newspapers:

An elderly German woman with a sore throat consulted her doctor homeopath who prescribed homeopathic remedies for her condition. These homeopathic treatments continued for several months without success. Ten months later, the patient changed her doctor and her new physician sent her straight away into hospital. There she was diagnosed with throat cancer. After 4 years of suffering, the woman died. The patient's relatives sued the homeopath who then claimed that the old woman had refused to be referred to a specialist and that the case notes provide proof for that claim. The relatives suspected that the case notes have been altered retrospectively. The judge suggested a 'good will' payment of 10,000 Euro, and the relatives had to pay 94% of the costs for the court proceedings.

Similar (but usually less dramatic) things happen regularly when an alternative therapist treats a seriously ill patient. <u>Newsweek</u> recently reported the story of a US herbalist charged with the death of a 13-year-old diabetic boy.[5] The therapist had replaced the boy's insulin with herbal remedies, and the child promptly died. The herbalist stated that god had guided him to use herbs rather than conventional medicine, and that he had successfully treated treat his own prostate cancer in this way. He had started treating the boy suffering from Type 1 diabetes after he met his mother at one of his seminars. When the boy subsequently became semi-comatose, Morrow told his parents to treat their son with his herbal remedies rather than insulin prescribed by the boy's doctors. The boy died only hours later. The medical examiner was quoted saying: "The allegations in this case underscore the serious health and safety risks of taking medical advice from someone who lacks a license and the proper training that goes with it... No family should have to suffer the tragedy of losing a child because of irresponsible, un-credentialed medical advice."

---

[2]Boucher and Robidoux (2014).

[3]Langworthy and le Fleming (2005).

[4]https://www.halternerzeitung.de/Nachrichten/Haltern/Web-Artikel-1289724.html.

[5]https://www.newsweek.com/herbalist-who-cured-cancer-herbs-charged-death-after-treating-boys-diabetes-836132.

5.4   Competence

Competence can, of course, be an issue in all professions. In medicine, lack of competence amounts to a serious ethical problem. Healthcare professionals have an ethical duty to be competent in what they are doing simply because incompetence endangers the safety of patients. In alternative medicine, lack of competence certainly is a frequent phenomenon.

How well should alternative practitioners be educated and trained to guarantee an adequate level of competence? The answer depends on what precisely they (are allowed to) do. Medical responsibility must always be matched to medical competence. If a massage therapist merely acts on the instructions of a doctor, she does not need to know the differential diagnosis of a headache, for instance. If, however, practitioners independently diagnose diseases (as many alternative practitioners do), they must have a knowledge-base that is suited to that task. If they use potentially harmful treatments (as some alternative practitioners do), they must be aware of the risks and be able to cope with potential emergencies that can arise from them. Any mismatch between responsibility and competence exposes patients to avoidable risks (see also previous section on neglect).

Uncritically teaching obsolete or nonsensical notions of vitalism, yin and yang, subluxation, detox, potentisation of homeopathics, millennia of experience etc. can be no sound basis for a competent healthcare professional. Education must be based on sound evidence; if not, it is in danger of being an exercise in brain-washing. In a nutshell: an education in nonsense is likely to result in nonsense.

In this context, a cognitive bias known as the 'Dunning-Kruger Effect' (DKE) or 'illusory superiority' has considerable relevance. The DKS means that the less you know, the less able you are able to recognize how little you know, and the less likely you are to recognize your limitations. Consequently, your confidence in yourself is inflated and you consider yourself more competent than you are. In other words, incompetence prevents the recognition of incompetence.

The relevance of the DKE to alternative medicine seems obvious. Here we are confronted with all sorts of practitioners who believe they know it all, who think they can treat any condition, tackle the 'root cause' of all ills, and who are bursting with confidence. Ironically, it is this exaggerated level of naïve confidence that tends to impress the gullible public who, in turn, give their full trust to such therapists.

But lack of competence in alternative medicine is not just a problem of clinicians, it also occurs regularly in research. One sign of this phenomenon is the proliferation of so-called 'pilot studies' of alternative therapies. A pilot or feasibility study is defined as a small-scale preliminary investigation to evaluate feasibility, time, cost, adverse events, and inform the study design of a full-scale research project. To qualify as a pilot study, an investigation needs to have an aim that is in line with the above-mentioned definition and, of course, its conclusions must be in accordance with this aim. One does not need to conduct much research to find that even these two elementary preconditions are not met by the plethora of pilot studies of alternative medicine. Three recent examples of incompetent pilot studies will have to suffice.

"Foot Reflexotherapy Induces Analgesia in Elderly Individuals with Low Back Pain: A Randomized, Double-Blind, Controlled Pilot Study."[6]

The aim of this study was "to evaluate the effects of foot reflexology on pain and postural balance in elderly individuals with low back pain." And the conclusions drawn by its authors were that "this study demonstrated that foot reflexology induced analgesia, but did not affect postural balance in elderly individuals with low back pain."

"Effect of Tai Chi Training on Dual-Tasking Performance That Involves Stepping Down among Stroke Survivors: A Pilot Study."[7]

The aim of this study was "to investigate the effect of Tai Chi training on dual-tasking performance that involved stepping down and compared it with that of conventional exercise among stroke survivors." And the conclusions read: "These results suggest a beneficial effect of Tai Chi training on cognition among stroke survivors without compromising physical task performance in dual-tasking."

"The Efficacy of Acupuncture on Anthropometric Measures and the Biochemical Markers for Metabolic Syndrome: A Randomized Controlled Pilot Study."[8]

The aim of this study was "to evaluate the efficacy of acupuncture over 12 weeks of treatment and 12 weeks of follow-up." And the conclusion: "Acupuncture decreases WC, HC, HbA1c, TG, and TC values and blood pressure in MetS."

It is obvious that these investigations are not 'pilot' studies as defined above. They are the result of incompetent researchers conducting pseudo-research for publication in low-quality journals run by incompetent editors. The sequence of events that lead to the publication of such studies is stereotypical:

1. A team of enthusiasts of alternative medicine with no or very little competence in conducting a clinical trial decide to do a bit of research.
2. They feel this would be nice as it promotes both their careers and their therapy.
3. They draw up a plan and start recruiting patients for their trial.
4. They soon notice that things are not as easy as they had imagined. They lack not just competence but also adequate funds and time.
5. Their study progresses thus slowly, and patient numbers remain low.
6. After several months, the would-be researchers had enough, and they stop the trial.
7. They improvise some statistical analyses with their data.
8. They write up the results, draw a positive conclusion and submit their paper for publication in a 3rd class journal. To get it accepted, they call it a 'pilot study' hoping that this title serves as an excuse for even the most obvious flaws in their work.

---

[6]de Oliveira et al. (2017).
[7]Chan and Tsang (2017).
[8]Han et al. (2017).

9. The journal's reviewers and editors are all proponents of alternative medicine who welcome any paper that seems to confirm their belief (which such studies invariably do).
10. Thus, the paper gets published.

Such pilot studies pollute the medical literature and misguide people who are unable or unwilling to look behind the smoke-screen. Enthusiasts of alternative medicine popularise these bogus trials, while hiding the fact that their results are unreliable. Journalists report about them, and many consumers assume any paper published in a 'peer-reviewed' medical journal must tell the truth. Such pilot studies are the result of embarrassing incompetence on several levels: researchers, funders, ethics committees, reviewers, journal editors. As they mislead the public, they can cause considerable harm and are a violation of medical ethics.

5.5 Truth

We are all under obligation to tell the truth. In healthcare, this moral obligation becomes an ethical imperative. Not telling the truth is likely to mislead patients and consumers and can thus cause considerable harm. Yet, in alternative medicine, the truth seems a flexible commodity. There are virtually hundreds of examples that I could quote in support this statement. Here just a few will have to suffice.

The following statements are from an article entitled 'An introduction to Homeopathy':[9]

1. "… a [homeopathic] remedy [is] made from a *natural* substance… in a tiny dose which has been 'potentised' to be effective."
2. "Homeopathy works by stimulating the body's own natural healing capacity."
3. "Today there are four homeopathic hospitals offering treatment under the National Health Service—in London, Glasgow, Liverpool and Bristol."
4. "Homeopathy can be used to treat the same wide range of illness as conventional medicine and may even prove successful when all other forms of treatment have failed."
5. "… the fact that the remedies are widely used on animals dismisses the idea that the success of a treatment is all in the mind."
6. "Occasionally, symptoms become worse on first taking a homeopathic medicine. This is called an 'aggravation' and is a good sign that the remedy is working."
7. "… some homeopathic remedies will successfully treat many people with the same symptoms. For example, arnica is usually used for muscular bruising …"

---

[9]https://www.weleda.co.uk/homeopathy?utm_medium=email&utm_source=apsis-anp-3.

These statements have one thing in common: they are not true! The truth would look differently:

1. Homeopathics can be made from any substance (including <u>Berlin Wall</u>) and not just natural ones. Moreover, the dose is often not 'tiny' but usually non-existent. Finally, the assumption that 'potentisation' renders remedies 'effective' is pure wishful thinking.
2. The notion that homeopathy works by stimulating the body's own natural healing capacity is at best wishful thinking; there is not a jot of evidence that it is true.
3. Today, there is not a single 'homeopathic hospital' in the NHS; they were all closed or changed their name.
4. The claim that homeopathy is a panacea is dangerous nonsense.
5. Usage of homeopathy in animals proves absolutely nothing.
6. 'Homeopathic aggravations' are a myth.
7. Homeopathic arnica is used for muscular bruising—but it is not 'successful' (i.e. effective) for that or any other condition.[10]

Some of these untruths are trivial, others are not. The important point is that these statements are false. Even more important is the fact that similar untruth abound; they even are being published by professional organisations of homeopaths. The UK Society of Homeopaths (SoH) is the organisation of 'professional' homeopaths in the UK. This some advice issued by the SoH:[11]

- *Aconite* "Great for shock, such as from fright, bad news or after having a fall. Also good for the onset of fever after exposure to acute cold, wind or heat."
- *Apis* "For bee or wasp stings and any allergic reaction which causes rapid swelling, redness and pain and where the affected area is puffy, white or rosy, feels hot and is better for cold compresses."
- *Arnica* "The classic remedy for trauma, injury and bruising. The typical arnica patient will tell you that they are fine but may well be confused or in shock. Also useful for fractures, strains after exertion such as lifting heavy objects and the early stages of a black eye and for jetlag."
- *Arsenicum* "This is a great remedy for food poisoning, especially from meat. The person will be very anxious and not easily pacified. The pains are often burning. Vomiting and diarrhoea accompanied by chills, exhaustion, and restless."
- *Belladonna* "Great for heatstroke or exhaustion, along with appropriate cooling and rehydration therapy, and for acute fevers or inflammations, which come on suddenly and lead to throbbing pain, redness and swelling. The skin is hot and red and the face flushed but, at the same time, the person can feel chilly and want to be covered."

---

[10]Ernst and Pittler (1998).
[11]http://files.constantcontact.com/314302f3101/110c7f00-35bc-4fe3-b09b-884f466e0475.pdf.

- *Ledum* "This is the first remedy to think of with puncture wounds and for bites and stings which fester. Good for twisted or sprained joints, especially ankles."
- *Nux Vomica* "The main remedy for hangover or indigestion from over-eating but also useful for food poisoning in which there is constant retching."
- *Urtica urens* "Very useful for skin conditions such as urticaria with raised lumps like nettle rash and great for 'prickly heat. Urtica can be used for minor burns and scalds as well where pains are stinging, like nettle rash, but not too sore to touch."

Such statements suggest that homeopaths do not know the truth, or just don't care. They do not seem to appreciate that shock, food poisoning and heat stroke can be life-threatening problems.

For what it's worth, I here is the truth about the above-listed remedies:

Aconite No evidence to justify the claims mentioned above.
Apis No evidence to justify the claims mentioned above.
Arnica Some evidence to show that Arnica does not work.[10]
Arsenicum No evidence to justify the claims mentioned above.
Belladonna No evidence to justify the claims mentioned above.
Ledum No evidence to justify the claims mentioned above.
Nux Vomica No evidence to justify the claims mentioned above.
Urtica urens No evidence to justify the claims mentioned above.

5.6 Conclusion

There are numerous and frequent ethical problems with alternative medicine. Only the most obvious ones were briefly discussed in this chapter. The discussion makes two things clear: medical ethics are flagrantly neglected in the realm of alternative medicine, and adhering to the rules of ethics would mean that most of alternative medicine would need to change drastically or stop altogether.

References

Boucher P, Robidoux S (2014) Lumbar disc herniation and cauda equina syndrome following spinal manipulative therapy: a review of six court decisions in Canada. J Forensic Leg Med 22:159–169

Chan WN, Tsang WW (2017) Effect of Tai Chi training on dual-tasking performance that involves stepping down among stroke survivors: a pilot study. Evid Based Complement Alternat Med 2017:9134173

de Oliveira BH, da Silva AQA, Ludtke DD, Madeira F, Medeiros GMDS, Parreira RB, Salgado ASI, Belmonte LAO, Cidral-Filho FJ, Martins DF (2017) Foot reflexotherapy induces analgesia in elderly individuals with low back pain: a randomized, double-blind, controlled pilot study. Evid Based Complement Alternat Med 2017:2378973

Ernst E, Pittler MH (1998) Efficacy of homeopathic arnica: a systematic review of placebo-controlled clinical trials. Arch Surg 133(11):1187–1190

Han M, Sun Y, Su W, Huang S, Li S, Gao M, Wang W, Wang F, Fang Z, Zhao H (2017) The efficacy of acupuncture on anthropometric measures and the biochemical markers for metabolic syndrome: a randomized controlled pilot study. Evid Based Complement Alternat Med 2017:8598210

Langworthy JM, le Fleming C (2005) Consent or submission? The practice of consent within UK chiropractic. J Manipulative Physiol Ther 28(1):15–24

Chapter 6
Other Issues

There are many other issues in alternative medicine which are worth mentioning. Here I will only elaborate on those that are most relevant in the context of this book. For further discussions, I refer you to another recent book of mine.[1]

6.1 Patient Choice

Patient choice is undoubtedly an important principle. But what exactly does it mean, and how does it apply to alternative medicine? One thing it does certainly not mean is that patients can arbitrarily chose any treatment that they happen to fancy, while expecting the public purse to pay for it.

Patients can, of course, always refuse to have a given therapy, if they so wish. Or they might opt for one evidence-based therapy instead of another. But this is probably where the dominance of the patient's wishes over medical knowledge ends—at least, if we only consider wishes paid for by the public purse. Yet, in discussions about patient choice, proponents of alternative medicine often ague that:

- They believe in evidence-based medicine (EBM) and are dedicated to its principles.
- They know that much of alternative medicine is not evidence-based.
- But they cannot ignore the many patients who want to use alternative treatments.
- The wish of a patient over-rules the medical evidence.
- Therefore, even treatments devoid of an evidence-base must be made available to patients who want them.

---

[1]https://www.amazon.co.uk/SCAM-So-Called-Alternative-Medicine-Societas/dp/1845409701/ref=pd_rhf_dp_p_img_2?_encoding=UTF8&psc=1&refRID=449PJJDXNTY60Y418S5J.

This is an alluring, yet deeply flawed line of thought. One cannot subscribe to EBM and, at the same time, administer implausible, disproven or unproven treatments. A patient's wish does not render a nonsensical treatment evidence-based. If we would accept this logic, we would sanction virtually any bogus therapy which would inevitably have two negative consequences:

- The cost of healthcare would rise.
- Many patients would not receive the best treatment available.

Neither of these consequences are in the best interest of anyone, except the alternative medicine industry. On reflection, therefore, patient choice is not a valid argument for disregarding scientific evidence.

6.2   Science Cannot Explain

The notion often expressed in defence of an alternative therapy that does not demonstrably generate more good than harm is that science cannot yet explain how it works. It is usually employed with the deepest of convictions by proponents of all sorts of alternative medicine who point out that science does not know or explain everything—and certainly not their (very special) therapy. Science is just not sophisticated enough, they say. In fact, only a few years ago, science could not even explain how Aspirin works, they might argue. And, just like Aspirin, their very special therapy—for example, energy healing (EH)—does evidently work and is supported by numerous, undeniable facts:

1. Patients get better after using EH (and surely patients don't lie).
2. Patients pay for EH (and who would pay for something that does not work?).
3. EH exists since hundreds of years (and ineffective therapies do not survive).
4. EH practitioners have tons of experience with EH (and they are the experts who know best).
5. EH is used by very important people and organisations (and they would not fall for bogus stuff).
6. EH is even reimbursed by some insurance companies (and they would not waste their money on something useless).

How can one respond to such deeply-felt arguments? In previous chapters, we have dealt with these issues before; therefore, I will make it short:

1. Getting better **after** receiving a therapy is not the same as getting better **because** of it.
2. Gullible people would pay for any rubbish.
3. An ancient history might just reveal the absence of a proper understanding of physiology and pathophysiology all those years ago.
4. What some call experience is just their inability to learn from mistakes.

5. Bungee-jumping and cigarette-smoking is also used by VIPs.
6. Insurance companies reimburse plenty of nonsense, simply because they want to be competitive.

But how can we refute the notion that science is not yet sufficiently advanced to explain EH? The simplest approach might be to explain that science has already tested EH and found it to be ineffective (see part 2 of this book). There really is nothing more to say.

And the often-quoted example of Aspirin is pure nonsense: true, a few decades ago, we did not know **how** it worked. But we always knew **that** it worked, because we conducted clinical trials that proved it. Their positive findings were the main reasons why scientists wanted to find out **how** it works, and eventually they did (John Vane even got a Nobel Prize for it).[2] Had the clinical trials of Aspirin not shown its effectiveness, nobody would have been interested in alleged mechanisms of action.

With EH, things are fundamentally different. Rigorous clinical trials of EH have been conducted, and the totality of this evidence fails to show that EH works. Therefore, chasing after a mechanism of action would be silly and wasteful. Yes, science cannot explain EH, but this is not because it is not yet sophisticated enough; it is because there is nothing to explain. EH has been disproven.

And what if EH stood for a therapy that has never been submitted to clinical trials? There is not a single rigorous clinical trial of crystal healing (CH), for instance. Does that mean CH-proponents are correct when claiming that CH does evidently work, and science simply cannot yet understand how?

No, like most of the untested alternative therapies, CH is not based on plausible assumptions. In fact, the implausibility of the underlying assumptions is the reason why such treatments have not been (and probably never will be) submitted to rigorous clinical trials. Why should anyone waste his time and our money running expensive tests on something that flies in the face of science and common sense? Arguably doing so would even be unethical.

With highly implausible therapies, like CH, we need no trials, and we do not need to fear that science is not yet sufficiently advanced to explain them. In fact, science is sufficiently advanced to affirm that there can be no explanation that is in line with the known laws of nature.

It is predictable that some fans of CH will not be satisfied with these arguments. They might respond to them by claiming that we need a 'paradigm shift'. They might insist that science cannot explain CH because it is stuck in the straight-jacket of an obsolete paradigm which does not cater for phenomena like CH. However, this last and desperate attempt makes no sense either. Paradigm shifts are not required because some deluded outsiders think so. They are needed, if data have been accumulating that cannot possibly be explained within the current paradigm. But this is clearly not the case in alternative medicine. We can explain all the experiences of CH-proponents, positive results of researchers and 'miracle' cures of

---

[2]https://en.wikipedia.org/wiki/John_Vane.

patients that are being reported. We know that their experiences are real, and we can be sure that their explanations of the experience are false. They are not due to the treatment per se but to other phenomena such as placebo effects, natural history, regression towards the mean, spontaneous recovery, etc.

So, whichever way we turn things, and whichever way enthusiasts of alternative therapies twist them, the argument that 'science cannot explain how my treatment works' is simply wrong.

6.3   Independent Replication

As we shall see in part 2 of this book, for many alternative therapies, there are several clinical trials testing their effectiveness. In the case of homeopathy, for instance, about 500 such studies exist. It is therefore not true to claim that no evidence exists. And, contrary to what sceptics regularly claim, some of them seem rigorous and do show positive results.

How is that possible? How can a rigorous trial of a homeopathic remedy that is too highly diluted to contain a single active molecule yield a positive result? As far as I can see, there are several possibilities:

1. Homeopathy does work after all, and we have not fully understood the laws of physics, chemistry etc. Most rational thinkers would discard this possibility outright. It is not that we don't quite understand homeopathy's mechanism; the fact is that we understand that there cannot be a mechanism that is in line with the laws of nature.
2. The trial in question only seems rigorous but, in fact, it is the victim of some undetected error or bias.
3. The result is due to chance. Of 500 trials, 25 would produce a positive result at the 5% probability level purely by chance.
4. The research is fraudulent.

By critically assessing a published trial, we are essentially attempting to determine which of these possibilities apply. But, of course, we usually rely on what the authors of the trial have put on paper. Published articles hardly ever provide all the details needed for this purpose, and we are often left speculating which of the explanations might apply. Scientists usually assume the result is false-positive due to the last three of the four possibilities listed above.

Naturally, this assumption is hard to accept for homeopaths; they merely conclude that scientists are biased against homeopathy and claim that, however rigorous a study of homeopathy might be, sceptics will not accept a positive result. And so, the debate continues without ever making progress (in the case of homeopathy, it has now raged for 200 years!).

Yet, there might be a way to settle the argument and arrive at a more objective verdict. We only need to remind ourselves of a crucially important principle in all science: independent replication. To be convincing, a scientific paper needs to provide evidence that the result are reproducible. In medicine, it is unquestionably wise to accept a finding only after it has been confirmed by independent researchers. Only if we have at least one (better several) independent replications, can we be reasonably sure that the result in question is true and not false-positive due to bias, chance, error or fraud.

An actual example might make this clearer. In a recent meta-analysis of trials of homeopathy, the authors found several studies that were both positive as well as rigorous.[3] These trials differ in many respects (e.g. remedies used, conditions treated) but they have one important feature in common: none has been independently replicated. Think of it: faced with a finding that, if true, would revolutionise much of medicine, scientists should jump with excitement. And yet, nobody seems to have taken the trouble to check whether these revolutionary findings are correct.

To explain this absurdity more fully, let us select just one of these positive and rigorous trials of homeopathy, one related to a common and serious condition: chronic obstructive pulmonary disease (COPD). The trial in question was published in 2005[4]—long enough ago for plenty of independent replications to emerge. Its results showed that "that potentized (diluted and vigorously shaken) potassium dichromate may help to decrease the amount of stringy tracheal secretions in COPD patients."[5]

If the authors are correct, their findings would improve the lives of thousands of seriously ill patients. So, why has this study not been replicated? A risk-free, cheap, universally available and easy to administer treatment for such a severe, often life-threatening condition would normally be picked up instantly. There should not be one, but dozens of independent replications by now. But instead there is a deafening silence.

Why? There is, I think, only logical explanation: independent replications were conducted but are not visible. Most likely, several researchers did try the treatment, found it does not work and soon dismissed it. Others might even have gone to the trouble of conducting a formal study and found the treatment to be ineffective. Subsequently they felt too embarrassed to submit it for publication—who would not laugh at them, if they said they studied a remedy that was diluted 1:100000000000000000000000000000000000000000000000000000000000000 and found it to be worthless? Others again might have written up their study and submitted it for publication but got rejected by reputable journals because the editors felt that comparing one placebo to another placebo amounts to pseudo-science.

Regardless of whether these speculations are correct or not, the undeniable truth is that there are no independent replications. Once a sufficiently long period of time has lapsed since the publication of such a paper and no replications of a 'sensational' finding have emerged, the finding becomes unbelievable—no rational

---

[3]Mathie et al. (2017).
[4]https://journal.chestnet.org/article/S0012-3692(15)31106-5/fulltext.
[5]https://en.wikipedia.org/wiki/John_Vane.

thinker can possibly believe such a result (I, for one, have not yet met an intensive care specialist who believes in the above-mentioned findings, for instance). Subsequently, the study in question is quietly dropped into the waste-basket of science where it no longer obstructs progress. In other words, the absence of independent replications is a most useful, effective and necessary 'self-cleansing' mechanism by which science rids itself of errors.

6.4   Alternative Medicine and Disease Prevention

Proponents of alternative medicine regularly claim that one strength of their approach is disease prevention and that conventional medicine neglects prevention almost completely. Both assumptions are demonstrably false.

During the 25 years of researching this subject, I have not seen any good evidence that a single alternative therapy might be effective in preventing any disease. Virtually everything we know today about disease prevention originates from conventional medicine and science. Thousands of rigorous research papers have been published that address prevention and, as far as I can see, they all come from the realm of conventional medicine. In support of this statement, here is a list of just 6 recent reviews on the subject.

- The first article is an update of the evidence for exercise as a prevention of heart failure. It concluded that "exercise provides protective benefit in preventing HF (primary prevention). With HF present: exercise improvement with training provides benefits in HF (secondary prevention). The prediction of future in HF patients: exercise impairment, as a leading characteristic of HF, is used as a prognostic factor."[6]
- The second is an update of the US Preventive Services Task Force on the benefits and harms of hormone therapy in reducing risks for chronic conditions. The authors found that "hormone therapy for the primary prevention of chronic conditions in menopausal women is associated with some beneficial effects but also with a substantial increase of risks for harms. The available evidence regarding benefits and harms of early initiation of hormone therapy is inconclusive."[7]
- The third article reviewed the evidence for Implantable Cardiac Defibrillators (ICDs). The authors stated that "individuals with stable ischemic heart disease (no recent myocardial infarction), especially those with inducible arrhythmias, seem to derive the highest mortality benefit from prophylactic ICD use."[8]
- The fourth investigated whether neuromuscular and proprioceptive training is effective in preventing knee and anterior cruciate ligament (ACL) injuries. Its

---

[6]Cattadori et al. (2018).

[7]Gartlehner et al. (2017).

[8]Sroubek and Buxton (2017).

authors concluded that "neuromuscular and proprioceptive training appeared to decrease the incidence of injury to the knee and specifically the ACL."[9]

- The fifth review summarized current evidence about real-world studies on apixaban for stroke prevention in atrial fibrillation. The authors concluded that "the use of apixaban in real-life is associated with an overall similar effectiveness in reducing stroke and any thromboembolic events when compared with warfarin. A better safety profile was found with apixaban compared with warfarin, dabigatran, and rivaroxaban."[10]

- Finally, the sixth article assessed the evidence of blood pressure (BP) lowering treatments as a means of reducing cardiovascular morbidity and mortality. The authors concluded that "primary preventive BP lowering is associated with reduced risk for death and CVD if baseline SBP is 140 mm Hg or higher. At lower BP levels, treatment is not associated with any benefit in primary prevention but might offer additional protection in patients with CHD."[11]

It follows that the often-voiced claim, that alternative medicine is strong on prevention, is quite simply not true. Proponents of alternative medicine like to talk about prevention (presumably because it is good for business), but when it comes to testing whether their interventions are effective preventative measures, all this talk turns out to be little more than wishful thinking. Even some of the most ardent proponents of integrative medicine admit that "by and large, the effectiveness of integrative approaches in health promotion or disease prevention is not fully elucidated; data derived from direct tests of integrative care models are promising but preliminary."[12]

6.5 Integrative Medicine

The Americans call it 'INTEGRATIVE MEDICINE', while, in the UK, we speak of 'INTEGRATED MEDICINE'. These terms sound convincing, authoritative and politically correct. INTEGRATIVE MEDICINE is said to be about 'the best of both worlds', but what is it really?

The BRITISH SOCIETY OF INTEGRATED MEDICINE defines it as follows: "Integrated Medicine is an approach to health and healing that provides patients with individually tailored health and wellbeing programmes which are designed to address the barriers to healing and provide the patient with the knowledge, skills and support to take better care of their physical, emotional, psychological and spiritual health. Rather than limiting treatments to a specific specialty, integrated medicine uses the safest and most effective combination of approaches and

---

[9]Dargo et al. (2017).

[10]Proietti et al. (2018).

[11]Brunström and Carlberg (2018).

[12]Ali and Katz (2015).

treatments from the world of conventional and complementary/alternative medicine. These are selected according to, but not limited to, evidence-based practice, and the expertise, experience and insight of the individuals and team members caring for the patient."[13]

Several things seem remarkable here. If the selected treatments are not limited to evidence, expertise, experience or insight, what are they based on? As we read on, we discover that, in integrated medicine, there are beliefs. To be precise, a total of 7 beliefs[14] hold that healthcare:

1. "Is individualised to the person—in that it takes into account their needs, insights, beliefs, past experiences, preferences, and life circumstances."
2. "Empowers the individual to take an active role in their own healing by providing them with the knowledge and skills to meet their physical and emotional needs and actively manage their own health."
3. "Attempts to identify and address the main barriers or blockages to a person experiencing their health and life goals. This includes physical, emotional, psychological, environmental, social and spiritual factors."
4. "Uses the safest, most effective and least invasive procedures wherever possible."
5. "Harnesses the power of compassion, respect and the therapeutic relationship."
6. "Focuses predominantly on health promotion, disease prevention and patient empowerment."
7. "Encourages healthcare practitioners to become the model of healthy living that they teach to others."

After reading this, one has good reasons to be confused:

1. All good medicine has always been 'individualised to the person', etc.
2. Patient empowerment is a key element in conventional medicine.
3. Holism is at the heart of any good health care.
4. Is there a form of medicine that focusses on unsafe, ineffective, unnecessarily invasive procedures?
5. Is there a type of healthcare that deliberately neglects compassion or disrespects the therapeutic relationship?
6. Disease prevention is a thing conventional medicine takes very seriously (see above).
7. Teaching by example is something that we all know is important (but some of us find it harder than others; see below).

Could it be that these 7 'beliefs' have been 'borrowed' from the mainstream? If so, what precisely is being integrated in integrated medicine? Proponents of integrated medicine claim it is about 'the best of both worlds', but is this true?

---

[13]http://www.bsim.org.uk/.
[14]Ali and Katz (2015).

To find out, I analysed all the presentations of the '3rd European Congress of Integrated Medicine' which took place in December 2010 in Berlin.[15] For this purpose, I read all the 222 abstracts and classified them according to their contents. The results showed that almost all the contributions were on unproven alternative therapies.

The abstracts from the International Congress on Integrative Medicine (ICIMH, Las Vegas, 2016) provided the opportunity to test whether this situation had changed.[16] There were around 400 abstracts which I analysed as before. Here are the results: mind-body therapies were the top subject with 49 papers, followed by acupuncture (44), herbal medicine (37), integrative medicine (36), chiropractic and other manual therapies (26), TCM (19), methodological issues (16), animal and other pre-clinical investigations (15) and Tai Chi (5). Thirty-six articles focussed specifically on integrative medicine. Most of these papers were about using alternative therapies as an add-on to conventional care. They focussed on the alternative therapies used and concluded that their 'integration' was followed by good results. None of these papers discussed integrative medicine and its assumptions critically, and none of these investigations cast any doubt on the assumption that integrative medicine is a positive thing.

Essentially, these two analyses published 6 years apart showed the same phenomenon: on the 'scientific level', integrated medicine is not about the 'best of both worlds'. It is almost exclusively about alternative therapies which, although their evidence-base is doubtful, advocates of integrated medicine aim to smuggle into the mainstream of healthcare.

And what about the routine practice of integrated medicine? If we search the Internet for clinics of integrative or integrated medicine, we find that, under this banner, every dubious treatment under the sun is being promoted at often exorbitant prices to the unsuspecting public. Integrated medicine therefore turns out to be a movement aimed at giving credibility to the use of unproven or disproven therapies in routine care. As such, it cannot be in the interest of anyone except those who are trying to make a living from selling quackery to the unsuspecting public.

6.6   Alternative Treatments for Children

Treating children with alternative medicine is more problematic than using it for adults. Firstly, children might not respond like adults. Consequently, the evidence from clinical trials with adults may not be transferable to children. Secondly, young children are not able to give informed consent (see previous chapter). Thirdly, most alternative practitioners lack the knowledge and training for treating children.

---

[15]Ernst (2012).
[16]Klatt et al. (2016).

Despite these problems, many alternative practitioners pride themselves of being particularly good at caring for children.

Two recent Canadian surveys, conducted in 2004 and 2014, assessed chiropractors' (DC) and naturopaths' (ND) knowledge, attitudes, and behaviour with respect to the paediatric patients.[17] Its results showed that, in 2014, 78% of DCs and 61% of NDs treared one or more paediatric patients per week. About half of DCs and one fifth of NDs reported they had received no hands-on clinical paediatric training. Yet, both DCs and NDs admitted treating even serious paediatric health concerns. The authors of this paper included two 'case studies' of conditions frequently treated by DCs and NDs:

Case study 1: Colic

"DC practitioners' primary treatment focus (314 respondents) would be to use spinal manipulation (78.3%) if physical assessment suggests utility, diet changes (14.6% for child, 6.1% for mom if breast feeding), and massage (16.9%). ND practitioners (95 respondents) would assess and treat primarily with diet changes (62% for child including prescribing probiotics; 48% for mom if breast feeding), homeopathy (46%), weak herbal or tea preparations (19%), and use topical castor oil (packs or massage) (18%). In 2014, 65.9% of DCs and 59% of NDs believe (somewhat or very much) that concurrent treatment by a medical practitioner would be of benefit; 64.0% of DCs and 60% of NDs would refer the patient to another health care practitioner (practitioner type not specified)."

Case study 2: Acute otitis media

"In 2014, almost all practitioners identified this as otitis media (in 2004, the DCs had a profession-specific question); DCs were more cautious about the value of their care for it relative to the NDs (DCs, 46.2% care will help patient very much, NDs, 95%). For treatment, DCs would primarily use spinal manipulation (98.5%) if indicated after assessment, massage (19.5%), dietary modifications (17.6%), and 3.8% would specifically refer to an MD for an antibiotic prescription. ND-preferred treatments were NHP products (79%), dietary modifications (66%), ear drops (60%), homeopathic remedies (18%), and 10% would prescribe antibiotics right away or after a few days. In 2014, 86.3% of DCs and 75% of NDs believe the patient would benefit (somewhat or very much) from concurrent treatment by a conventional medical practitioner; 81.7% of DCs and 58% of NDs would refer the patient to another health care provider."

The authors of this paper concluded that "the majority of responding DCs and NDs see infants, children, and youth for a variety of health conditions and issues, but self-assess their undergraduate paediatric training as inadequate. We encourage augmented paediatric educational content be included as core curriculum for DCs and NDs and suggest collaboration with institutions/organizations with expertise in

---

[17]Porcino et al. (2017).

paediatric education to facilitate curriculum development, especially in areas that affect patient safety."[18]

Even though alternative practitioners are not adequately educated or trained to treat children, they often do so. Moreover, their therapeutic repertoire is inadequate for treating seriously sick children effectively and responsibly. Only very few paediatric conditions are effectively treatable with alternative therapies. To these concerns, we must add that many alternative practitioners advise against immunising children.[19] Harm to children and to society at large is thus almost inevitable.

6.7 How to Advise Consumers

Many patients and consumers seek advice on alternative medicine from their doctor, nurse, pharmacist, midwife etc. Yet, conventional healthcare professionals are often ill-prepared to deal with the current boom in alternative medicine and thus uncertain about advising them. How should they react? What can patients expect?

Consider a scenario where a patient asks her doctor: "What about therapy xy for my condition? My friend suffers from the same problem as I, and she says the treatment works very well." There are essentially four options for providing advice:

A. Uncompromisingly negative

For conventional healthcare providers, it can be tempting to be wholly dismissive and simply state that all alternative medicine is nonsense. If it were any good, it would have been adopted by conventional medicine. Therefore, alternative medicine is never an alternative.

Even if all of this were true—in part 2 of this book we shall see that it is not—the uncompromisingly negative approach is not helpful. Patients deserve more understanding of their position. If their doctor offends them, they simply go elsewhere. Not only would the doctor then lose a patient, but he would run a high risk of exposing his patient to a practitioner who promotes quackery. The dismissive approach helps nobody.

B. Evidence-based

The doctor might consider their patient's question and reply to it by explaining what the current best evidence tells us about the therapy in question. This can be done with empathy and compassion. For instance, he might explain that the treatment in question lacks a scientific basis, that it has been tested in clinical trials which failed to show that it works. The doctor should then explain what effective treatments do exist and discuss a reasonable treatment plan with his patient.

---

[18]http://www.bsim.org.uk/.

[19]Schmidt and Ernst (2003).

The problem with this approach is that most conventional doctors are clueless about the evidence relating to the plethora of alternative therapies. Therefore, an honest discussion around the current best evidence is often not possible. (This, by the way, is one reason why this book, even though primarily written for lay people, might be a valuable text also for conventional healthcare professionals.)

C. Open-minded

Today, many doctors seem to employ this is the approach as a default position. They basically tell their patient that there is not a lot of evidence for the treatment in question. However, it seems harmless enough, and therefore—if the patient is keen on it—why not? This type of response is often given regardless of the therapy in question and ignores the evidence—as we will see in part 2 of this book, some alternative treatments do work, some don't, some are safe, some aren't.

Condoning alternative medicine in this way gives the impression of being 'open-minded' and 'patient-centred'. It has the considerable advantage that it does not require any hard work, such as informing oneself about the current best evidence. Its disadvantage is that it neither correct, nor professional, nor ethical.

D. Uncritically promotional

Some doctors go even one decisive step further. Under the banner of 'integrated medicine' (see above), they openly recommend using 'the best of both worlds' as being 'holistic', 'empathetic', 'patient-centred', etc. By this, they usually mean employing as many unproven or disproven treatments as alternative medicine has to offer.

This approach might give the impression of being 'modern' and 'in tune' with the wishes of patients. Its disadvantages are, however, obvious. Introducing bogus treatments into clinical routine can only render it less effective, more expensive, and less safe. It is not in the best interest of patients and arguably unethical.

The conclusion is, I think, clear: professional advice must be responsible. To be responsible, it has to be based on reliable evidence. The following part of this book is all about the evidence for or against 150 different alternative therapies and diagnostic methods.

References

Ali A, Katz DL (2015) Disease prevention and health promotion how integrative medicine fits. Am J Prev Med 49(5):S230–S240

Brunström M, Carlberg B (2018) Association of blood pressure lowering with mortality and cardiovascular disease across blood pressure levels: a systematic review and meta-analysis. JAMA Intern Med 178(1):28–36

Cattadori G, Segurini C, Picozzi A, Padaletti L, Anzà C (2018) Exercise and heart failure: an update. ESC Heart Fail 5(2):222–232

Dargo L, Robinson KJ, Games KE (2017) Prevention of knee and anterior cruciate ligament injuries through the use of neuromuscular and proprioceptive training: an evidence-based review. J Athl Train 52(12):1171–1172

Ernst E (2012) Integrated medicine. J Intern Med 271(1):25–28

Gartlehner G, Patel SV, Feltner C, Weber RP, Long R, Mullican K, Boland E, Lux L, Viswanathan M (2017) Hormone therapy for the primary prevention of chronic conditions in postmenopausal women: evidence report and systematic review for the US preventive services task force. JAMA 318(22):2234–2249

Klatt M, Huerta T, Gascon G, Sieck C, Malarkey W (2016) The international congress on integrative medicine and health (ICIMH). J Altern Complement Med 22(6):A1–A142

Mathie RT, Ramparsad N, Legg LA, Clausen J, Moss S, Davidson JR, Messow CM, McConnachie A (2017) Randomised, double-blind, placebo-controlled trials of non-individualised homeopathic treatment: systematic review and meta-analysis. Syst Rev. 6 (1):63

Porcino A, Solomonian L, Zylich S, Gluvic B, Doucet C, Vohra S (2017) Pediatric training and practice of Canadian chiropractic and naturopathic doctors: a 2004–2014 comparative study. BMC Complement Altern Med 17:512

Proietti M, Romanazzi I, Romiti GF, Farcomeni A, Lip GYH (2018) Real-world use of apixaban for stroke prevention in atrial fibrillation: a systematic review and meta-analysis. Stroke 49 (1):98–106

Schmidt K, Ernst E (2003) MMR vaccination advice over the Internet. Vaccine 21(11–12):1044–1047

Sroubek J, Buxton AE (2017) Primary prevention implantable cardiac defibrillator trials: what have we learned? Card Electrophysiol Clin 9(4):761–773

Chapter 7
Diagnostic Techniques

7.1 Applied Kinesiology

(related modalities: chiropractic, Vega test)

Applied kinesiology is a method employed for diagnosing diseases and for identifying possible alternative treatments. Its proponents claim to pick up subtle signals via manual muscle testing reflecting the body's energetic balance.

1. Applied kinesiology was developed in 1964 by George J. Goodheart, Jr. (1918–2008), a US chiropractor. Today it has become a popular around the world.
2. The underlying assumption is that, by manually assessing a person's relative muscular weakness, an answer as to the question whether a given remedy is therapeutic for that individual can be obtained. The assumptions upon which applied kinesiology are based are out of line with our present understanding of how our bodies function; in other words, they lack plausibility.
3. Most practitioners using applied kinesiology are chiropractors, but some naturopaths, medical doctors, dentists, nutritionists, physiotherapists, massage therapists, nurses and other clinicians also employ the method.
4. The range of conditions claimed to be diagnosable with applied kinesiology is virtually limitless.
5. Therapists who diagnose by means of applied kinesiology would subsequently employ variety of treatments, such as joint manipulations or mobilizations, myofascial therapies, cranial techniques, acupuncture, clinical nutrition and dietary management, counselling, detox, reflexology and homeopathy.
6. Several scientific tests of applied kinesiology have been published, but most of them are of poor quality and therefore not reliable. The only systematic review on this subject (published by known proponents of alternative medicine,) included 22 original studies and concluded that "there is insufficient evidence

© Springer Nature Switzerland AG 2019
E. Ernst, *Alternative Medicine*,
https://doi.org/10.1007/978-3-030-12601-8_7

for diagnostic accuracy within kinesiology, the validity of muscle response and the effectiveness of kinesiology for any condition."[1]

7. Even though applied kinesiology itself is unlikely to cause harm (other than to the patient's bank balance), it is likely to lead to false-positive and false-negative diagnoses. This would obviously be harmful and, in extreme cases, could even cost a patient's life.

Plausibility	
Efficacy	
Safety	
Cost	
Risk/benefit balance	

7.2 Dowsing

(related modalities: bioresonance)

Dowsing is a common but unproven method for divining water and other materials. In alternative medicine, it is sometimes used as a technique for diagnosing diseases or the causes of health problems.

1. Dowsers employ a motor automatism, amplified through a pendulum, divining rod or similar device. The effect is that the device seemingly provides an independent, visible reaction, while the dowser is, in fact, its true cause.
2. Dowsing is used by some homeopaths as an aid to prescribe the optimal remedy and as a tool for identify a miasm or toxin load.
3. The assumptions upon which dowsing is based lack plausibility.
4. Dowsing has not often been submitted to clinical trials.
5. All rigorous attempts to test water dowsing have failed, and it is no longer considered a viable method for this purpose.
6. The only randomized double-blind trial that has tested whether homeopaths are able to distinguish between a homeopathic remedy and placebo by dowsing

---

[1]Hall et al. (2008).

failed to show that it is a valid method. Its authors (well-known homeopaths) drew the following conclusion: "These results, wholly negative, add to doubts whether dowsing in this context can yield objective information."[2]

7. If dowsing is employed for differentiating between truly effective treatments (rather than homeopathic remedies), the risk of false choices would be intolerably high, and serious harm would inevitably be the result.

Plausibility	👎
Efficacy	👎
Safety	👎
Cost	👍
Risk/benefit balance	👎

7.3 Hair Analysis

(related modalities: none)

Hair analysis is used in conventional medicine typically to estimate a person's long-term exposure to toxins.[3] In alternative medicine, it is sometimes employed for diagnosing other conditions. Table below refers to the alternative use of hair analysis.

1. Hair analysis uses a sample of hair for a chemical analysis of its content. As hair grows slowly, such an analysis would provide information about exposures of past weeks or months.
2. Proponents of alternative hair analysis claim that they can identify nutritional deficiencies, autism and other diseases with this method.
3. An investigation into hair analysis found that the detection of "aluminium in hair is of no value in environmental medicine. For assessment of cadmium and inorganic arsenic exposure hair analysis is only suitable as a screening method based on large populations. Monitoring of lead in hair is a valuable screening

---

[2]McCarney et al. (2002).

[3]Joksić and Katz (2014).

method also for small groups, especially for children. Based on toxicokinetics and under consideration of practicability the optimal biomarker of methylmercury exposure is the hair concentration. For other mercury compounds hair analysis is of lower significance. Nicotine and cotinine measurements in hair provide a practical and proper method for estimating environmental tobacco smoke exposure and to validate smoker status in epidemiological studies."[4]

4. A systematic review of 66 studies concluded that "the profile of hair mineral imbalance might be useful as a diagnostic tool for the early diagnosis of many diseases. However, it seems that there is a need to standardize sample preparation procedures, in particular washing and mineralization methods."[5]

5. However, another systematic review disclosed a lack of standardisation and concluded that "it is necessary to elaborate the standard procedures and furtherly validate hair mineral analysis and deliver detailed methodology. Only then it would be possible to provide meaningful reference ranges and take advantage of the potential that lies in Hair Mineral Analysis as a medical diagnostic technique."[6]

6. An investigation into the reliably of 7 different laboratories offering hair analysis found that "hair mineral analysis from these laboratories is unreliable. Therefore, we must recommend to refrain from using such analysis to assess individual nutritional status or suspected environmental exposure."[7] Several further tests have arrived at similar conclusions which means that alternative hair analysis lacks reliability.

7. Hair analysis as used in alternative medicine is prone to false-positive and false-negative diagnoses both of which can cause considerable harm.

Plausibility	👎
Efficacy	👎
Safety	👎
Cost	👎
Risk/benefit balance	👎

[4]Wilhelm and Idel (1996).
[5]Wołowiec et al. (2013).
[6]Mikulewicz et al. (2013).
[7]Drasch and Roider (2002).

7.4   Iridology

(related modalities: none)

Iridology is a diagnostic method based on the belief that pigmentations on specific spots of the iris of patients provide diagnostic clues as to the health of their organs.

1. Iridology was invented by a Hungarian homeopath in the late 19th century who thought to observe changes in the iris of an owl after the animal had broken a leg.
2. Iridologists believe that the iris is a 'mirror of our body'. Any relevant abnormality on the right half of the body will reveal itself on the right iris and problems on the left side will show up on the left iris.
3. They assume that the iris is linked via multiple nerve connections to all organs and believe that any bodily malfunction will thus be represented as abnormalities of pigmentation on the iris.
4. These assumptions are not in keeping with basic anatomy or physiology and thus lack plausibility.
5. Iridologists have produced detailed maps of the iris where each iris is divided in 60 sectors (much like the face of a clock) and each segment is related to an inner organ or bodily function (for instance, heart diseases are thus seen in the left iris somewhere between two and three o'clock). Iridologists either study the iris in situ or they produce high-quality colour photographs of both irides for detailed inspection.
6. Several studies have tested the validity of iridology. A systematic review of these data concluded that "the validity of iridology as a diagnostic tool is not supported by scientific evaluations. Patients and therapists should be discouraged from using this method."[8]
7. Ophthalmologists have repeatedly warned not to use iridology because can cause considerable harm through false-positive or false-negative diagnoses.[9] A false-positive diagnosis would mean that a patient is diagnosed with a condition that she does not have. This would cause unnecessary anxiety and expense. A false-negative diagnosis would mean that a patient is given a clear bill of health, while in truth she is affected by a disease. This would mean she loses valuable time to get an effective therapy; in the worst-case scenario, this could hasten her death.

---

[8]Ernst (1999).

[9]https://www.aerzteblatt.de/nachrichten/97971/Augenaerzte-warnen-vor-sogenannter-Irisdiagnostik.

Plausibility	👎
Efficacy	👎
Safety	👎
Cost	👎
Risk/benefit balance	👎

7.5 Kirlian Photography

(related modalities: radionics)

Kirlian photography is used in alternative medicine as a diagnostic tool. It is a method for photographing patients 'aura' developed by the Russian Semyon Davidovich Kirlian (1898–1978).

1. While observing a demonstration of a high-frequency electrotherapy device, Kirlian noticed that there was a small flash of light between the machine's electrodes and the patient's skin. Subsequently, he wondered, if he could photograph this phenomenon.
2. After experimenting with similar devices, he was able to take a photograph of an apparent energy discharge of his own hand.
3. Together with his wife, he perfected the method using a high-frequency oscillator or spark generator that operated at 75–200 kHz. The resulting pictures were often of fascinating beauty and captured the interest of many scientists and lay-people alike.
4. In 1949, the Kirlians received a patent on their device under the title "a method of photographing by means of high-frequency currents."
5. Kirlian then started claiming that his photographs were pictures of a human aura and that they provided an indication of health and disease.[10] Kirlian proposed, for instance, his photographs were a physical proof of the life force or aura surrounding all living beings. This claim was said to be supported by experiments by the Kirlians that involved cutting part of a leaf off—the Kirlian images of such leaves, it was said, still showed the leaves as whole, as though the

---

[10]Treugut et al. (2000).

cutting had never happened. During the 1960s, Kirlian photography became fashionable in the West and part of the New Age counter-culture.

6. The assumptions that Kirlian photography are more than simple electrical discharges lack plausibility.[11]

7. Several studies of Kirlian photography have been published. Most lack enough scientific rigour to be meaningful. The totality of this evidence provides no sound evidence that Kirlian photography is of any use in diagnosing human health. One review, for instance, concluded that the data "currently offer insufficient reliable research evidence concerning their use as diagnostic or imaging alternatives."[12] Because it is not a reliable diagnostic method, Kirlian photography risks false-positive and false-negative diagnoses, both of which can cause considerable harm.

Plausibility	👎
Efficacy	👎
Safety	👍
Cost	👍
Risk/benefit balance	👎

7.6   Live Blood Analysis

(related modalities: none)

Live blood analysis is a diagnostic method that has become popular with some alternative practitioners.

1. The technique involves the patient giving a small blood sample which is then placed under a dark field microscope. Subsequently, the patient can often see his blood cells magnified on a screen and is given all sorts of explanations for the phenomena observed.

2. To many lay people, this procedure appears to be 'high tech' and 'cutting edge' science.

---

[11]Stanwick (1996).

[12]Duerden (2004).

3. Alternative practitioners use the method to diagnose a wide range of conditions. Frequently, they then sell supplements and other therapies to remedy them.
4. Live blood analysis is based on the assumption that the visible phenomena of fresh blood (e.g. red cell aggregation) is indicative for specific diseases and specific treatments to cure them. This assumption is not plausible, and the reliability of the method has never been verified. The results of the only two studies suggest that the method is not reliable.[13,14]
5. Live blood analysis is thus likely to produce false-positive and false-negative diagnoses. A false-positive diagnosis is a condition which the patient does not have. This means she will receive treatments that are not necessary, potentially harmful and financially wasteful.
6. A false-negative diagnosis would mean that the patient is told she is healthy, while in fact she is not. This can cost valuable time to start an effective therapy and, in extreme cases, it can hasten the death of that patient.
7. Live blood analysis is not a reliable diagnostic method; in fact, it is little more than a tool to impress patients and take their money.

Plausibility	👎
Efficacy	👎
Safety	👎
Cost	👎
Risk/benefit balance	👎

7.7   Pulse Diagnosis

(related modalities: Ayurvedic medicine, tongue diagnosis, Traditional Chinese Medicine)

Pulse diagnosis is the technique used in Traditional Chinese Medicine (TCM) and several other Asian traditions to identify the cause of ill health by feeling the pulse of a patient.

---

[13]https://www.karger.com/Article/Abstract/85212.

[14]Teut et al. (2006).

1. Conventional clinicians feel the pulse to check the regularity and frequency of the heart-beat. This conventional form of pulse-taking is evidently useful and excluded from this discussion.
2. TCM practitioners aim to feel other qualities of the pulse and believe they provide information about a patient's state of health.
3. One proponent, for instance, claims that "Chinese Pulse Diagnosis is considered to be the most accurate way to detect patterns of ill health by reading subtle signs of distress within the body. The art of pulse diagnosis involves interpreting the flow of blood through the radial artery at the wrists. In the hands of an expert practitioner, the pulse can reveal many … common health concerns."[15]
4. In Ayurvedic medicine too, the examination of the pulse is used for identifying energy imbalances of prana, tejas, and ojas.
5. Pulse diagnosis first emerged in China at a time when there was little understanding as to how the human body functions; it is based on obsolete concepts and has no basis in human physiology. In other words, it is not plausible.
6. It is thus understandable that the validity of pulse diagnosis has not been submitted to extensive scientific tests. In one study, the reliability of pulse diagnosis was tested by letting several experienced clinicians diagnose the same patients and comparing their findings. The authors concluded that "the interobserver reliability in making a pulse diagnosis in stroke patients is not particularly high when objectively quantified. Additional research is needed to help reduce this lack of reliability for various portions of the pulse diagnosis."[16]
7. The risks of pulse diagnosis consist in arriving at false-positive and false-negative diagnoses and can therefore be considerable.

Plausibility	👎
Efficacy	👎
Safety	👎
Cost	👍
Risk/benefit balance	👎

---

[15]http://acupuncturewellness.net/treatments/pulse-diagnosis/.
[16]Ko et al. (2013).

7.8   Radionics

(related modalities: bioresonance, dowsing)

Radionics is an umbrella term for a range of techniques used in alternative medicine which are based on the idea that disease can be diagnosed and treated by using electromagnetic radiation.

1. The current fashion of radionics started in the early 1900s when Albert Abrams (1864–1924) became a millionaire by leasing his radionic machines to the public.
2. Today there are numerous devices that rely on radionics and are promoted to diagnose illness, prevent disease and treat various health conditions.
3. In addition, there is a range of radionic modalities that does not use any devices. Practitioners who employ dowsing rods or pendula, for instance, claim to have paranormal abilities to detect 'radiation' or 'aura' within a patient's body, a phenomenon which they call radiesthesia.
4. The underlying concept is that a healthy person supposedly has certain energy frequencies that define health. An unhealthy person is claimed to exhibit different energy frequencies than a healthy one. Thus, by comparing the two, it is assumed to be possible to arrive at more or less specific diagnoses.
5. By "balancing" their discordant frequencies practitioners furthermore claim to be able to restore health. One proponent, for instance, claims that "radionics is an energy healing technique in which our natural intuitive faculties are used both to discover the disturbances underlying illness and to encourage the return of a normal energetic field that supports health. It is independent of the distance between practitioner and patient. Radionics can be used to help humans and animals and in agriculture by means of electronic radionic instruments which amplify and 'broadcast' the healing signal to the subtle energy field of the patient."[17]
6. The principles of radionics are neither sound nor plausible, and the field of radionics has some of the hallmarks of a cult.
7. The numerous and often far-reaching health claims of radionics are not based on reliable scientific evidence. Virtually all the scientific tests that have been conducted have shown the claims of radionics proponents to be bogus.[18] Therefore the dangers of false-positive and false negative diagnoses or ineffective treatments of treatable conditions is undeniable.

---

[17]https://www.holistictherapypractice.com/online/9/Therapy-Services/Radionics.html.
[18]Chesney (2006).

Plausibility	👎
Efficacy	👎
Safety	👍
Cost	👎
Risk/benefit balance	👎

7.9   Tongue Diagnosis

(related modalities: pulse diagnosis, Traditional Chinese Medicine)

Tongue diagnosis is a method for identifying disease used in Traditional Chinese Medicine (TCM). It is fundamentally different from the diagnostic clues which conventional doctors might obtain from examining their patients' tongues.

1. Tongue diagnosis has a long history in China. It was developed at a time when our knowledge of physiology was still woefully incomplete.
2. TCM-practitioners look at the tongue of patients to evaluate its qualities such as colour, coating, shape, presence or absence of cracks.
3. They also use maps where specific areas of the tongue are supposed to correspond to specific organs of the body.
4. From this information, practitioners take diagnostic clues and guidance as to what the best therapy might be. One typical article by proponents of tongue diagnosis, for instance, claims that "the tongue has many relationships and connections in the body, both to the meridians and the internal organs. It is therefore very useful and important during inspection for confirming TCM diagnosis. It can present strong visual indicators of a person's overall harmony or disharmony. The tongue has a special relationship with the Heart, in that the Heart opens to the tongue. The tongue is said to be an "offshoot" of the Heart, or "flowers" into the Heart."[19]

---

[19]https://www.sacredlotus.com/go/diagnosis-chinese-medicine/get/tongue-diagnosis-chinese-medicine.

5. The assumptions underlying tongue diagnosis are not in line with our current knowledge of anatomy, physiology, pathophysiology etc. In other words, they are not plausible.
6. There is no good evidence that tongue diagnosis can reliably identify any disease or condition.[20,21,22]
7. Tongue diagnosis can cause considerable harm by producing false-positive or false-negative diagnoses. In the former case, patients would be diagnosed with a condition that they do not have and subsequently receive treatments that are needless. In the latter case, patients would be given the 'all clear', while in fact they are ill. Consequently, they would lose valuable time to get cured.

Plausibility	👎
Efficacy	👎
Safety	👎
Cost	👍
Risk/benefit balance	👎

7.10   Vega Test

(related modalities: Bioresonance, Traditional Chinese Medicine)

The Vega test (or electrodermal testing) involves an impressive-looking yet technically very simple electronic device used by some alternative practitioners for diagnosing diseases.

1. The Vega test is a development based on the electroacupuncture according to Voll. It was originally developed as an aid in prescribing homeopathic remedies. According to one proponent, "Vega Testing is a synthesis of age old Chinese medical knowledge and cutting-edge western technology."[23]

---

[20]Liu et al. (2003).

[21]Yue and Liu (2004).

[22]Wei et al. (2002).

[23]https://maureenfinck.com/vega-testing/.

2. Today, the Vega test is popular predominantly for diagnosing allergies. More than 500 devices are thought to be currently used in the UK alone.[24] A proponent argued that the method "achieves the greatest rate of diagnostic success in cases of functional disturbances."[25]

3. The Vega test is based on the assumption that changes in electrical impedance of the skin occur at the site of an acupuncture point in response to substances placed in an electrical circuit. The suggested mechanism of the Vega test has been summarised as "quantum biology" .[26]

4. The Vega test proponents' use of pseudoscientific language cannot hide the fact that it lacks plausibility.

5. The only rigorous test of the Vega machine available to date was published by proponents of this method. It concluded that it "cannot be used to diagnose environmental allergies."[27] A less formal assessment was performed by the BBC in 2003 and showed that the results obtained with the Vega test lacked reliability.[28]

6. Several medical associations have advised against using the Vega test, including the National Institute for Health and Clinical Excellence, the Australian College of Allergy, the Australasian Society of Clinical Immunology and Allergy, the American Academy of Allergy, Asthma and Immunology and the Allergy Society of South Africa.

7. The risks of the Vega test consist in arriving at false-positive and false-negative diagnoses both of which can cause considerable harm to the patient in question.

Plausibility	👎
Efficacy	👎
Safety	👎
Cost	👎
Risk/benefit balance	👎

---

[24]Lewith et al. (2001).

[25]http://www.naturaltherapycenter.com/vega-testing/.

[26]Hall et al. (2008).

[27]Hall et al. (2008).

[28]http://www.bbc.co.uk/insideout/south/series2/food_sensitivity_allergy_vega_tests.shtml.

References

Chesney CJ (2006) Radionics and repeatability. Vet Rec 158(24):839–840

Drasch G, Roider G (2002) Assessment of hair mineral analysis commercially offered in Germany. J Trace Elem Med Biol 16(1):27–31

Duerden T (2004) An aura of confusion Part 2: the aided eye–"imaging the aura?". Complement Ther Nurs Midwifery 10(2):116–123

Ernst E (1999) Iridology: a systematic review. Forsch Komplementarmed 6(1):7–9

Hall S, Lewith G, Brien S, Little P (2008) A review of the literature in applied and specialised kinesiology. Forsch Komplementmed 15(1):40–46

Joksić AŠ, Katz SA (2014) Efficacy of hair analysis for monitoring exposure to uranium: a mini-review. J Environ Sci Health A Tox Hazard Subst Environ Eng 49(13):1578–1587

Ko MM, Park TY, Lee JA, Choi TY, Kang BK, Lee MS (2013) Interobserver reliability of pulse diagnosis using traditional Korean medicine for stroke patients. J Altern Complement Med 19 (1):29–34

Lewith GT, Kenyon JN, Broomfield J, Prescott P, Goddard J, Holgate ST (2001) Is electrodermal testing as effective as skin prick tests for diagnosing allergies? A double blind, randomised block design study. BMJ 322(7279):131–134

Liu Q, Yue XQ, Ling CQ (2003) Researches into the modernization of tongue diagnosis: in retrospect and prospect. Zhong Xi Yi Jie He Xue Bao 1(1):66–70

McCarney R, Fisher P, Spink F, Flint G, van Haselen R (2002) Can homeopaths detect homeopathic medicines by dowsing? A randomized, double-blind, placebo-controlled trial. J R Soc Med 95(4):189–191

Mikulewicz M, Chojnacka K, Gedrange T, Górecki H (2013) Reference values of elements in human hair: a systematic review. Environ Toxicol Pharmacol 36(3):1077–1086

Stanwick M (1996) Aura photography: mundane physics or diagnostic tool? Nurs Times 92 (25):39–41

Teut M, Lüdtke R, Warning A (2006) Reliability of Enderlein's darkfield analysis of live blood. Altern Ther Health Med 12(4):36–41

Treugut H, Köppen M, Nickolay B, Füss R, Schmid P (2000) Kirlian photography: accidental or person-specific pattern? Forsch Komplementarmed Klass Naturheilkd 7(1):12–16

Wei BG, Shen LS, Wang YQ, Wang YG, Wang AM, Zhao ZX (2002) A digital tongue image analysis instrument for traditional Chinese medicine. Zhongguo Yi Liao Qi Xie Za Zhi, 26 (3):164–166, 169

Wilhelm M, Idel H (1996) Hair analysis in environmental medicine. Zentralbl Hyg Umweltmed 198(6):485–501

Wołowiec P, Michalak I, Chojnacka K, Mikulewicz M (2013) Hair analysis in health assessment. Clin Chim Acta 419:139–171

Yue XQ, Liu Q (2004) Analysis of studies on pattern recognition of tongue image in traditional Chinese medicine by computer technology. Zhong Xi Yi Jie He Xue Bao 2(5):326–329

Chapter 8
Medicines and Oral Treatments

8.1 Agrohomeopathy

(related modalities: homeopathy, homotoxicology)

Agrohomeopathy is the use of homeopathic remedies and homeopathic princi-ples in the treatment of diseases of plants.

1. Agrohomeopathy seems to be popular, particularly in India and Italy, where there even is a 'Laboratory of Agrohomeopathy'. Dozens of books are available on the subject.
2. Proponents of agrohomeopathy claim that it is an effective, chemical free, non-toxic method of growing plants. They even organise international confer-ences of the subject.
3. Proponents believe that agrohomeopathy renders plants resistant to disease by strengthening them 'from the inside out'.
4. Agrohomeopathy, they say, can even treat a trauma retained in the 'biological memory' of the plant resulting from conditions such as forced hybridization, moving to places outside their natural habitats, or exaggerated fertilization.
5. There is no evidence that any of these assumptions are correct. Plant models are sometimes used by homeopaths for investigating basic research questions relating to homeopathic preparations,[1] but there are no reliable trials of home-opathy as a treatment of diseases of plants. The many books on agrohomeopathy are largely devoid of scientific evidence.
6. There is no rational basis for agrohomeopathy. Samuel Hahnemann, the founder of homeopathy, made no recommendations for treating plants with homeopathic remedies.
7. Agrohomeopathy can cause harm in at least two different ways. Firstly, it costs money and therefore is harmful to consumers' bank balance. Secondly, if people

---

[1]Jäger et al. (2015).

© Springer Nature Switzerland AG 2019
E. Ernst, *Alternative Medicine*,
https://doi.org/10.1007/978-3-030-12601-8_8

treat diseases of plants with homeopathy instead of using effective agents, the diseases will spread unhindered.

Plausibility	👎
Efficacy	👎
Safety	👍
Cost	👎
Risk/benefit balance	👎

8.2   Alkaline Diet

(related modalities: none)

There are many dietary fads, too many to discuss them all in this book. They are usually promoted by VIPs who claim to have lost weight or healed an illness by using them. These diets have in common that they are not supported by good evidence. The 'Alkaline Diet' is no exception; it is based on the assumption that some foods make our body acid which is said to be bad for our general health and the cause of a range of diseases.

1. Acidity is quantified by a measure called 'pH' which ranges from 0 to 14. A pH of 0 is totally acid, and 14 is completely alkaline. The acidity of our body varies by location; the stomach, for instance, must be quite acid to function adequately, while the pH of our blood is neutral and tightly regulated by extremely powerful mechanisms keeping it in the narrow range between 7.35 and 7.40.
2. Food has therefore hardly any influence on the acidity of the blood of a healthy individual.
3. If a patient's blood pH would ever go outside the range of 7.35 and 7.45, she would be seriously ill and require intensive care to save her life.
4. Proponents of the Alkaline diet claim that the bodies of many people is too acid. This claim is demonstrably false.
5. They also assume that certain foods, like dairy products or meat, render our bodies acid. This is notion also not true.

6. They furthermore claim that other foods, like fruits, vegetables, tofu and nuts make our bodies more alkaline. This is false too.
7. The Alkaline diet allegedly has powerful effects on our health and can treat or prevent a range of conditions. There is no good evidence for these assumptions to be correct.[2,3] The Alkaline diet is at best useless, at worse it can even cause harm through malnutrition.

Plausibility	👎
Efficacy	👎
Safety	👎
Cost	👎
Risk/benefit balance	👎

8.3 Aloe Vera

(related modalities: none)

Aloe vera is a plant that belongs to the *Liliaceae* family. It is amongst the most popular herbal remedies and is being promoted for a wide range of conditions. Therefore it is one of the few herbal remedies with a dedicated chapter in this book.

1. There are many aloe species; for medicinal purposes, *Aloe barbadensis* is the most commonly used.
2. The name Aloe derives from the Arabic word "Alloeh" which means shining bitter substance while "vera" is Latin and means true.
3. Aloe vera contains more than 200 different pharmacologically active substances, including minerals and vitamins, various polysaccharides and phenolic chemicals, notably anthraquinones.[4] They are said to have immunomodulatory, anti-viral, anti-bacterial, anti-inflammatory, anti-tumour, anti-arthritic, anti-cancer, anti-diabetic and wound-healing properties.

---

[2]Schwalfenberg (2012).
[3]Fenton and Fenton (2016).
[4]Radha and Laxmipriya (2014).

4. There are two fundamentally different types of Aloe vera preparations. Aloe vera gel is used topically and is made of mucillaginous centre of the plant's leaf. Aloe vera pills are used orally and are made from the plant's peripheral bundle sheath cells.

5. Ingestion of Aloe vera preparations has been associated with diarrhoea, hypokalaemia, kidney failure, phototoxicity, allergic reactions and hepatitis. Aloe vera whole leaf extract also has carcinogenic activity in rats.[5]

6. Aloe vera have been traditionally used for an extremely wide range of conditions. For most of them, there is no good evidence. For some conditions, aloe vera preparations have been tested in several clinical trials. These are often of poor-quality and produced contradictory results. Authorative reviews arrive at disappointing conclusions: "There is currently an absence of high quality clinical trial evidence to support the use of Aloe vera topical agents or Aloe vera dressings as treatments for acute and chronic wounds."[6] "There is no strong evidence for preventing or treating infusion phlebitis with external application of Aloe vera."[7]

7. Considering the documented risks and the absence of good evidence for efficacy, the risk/benefit balance for Aloe vera preparations cannot be positive.

Plausibility	👍
Efficacy	👎
Safety[a]	👎
Cost	👍
Risk/benefit balance	👎

[a]Oral remedies

---

[5]Guo and Mei (2016).

[6]Dat et al. (2012).

[7]Zheng et al. (2014).

8.4 Antineoblasons

(related modalities: urine therapy, alternative cancer cures)

Antineoblastons are treatments which were originally developed by Dr. S. R. Burzinski in the 1970s and are being promoted as 'alternative cancer cures'.

1. Burzinski is a Polish physician who moved to the US in 1970 and later opened his cancer clinic in Texas. He and his work have been controversial ever since and attracted numerous law suits. In 2017, the Texas Medical Board recommended Burzynski's medical license be revoked and a fined him $360,000 for billing irregularities and other violations.
2. Antineoblastons are chemicals found in our blood and urine; they are claimed to be regulators of cell differentiation which have shown anti-cancer activity in test-tube experiments.[8]
3. Proponents of this treatment often point out that the medicinal use of urine has been known for centuries in ancient Egypt, Greece, Rome, India and North and Central America.
4. Several preliminary, uncontrolled studies seemed to suggest positive effects in cancer patients. However, these investigations were conducted by Burzinski's own research group, had serious methodological flaws, and have never been independently replicated.
5. Controlled clinical trials by independent scientists are scarce and fail to show a survival benefit.[9] In 2013, the US National Cancer Institute stated that "no phase III randomized, controlled trials of antineoplastons as a treatment for cancer have been conducted. Publications have taken the form of case reports, phase I clinical trials, toxicity studies, and phase II clinical trials."[10]
6. Antineoplastons can cause a range of adverse effects, including: anaemia, tiredness, headaches, nausea, tiredness, allergic reactions, fever and seizures.
7. The therapy is exceedingly expensive (around US$ 10,000 per month).

Plausibility	👎
Efficacy	👎
Safety	👎

(continued)

---

[8]Korman (2014).

[9]Ogata et al. (2015).

[10]https://www.cancer.gov/about-cancer/treatment/cam/hp/antineoplastons-pdq#section/all.

(continued)

Cost	👎
Risk/benefit balance	👎

8.5 Antioxidants

(related modalities: dietary supplements)

Antioxidants are substances that act as electron donors and thus might inhibit oxidation of free radicals and thus prevent or delay some types of degenerative diseases.

1. Antioxidants became well-known (and much-hyped by the media) in the 1990s after we learnt about the damage done by free radicals and the potential of antioxidants to neutralise their harmful effects.
2. There are probably thousands of substances, natural and synthetic, that have antioxidant activity. Antioxidants are found in many foods, particularly fruits and vegetables.
3. Antioxidants are now commercially available as dietary supplements containing ingredients such as beta-carotene, lutein, lycopene, manganese, phenols, polyphenols and selenium as well as vitamins A, C or E. Each antioxidant has its unique set of chemical behaviours and biological properties.[11]
4. Antioxidants seem to have evolved as parts of elaborate networks in which each substance plays slightly different roles. This means that no single substance can do the work of the all antioxidants.
5. There is good evidence that eating a diet rich in vegetables and fruits lowers risks of certain diseases. But it is less clear whether this is because of their high antioxidants content or some other factors.
6. After initially promising findings, much (but not all) of the long-term evidence on antioxidants turned out to be disappointing. In most instances antioxidant supplements did not prevent disease.[12]

   - The Women's Health Study demonstrated that vitamin E supplements did not reduce the risk of heart attack, stroke, cancer, age-related macular degeneration, or cataracts.

---

[11]Siti et al. (2015).

[12]https://nccih.nih.gov/health/antioxidants/introduction.htm#science.

- The Women's Antioxidant Cardiovascular Study found no beneficial effects of vitamin C, vitamin E, or beta-carotene supplements on cardiovascular events or diabetes or cancer or cognitive function.
- The Physicians' Health Study II found that neither vitamin E nor vitamin C supplements reduced the risk of major cardiovascular events, cancer, or cataracts.
- The Selenium and Vitamin E Cancer Prevention Trial showed that selenium and vitamin E supplements, taken alone or together, did not prevent prostate cancer. And a 2011 updated analysis from this trial concluded that vitamin E supplements increased the occurrence of prostate cancer.
- One of the few enduringly encouraging findings comes from the Physicians' Health Study which found that taking beta-carotene was associated with a modest reduction in the rate of cognitive decline.[13]

7. Even though antioxidants are usually promoted as safe, they are not entirely risk-free. For instance, high doses of beta-carotene may increase the risk of lung cancer in smokers. High doses of vitamin E may increase risks of prostate cancer and stroke. Some antioxidant supplements also interact with certain medicines, for instance with anti-cancer drugs.[14]

Plausibility	👍
Efficacy	👎
Safety	👎
Cost	👍
Risk/benefit balance	👎

8.6   Arnica

(related modalities: herbal medicine, homeopathy)

Arnica (*Arnica montana L.*) is a plant that grows mainly in Siberia and central Europe, as well as temperate climates in North America. The flowers of the plant have a long history of use in folk medicine (Fig. 8.1).

---

[13]Grodstein et al. (2007).

[14]Lemmo (2015).

Fig. 8.1 Arnica, drawn by
Franz Eugen Köhler, Köhler's
Medizinal-Pflanzen

1. There are two fundamentally different types of arnica products: herbal and
   homeopathic remedies. (The table below refers only to homeopathic arnica
   preparations.)
2. Herbal arnica extracts have been reported to possess antibacterial, antitumor,
   antioxidant, anti-inflammatory, antifungal and immunomodulatory activity.
   A wide range of chemical compounds including sesquiterpene lactones and their
   short-chain carbonic acid esters, flavonoids, carotenoids, essential oils, diter-
   penes, arnidiol, pyrrolizidine alkaloids, coumarins, phenolic acids, lignans and
   oligosaccharides, are found in different parts of the plant.[15] Because arnica
   causes adverse effects such as stomach pain, diarrhoea, and vomiting, herbal
   preparations (which contain substantial amounts of ingredients) are not for oral
   but only for external use.[16] There is some (but not very convincing) evidence
   that herbal arnica creams are effective.[17]
3. Most arnica preparations that are currently for sale are homeopathic preparations. That means they are so highly diluted that they no longer contain relevant

---

[15]Kriplani et al. (2017).

[16]Toxicology IJO (2001).

[17]Ho et al. (2016).

amounts of molecules from the plan. Therefore, they can safely be taken by mouth.

4. In clinical homeopathy, arnica is the standard remedy for cuts and bruises. Confusingly, both external and oral homeopathic arnica preparations exist, but the latter are much more popular.

5. Several trials, some of good methodological quality, have tested the effectiveness of homeopathic arnica. The totality of this evidence fails to show that homeopathic arnica is more effective than a placebo. A systematic review of all 8 clinical trials concluded that "the claim that homeopathic arnica is efficacious beyond a placebo effect is not supported by rigorous clinical trials."[18]

6. Because homeopathic preparations are unlikely to contain even a single molecule of arnica, there is hardly any risk of side-effects (unless, of course, the batch has been contaminated which does occasionally happen with sub-standard quality control).

7. As homeopathic arnica has not been shown to be effective, a risk/benefit analysis cannot arrive at a positive conclusion.

Plausibility	👎
Efficacy	👎
Safety	👍
Cost	👍
Risk/benefit balance	👎

8.7   Bach Flower Remedies

(related modalities: homeopathy, homotoxicology, anthroposophical medicine)

Bach flower remedies were invented in the 1920s by Dr. Edward Bach (1886–1936), a doctor homeopath who had previously worked in the London Homeopathic Hospital. They have since become very popular in Europe and beyond.

---

[18]Ernst and Pittler (1998).

1. Bach flower remedies are clearly inspired by homeopathy; however, they are not the same because they do not follow the 'like cures like' principle and neither are they potentised.
2. They are manufactured by placing freshly picked specific flowers or parts of plants in water which is subsequently mixed with alcohol, bottled and sold.
3. Like most homeopathic remedies, they are highly dilute and thus do not contain therapeutic amounts of the plant printed on the bottle.
4. Bach developed 38 different remedies, each corresponding to an emotional state which he believed to be the cause of all illness:

Agrimony—mental torture behind a cheerful face
Aspen—fear of unknown things
Beech—intolerance
Centaury—the inability to say 'no'
Cerato—lack of trust in one's own decisions
Cherry Plum—fear of the mind giving way
Chestnut Bud—failure to learn from mistakes
Chicory—selfish, possessive love
Clematis—dreaming of the future without working in the present
Crab Apple—the cleansing remedy, also for self-hatred
Elm—overwhelmed by responsibility
Gentian—discouragement after a setback
Gorse—hopelessness and despair
Heather—self-centredness and self-concern
Holly—hatred, envy and jealousy
Honeysuckle—living in the past
Hornbeam—procrastination, tiredness at the thought of doing something
Impatiens—impatience
Larch—lack of confidence
Mimulus—fear of known things
Mustard—deep gloom for no reason
Oak—the plodder who keeps going past the point of exhaustion
Olive—exhaustion following mental or physical effort
Pine—guilt
Red Chestnut—over-concern for the welfare of loved ones
Rock Rose—terror and fright
Rock Water—self-denial, rigidity and self-repression
Scleranthus—inability to choose between alternatives
Star of Bethlehem—shock
Sweet Chestnut—extreme mental anguish, when everything has been tried and there is no light left
Vervain—over-enthusiasm
Vine—dominance and inflexibility
Walnut—protection from change and unwanted influences
Water Violet—pride and aloofness

White Chestnut—unwanted thoughts and mental arguments
Wild Oat—uncertainty over one's direction in life
Wild Rose—drifting, resignation, apathy
Willow—self-pity and resentment
Rescue Remedy, a combination remedy made up of five different remedies, is promoted against anxiety and stress.

5. There are only few clinical trials of Bach flower remedies. Collectively, they fail to show that they are effective beyond placebo. A systematic review of all 7 studies concluded that "the most reliable clinical trials do not show any differences between flower remedies and placebos."[19]
6. Since they do not contain any pharmacologically active molecules (other than alcohol), Bach flower remedies are unlikely to cause adverse effects other than those to the consumer's wallet.
7. Considering that Bach flower remedies are not effective, their risk/benefit balance cannot be positive.

Plausibility	👎
Efficacy	👎
Safety	👍
Cost	👎
Risk/benefit balance	👎

8.8 Berlin Wall

(related modalities: homeopathy)

Berlin wall (*Murus Berlinensis*) is a homeopathic remedy that is commercially available.[20] Even though it is rarely used, it has become famous and is therefore discussed here (Fig. 8.2).

---

[19]Ernst (2010a).

[20]https://www.helios.co.uk/shop/berlin-wall.

Fig. 8.2 Berlin wall as a commercially available homeopathic remedy. *Photo credit* Simon Singh. 100 ml of the remedy in 'medicating potency' currently costs £64.50 (see www.ainsworths. com/index.php?node= RemedyStore2\&_action= agent.add\&remedy=18379)

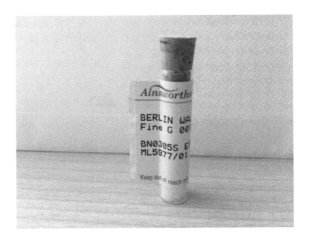

1. The main reason for its fame is that it demonstrates certain, little-known characteristics of homeopathy in exemplary fashion:

   - Homeopathic remedies can be made not just from natural material. It is thus misleading to call homeopathy a natural treatment.
   - In fact, homeopathic remedies can be produced from anything, even from immaterial things like X-rays or vacuum.
   - Berlin wall demonstrates clearly how a homeopathic remedy is produced and what the thinking behind this process is (see below).
   - Berlin wall is one of the most bizarre remedies in the realm of homeopathy.

2. Berlin wall is used in homeopathy according to the 'like cures like' principle.
3. Like all homeopathic remedies, Berlin wall has been submitted to a 'proving'.
4. In such a test, healthy volunteers would ingest samples of the remedy and then record all the symptoms they experience following its administration.
5. In the case of Berlin wall, the symptoms recorded included:[21]

   - Feeling of being forsaken.
   - Oppression.
   - States of possession.
   - Children of ambitious parents who are pushed.
   - Indescribable evil/darkness.
   - Suspicious, uneasy, shifty eyes; cannot look you in the eye.
   - Frequent weeping, tears just flow; sense of numbness or despair over them.
   - Deep grief which cannot be accessed, unspoken, but it hangs in the air.
   - Depression, sense of blackness, total isolation, aloneness, despair.
   - Panic.
   - Deceit.

---

[21]http://www.interhomeopathy.org/berlin_wall.

6. This means that patients who complain about such symptoms might receive Berlin wall from their homeopath.
7. Some homeopaths have published case reports of patients improving with this remedy.[22] There is, however, no reliable evidence that Berlin wall has any health effects beyond placebo.

Plausibility	👎
Efficacy	👎
Safety	👍
Cost	👎
Risk/benefit balance	👎

8.9   Carctol

(related modalities: Alkaline diet, alternative cancer cures, Ayurvedic medicine, herbal medicine)

Carctol is the trade-name of an 'alternative cancer cure' designed by Dr. Nandlal Tiwari, an Ayurvedic practitioner from India, who has been promoting his remedy for the last 30 years.

1. Carctol is claimed to be a cure for all types of cancer at all stages of the disease, even when conventional treatments can no longer offer a cure. A plethora of Carctol promotional websites claim that 30–40% of all patients will respond to Carctol.
2. One 560-mg capsule of Carctol contains Hemidesmus indicus (roots): 20 mg/ Tribulas terrestris (seeds): 20 mg/Piper cubeba Linn. (seeds): 120 mg/Ammani vesicatoria (plant): 20 mg/Lepidium sativum Linn. (seeds): 20 mg/Blepharis edulis (seeds): 200 mg/Smilax china Linn. (roots): 80 mg/Rheumemodi wall (roots): 20 mg.[23]

---

[22]https://hpathy.com/clinical-cases/a-case-for-berlin-wall/.

[23]https://www.carctol.in/about.html.

3. While taking Carctol, patients are advised to

   - avoid acid food,
   - follow a vegetarian diet,
   - drink up to 5 l of boiled water per day,
   - avoid alcohol,
   - avoid fried foods.

4. No evidence exists to show or to suggest that Carctol helps cancer patients in any way.[24]
5. Dr. Tiwari seems to think that Carctol depletes the body of acidity. This, he claims, creates an alkaline environment which kills cancer cells. Carctol is claimed to act slowly, and several months of treatment are advised. This means, of course, that the total costs for this treatment are high.
6. The theory that supposedly underpins Carctol is both implausible and unproven.
7. Despite the negative evidence, Carctol has been heavily promoted. One UK newspaper, for instance, published a full-page feature on Dr. Daniel, a promoter of Carctol, entitled *'I've seen herbal remedy make tumours disappear, says respected cancer doctor'*.[25]

Plausibility	👎
Efficacy	👎
Safety	👎
Cost	👎
Risk/benefit balance	👎

8.10 Cease Therapy

(related modalities: homeopathy, homotoxicology)

CEASE was developed by Dr. Tinus Smits (1946–2010) in the Netherlands. The name stands for "Complete Elimination of Autistic Spectrum Expression."

---

[24]Ernst (2009).

[25]https://www.telegraph.co.uk/news/uknews/3310370/Ive-seen-herbal-remedy-make-tumours-disappear-says-respected-cancer-doctor.html.

1. Smits had practised as a lay-homeopath for many years before he decided to study medicine.
2. He developed his own theories about autism (see below) and published several books about his theory.
3. In his experience (Smits never published a scientific paper in the peer-reviewed literature), autism is caused by an accumulation of different causes. About 70% is allegedly due to vaccines, 25% to toxic medication and other toxic substances, 5% to other diseases.
4. According to the 'like cures like' principle of homeopathy, Smits claimed that autism must be cured by applying homeopathic doses of the substances which allegedly caused the condition. Step by step all assumed causative factors (vaccines, regular medication, environmental toxic exposures, effects of illness, etc.) are 'detoxified' with the homeopathically prepared substances that were administered prior to the onset of autism and are suspected to have caused the condition. Smits and his followers believe that this procedure clears out the energetic field of the patient from the imprint of toxic substances or diseases.
5. One problem with this concept is that it flies in the face of science.
6. Another, perhaps even more important problem is that there is no evidence that the CEASE therapy is clinically effective.
7. Despite all this, many homeopaths have adopted the CEASE therapy. The UK 'Society of Homeopaths' issued a statement saying: "... members should be aware the title, meaning 'Complete Elimination of Autistic Spectrum Expression' is misleading. RSHoms must not suggest that they are capable of a complete cure of autism as this would be unethical and in breach of the Code of Ethics. The Society does not endorse any aspects of CEASE therapy contrary to NHS guidance and nor should RSHoms..."[26]

Plausibility	👎
Efficacy	👎
Safety	👍
Cost	👎
Risk/benefit balance	👎

---

[26]https://homeopathy-soh.org/resources/position-statements/.

8.11   Chelation Therapy

(related modalities: detox)

Chelation therapy is a well-established conventional treatment for certain acute intoxications (e.g. heavy metal) and, for that purpose, it can be life-saving. In alternative medicine, it is used for all sorts of illnesses and for 'detox'. This discussion is exclusively on this alternative form of chelation therapy.

1. The principle of chelation therapy is to inject a chemical called EDTA into the veins which binds ions that subsequently can be excreted.
2. Alternative practitioners promote chelation for a wide range of conditions ranging from arthritis to cardiovascular disease.
3. However, these claims are both implausible and not evidence-based. Several systematic reviews of the best evidence concluded less than optimistically:

   • "...more controlled studies are required to determine the efficacy of chelation therapy in cardiovascular disease before it can be used broadly in the clinical setting."[27]
   • "The best available evidence does not support the therapeutic use of EDTA chelation therapy in the treatment of cardiovascular disease."[28]
   • "Given the potential of chelation therapy to cause severe adverse effects, this treatment should now be considered obsolete."[29]
   • "The available data do not support the use of chelation in cardiovascular diseases."[30]

4. A recent trial generated more encouraging findings and concluded that "among stable patients with a history of MI, use of an intravenous chelation regimen with disodium EDTA, compared with placebo, modestly reduced the risk of adverse cardiovascular outcomes, many of which were revascularization procedures. These results provide evidence to guide further research but are not sufficient to support the routine use of chelation therapy for treatment of patients who have had an MI."[31] Yet, this study has been heavily criticised for a multitude of methodological weaknesses.
5. Chelation therapy can dramatically alter the electrolyte levels in our blood which carries serious risks. Several fatalities are on record.
6. Chelation therapy it is expansive; often the costs amount to several US$ 10,000 for one series of treatments.
7. Considering its risks and the doubtful effectiveness of alternative chelation therapy, its risk/benefit balance fails to be positive.

---

[27]Elihu et al. (1998).
[28]Seely et al. (2005).
[29]Ernst (2000).
[30]Shrihari et al. (2006).
[31]Lamas et al. (2013).

Plausibility	👎
Efficacy	👎
Safety	👎
Cost	👎
Risk/benefit balance	👎

8.12   Chinese Herbal Medicine

(related modalities: herbal medicine, Reishi, Traditional Chinese Medicine)

Chinese herbal medicine has recently has become popular in the West, not least because the Chinese government is promoting it aggressively, as it is one of the most important export articles for China. The global annual market is estimated to currently amount to around US$ 50 billion[32] (Fig. 8.3).

1. Chinese herbal medicine has a long history in China and is still being used there in parallel with conventional medicine. The remedies employed are usually administered orally as decoctions (teas) or capsules, or topically as creams or plasters, less frequently also by injection.
2. There are thousands of plants used medicinally. In Chinese herbal medicine, herbal ingredients are typically combined in mixtures that contain a multitude of different plants. The ancient Chinese literature recorded more than 100,000 medicinal recipes some of which also contain non-botanical ingredients such as minerals and animal parts (see chapter on Rhino horn). Generalisations across all Chinese herbal medicines are therefore highly problematic.
3. Most of the research into Chinese herbal medicines is published in Chinese, and there are several reasons to be sceptical about its reliability; fraud seems to be rife and Chinese researchers publish only positive results.[33]

---

[32]Cyranoski (2018).
[33]Tang et al. (1999).

Fig. 8.3 Chinese Herbal
Medicine became big
business in the US during the
early 20th century. *Source* US
National Library of Medicine

M. J. YEM, **Manager**

Chinese Medical Co.

955 South Hill Street
Los Angeles, California

(Over)

4. In recent years, a plethora of reviews of these studies was published in English.
   The conclusions are usually encouraging, however, because the primary studies'
   lack reliability, caution is advised.
5. China's drug regulator gets more than 230,000 reports of adverse effects from
   traditional treatments each year,[34] and it is clear that Chinese herbal medicines
   carry multiple risks:

   - one or more ingredients may be toxic,
   - some have been shown to be contaminated with toxic materials such as
     heavy metals,

---

[34]Cyranoski (2018).

- others are adulterated with synthetic drugs such as steroids,
- and others again can interact with prescription drugs taken concomitantly.[35,36,37]

6. The 2015, Nobel Prize in Physiology and Medicine was awarded to Youyou Tu for her contributions in discovering the Chinese herb artemisinin as a treatment of malaria. However, calling this a triumph of Chinese herbal medicine would be mistaken:

   - artemisinin was not employed as an anti-malaria drug in Traditional Chinese Medicine,
   - using a single herb is not characteristic for Chinese herbal traditions,
   - employing a single ingredient (such as artemisinin) from the total range of ingredients in a plant is, by definition, not herbal medicine but conventional pharmacology.

7. Considering the multitude of Chinese herbal recipes, their mostly unknown efficacy and their potential for causing harm, the risks of Chinese herbal medicine do not outweigh the benefits.

Plausibility	👍
Efficacy	👎
Safety	👎
Cost	👎
Risk/benefit balance	👎

8.13   Chondroitin

(related modalities: dietary supplements, glucosamine)

Chondroitin is a substance that occurs naturally in our body. It has become a popular dietary supplement. Chondroitin is often combined with glucosamine and promoted as a natural treatment for osteoarthritis.

---

[35]Nortier et al. (2000).

[36]Posadzki et al. (2013).

[37]Ernst (2004).

1. Chondroitin sulfate proteoglycans are peri-cellular and extracellular substances that are involved in numerous biological phenomena. Their diverse functions can be attributed to their structural variability.[38]
2. Chondroitin sulfate is an important component of the cartilage in our joints and is responsible for its resistance to mechanical wear and tear.
3. Chondroitin supplements are produced from extracts of cartilaginous cow and pig tissues; they are thus not suited for vegetarians.
4. The results of clinical trials, many of which are methodologically weak, are mixed. A Cochrane review concluded that "chondroitin (alone or in combination with glucosamine) was better than placebo in improving pain in participants with osteoarthritis in short-term studies. The benefit was small to moderate with an 8 point greater improvement in pain (range 0–100) and a 2 point greater improvement in Lequesne's index (range 0–24), both seeming clinically meaningful."[39]
5. Some epidemiological studies have shown *a protective association between use of glucosamine and chondroitin and risk of colorectal cancer.*[40]
6. Chondroitin supplements seem to be safe; side effects are rare and usually mild. Some people have reported headaches, allergic reactions and diarrhoea. People suffering from clotting disorders should be cautious, as chondroitin may have anticoagulant activities.
7. Chondroitin can interact with a range of prescribed medications and therefore should not be taken without professional advice by patients who also take other drugs. There is a risk of contamination of chondroitin preparations; it is therefore advisable to purchase only from reputable sources.

Plausibility	👍
Efficacy	👍
Safety	👍
Cost	👎
Risk/benefit balance	👍

[38]Mikami and Kitagawa (2013).

[39]Singh et al. (2015).

[40]Kantor et al. (2016).

8.14 Colloidal Silver

(related modalities: dietary supplements)

The medicinal use of silver has a long history. With the current boom in alternative medicine, it has seen a remarkable revival.

1. Silver is toxic for bacteria, algae, and fungi. These effects are based on its ability to irreversibly damage key enzyme systems in the cell membranes of these pathogens.
2. The use of silver in wound dressings, creams, and as an antibiotic coating on medical devices was therefore wide-spread. In recent decades, it has become less important due to the emergence of more powerful antibiotics and antiseptics.
3. In alternative medicine, silver has made a renaissance in the form of colloidal silver. It is currently being promoted for a range of conditions including serious diseases such as AIDS, cancer, diabetes and tuberculosis.
4. Contrary to many statements from manufacturers, humans have no dietary requirement for silver, and hence there is no such thing as a 'silver deficiency'.
5. One review assessed the evidence for colloidal silver and *emphasized the lack of established effectiveness and potential toxicity of these products.*[41]
6. After oral intake, colloidal silver is distributed to all organs with the highest levels being observed in the intestines and the stomach. In the skin, silver induces a blue-grey discoloration known as argyria.[42]
7. In 1999, the U.S. Food and Drug Administration banned colloidal silver sellers from claiming any therapeutic or preventive value for their products; yet silver-containing preparations continue to be promoted as alternative remedies, often at considerable costs.

Plausibility	👎
Efficacy	👎
Safety	👎
Cost	👎
Risk/benefit balance	👎

---

[41]Fung and Bowen (1996).
[42]Hadrup and Lam (2014).

8.15   Dietary Supplements

(related modalities: herbal medicine)

Dietary (or food or nutritional) supplements or nutraceuticals form a category of remedies that, in most countries, is poorly regulated and not allowed to make significant health claims. Supplements can contain all sorts of ingredients, from minerals and vitamins to plants and animal products. Therefore, generalisations across all types of supplements are impossible.

1. Dietary supplements are marketed in several forms, such as tablets, capsules, powders, and liquids. The therapeutic claims that are being made for them (even though such claims are usually forbidden) range from weight loss to ant-aging, and from curing erectile dysfunction to preventing cardiovascular disease.[43]
2. Although they are usually promoted as natural and safe, dietary supplements do not have necessarily either of these qualities. For example, the following behaviours could lead to harmful—even life-threatening—consequences.

   - Combining one supplement with another supplement or with prescribed medicines
   - Substituting supplements for prescription medicines
   - Taking too much of some supplements, such as vitamin A, vitamin D, or iron

3. Examples of some of the currently most popular supplements include:

   - Calcium
   - Echinacea
   - Fish Oil
   - Ginseng
   - Glucosamine and/or
   - Chondroitin Sulphate
   - Garlic
   - Vitamin D
   - St. John's Wort
   - Saw Palmetto
   - Ginkgo
   - Green Tea

4. Some supplements are unquestionably effective. An example of this category is the herbal supplement St John's Wort (see there). And one review concluded, for instance, that for blood pressure control "a very large body of evidence supports the use of potassium, L-arginine, vitamins C and D, cocoa flavonoids,

---

[43]Cohen and Ernst (2010).

beetroot juice, some probiotics, coenzyme Q10, controlled-release melatonin, aged garlic extract."[44]

5. Many other supplements are not supported by sound evidence. Examples of this category include most vitamins for healthy individuals consuming a balanced diet or the popular herbal supplement evening primrose oil (see there).

6. Other supplements again can contain toxic material. One review, for instance, showed that, in herbal supplements, "47 toxic compounds in 55 species from 46 plant families were found to demonstrate harmful effects due to hepatic, cardiovascular, central nervous system, and digestive system toxicity."[45]

7. Poor regulation in many countries means that supplements may not contain what it says on the label. Numerous investigations have shown that some commercially available supplements fail to contain the amount of the ingredient claimed by the manufacturer. Similarly, supplements have been shown repeatedly to be contaminated with toxic materials or adulterated with synthetic drugs.[46]

Plausibility	👎
Efficacy	👎
Safety	👎
Cost	👎
Risk/benefit balance	👎

8.16 Essential Oils

(related modalities: aromatherapy, herbal medicine)

Essential oils have their name not from being essential for health or anything else, but from the fact that they are based on the essences of plants.

1. Essential oils are produced by steam distillation of the respective plants. A more suitable name would be volatile oil, as these oils completely evaporate in air.

2. They are commonly used in cosmetics, perfumes, food and sometimes also as pesticides and antiseptics.

---

[44]Sirtori et al. (2015).
[45]Hudson et al. (2018).
[46]Posadzki et al. (2013).

3. In alternative medicine, they are employed as aromatherapy oils and usually applied via a gentle massage, less frequently by inhalation or as an additive to bathwater.
4. Aromatherapists tend to make very specific therapeutic claims for their oils. Five examples must suffice:

   • Bergamot is extracted from the Citrus Beragamia tree, a native of Southeast Asia. Aromatherapists recommend it to treat stress, depression, anxiety, anorexia, infections and eczema. It is also used to stimulate the liver, digestive system and spleen, and provide an overall lift to those suffering from a general malaise.
   • There are two types of Chamomile plants, the Roman Chamomile and German Chamomile, and aromatherapy oils can be extracted from both varieties. Chamomile is recommended as a calming agent, as well as for its antibiotic, antiseptic, analgesic, and antidepressant qualities.
   • Eucalyptus is said to be an agent against respiratory diseases and lack of concentration, as an antiseptic, antispasmodic, decongestant, diuretic and stimulant as well as against migraines and fevers.
   • Lavender is said to have relaxant, sedative, antiseptic, antidepressant, anti-inflammatory decongestant, deodorant and diuretic properties.
   • Ylang-Ylang is recommended for reducing stress and as an aphrodisiac. It is also used to soothe headaches, nausea, skin conditions, stimulate hair growth, reduce high blood pressure and fight intestinal problems.

5. Few of these claims are supported by sound evidence. The relaxing effects of aromatherapy are mostly due to the massage and largely unrelated to the oils.[47]
6. One overview showed that "due to a number of caveats, the evidence is not sufficiently convincing that aromatherapy is an effective therapy for any condition."[48]
7. Essential oils must not be applied undiluted to the skin or taken by mouth. They can cause adverse effects such as skin irritation and allergic reactions; even one fatality is on record.[49]

Plausibility	
Efficacy	
Safety	

(continued)

---

[47]Perry et al. (2012).
[48]Lee et al. (2012).
[49]Posadzki et al. (2012).

(continued)

Cost	👎
Risk/benefit balance	👎

8.17 Essiac

(related modalities: alternative cancer cures, dietary supplements, herbal medicine)

Essiac is an herbal mixture invented by the Canadian nurse Rene Caisse (1888–1978). The remedy has been heavily promoted as an alternative cancer cure and has been popular since many decades.

1. Essiac has its name from spelling Caisse backwards.
2. Caisse claims to have been given the formula for Essiac by a patient she treated in 1922, a claim that has never been independently verified. Caisse also invented a similar product called 'Flor Essence'.
3. Essiac is for oral consumption in the form of a tea. It contains four herbal ingredients, but its precise formula is a secret.
4. Contrary to many claims, there is no good evidence to suggest that Essiac cures any form of cancer. A review of data from an incomplete Canadian study showed no clear evidence of improved survival in cancer patients taking Essiac. The Canadian government also reviewed information on 86 cancer patients who had taken Essiac. The researchers reported that it was not clear, if any changes in the patients' conditions were caused by Essiac.[50] A review concluded that "there is a lack of both safety and efficacy data for Essiac and essiac formulations."[51]
5. Test-tube experiments have been conducted and the authors concluded that they found "significant antioxidant and immunomodulatory properties, as well as neoplastic cell specific cytotoxicity consistent with the historical properties ascribed to this compound. Importantly, significant CYP450 and fibrinolysis inhibition were also observed."[52]
6. All attempts to get Essiac and related products registered as an anti-cancer drug have failed. Today, Essiac is marketed as a dietary supplement by numerous companies which all produce similar or identical preparations. Medicinal claims are illegal for such supplements.

---

[50]https://www.ncbi.nlm.nih.gov/books/NBK66020/.

[51]Ulbricht et al. (2009).

[52]Seely et al. (2007).

7. Essiac can cause nausea and vomiting; it might also interact with prescribed drugs. The greatest risk, however, is that patients follow the advice of some therapists and use Essiac as an alternative to conventional cancer treatments. This would be a sure way to hasten death.

Plausibility	
Efficacy	
Safety	
Cost	
Risk/benefit balance	

8.18   Evening Primrose

(related modalities: dietary supplements, herbal medicine)

Evening primrose oil is amongst the best-selling herbal remedies of all times. It is marketed in most countries as a dietary supplement.

1. Evening primrose is native to North America and was used therapeutically by Indians mainly for minor cuts and bruises.
2. Today, evening primrose oil is being promoted for eczema, rheumatoid arthritis, premenstrual syndrome, breast pain, menopause symptoms, and many other conditions.
3. The oil is produced from the seeds of the plant which contain large amounts cis-gamma-linolenic acid that potentially has therapeutic properties.
4. Evening primrose oil has been extensively tested in clinical trials for a wide range of conditions, including eczema, postmenopausal symptoms, asthma, psoriasis, cellulite, hyperactivity, multiple sclerosis, schizophrenia, obesity, chronic fatigue syndrome, rheumatoid arthritis, and mastalgia. In fact, there are not many herbal remedies that have been submitted to such a sizable amount of clinical trials.
5. The results of these investigations fail to show that evening primrose oil is effective for any condition except possibly eczema. A 2006 review found that, in this condition, it "has a simultaneous, beneficial effect on itch/pruritus, crusting, oedema and redness (erythema) that becomes apparent between 4 and 8 weeks after treatment is initiated. However, the magnitude of this effect is reduced in

association with increasing frequency of potent steroid use."[53] These findings were, however, contradicted by a Cochrane review of 2013 concluding that supplements of "evening primrose oil lack effect on eczema; improvement was similar to respective placebos used in trials."[54]

6. Evening primrose oil can cause mild, transient adverse effects, which are mainly gastrointestinal. The adverse effects of long-term use are unknown. A case report suggested that, if is taken for prolonged periods of time (more than one year), there is a potential risk of inflammation, thrombosis, and immunosuppression. One study also found that evening primrose oil may increase the risk of bleeding for people on the anti-coagulant warfarin.[55] Furthermore, it has the potential to interact with several common prescription drugs.

7. Evening primrose oil seems to be a prime example for the fact that, in alternative medicine, the commercial success of a remedy is not necessarily determined by the strength of the evidence but by the intensity and cleverness of the marketing activities.

Plausibility	
Efficacy	
Safety	
Cost	
Risk/benefit balance	

8.19 Feverfew

(related modalities: dietary supplements, herbal medicine)

Feverfew (*Tanacetum parthenium*) is a plant that belongs to the daisy family. It is a popular herbal remedy that has been used medicinally since millennia, particularly for pain, fever and women's ailments. The word "feverfew" comes from the Latin word febrifugia (fever reducer).

---

[53]Morse and Clough (2006).

[54]Bamford et al. (2013).

[55]Bamford et al. (2013).

1. Feverfew's main pharmacologically active principle is believed to be a chemical called parthenolide. It has a range of pharmacological activities, including analgesic and anti-inflammatory activities.
2. Today, feverfew is used mainly for the treatment of two conditions: migraine and rheumatoid arthritis. Many dietary supplements containing feverfew are currently commercially available. The plant can also be grown by consumers in their gardens and be taken as a tea.
3. A Cochrane review of feverfew for migraine prevention included 6 clinical trials. Collectively, their results were encouraging, but we concluded that this "low-quality evidence needs to be confirmed in larger rigorous trials with stable feverfew extracts and clearly defined migraine populations before firm conclusions can be drawn."[56]
4. For rheumatoid arthritis, there is even less evidence. The results of the most rigorous study revealed "no apparent benefit from oral feverfew in rheumatoid arthritis."[57]
5. Feverfew is also sometimes recommended for psoriasis, allergies, asthma, tinnitus, dizziness, nausea, and vomiting. However, the evidence for these conditions is weak or non-existent.
6. About 20% of users experience adverse effects after taking feverfew, the most serious of which is mouth ulceration. Feverfew can also induce more widespread inflammation of the oral mucosa and tongue, sometimes with lip swelling and loss of taste.
7. Feverfew may inhibit the activity of blood platelets, therefore individuals taking blood-thinning medications, such as aspirin or warfarin, should be cautious and consult a health care provider before taking this herbal remedy.[58] Abrupt discontinuation of feverfew by a migraineur is said to cause a rebound phenomenon with severe headaches.

Plausibility	👍
Efficacy	👍 a
Safety	👎

(continued)

---

[56]Wider et al. (2015).

[57]Pattrick et al. (1989).

[58]Pareek et al. (2011).

(continued)

Cost	
Risk/benefit balance	[a]

[a]For migraine prevention

8.20   Fish Oil

(related modalities: dietary supplements)

Fish oil (omega-3) preparations are extremely popular and amongst the best-researched dietary supplements.

1. During the 1970s, two Danish scientists, Bang and Dyerberg, noticed that Greenland Eskimos had a markedly lower prevalence of coronary artery disease than mainland Danes.
2. They also noted that their diet contained large amounts of seal and whale blubber and suggested that this 'Eskimo-diet' was a key factor in the lower prevalence of coronary heart disease.
3. Subsequently, a flurry of research stared to investigate the phenomenon, and it was discovered that the 'Eskimo-diet' contained unusually high concentrations of omega-3 polyunsaturated fatty acids from fish oils (seals and whales feed predominantly on fish).
4. Initial research also demonstrated that the regular consumption of fish oil had a multitude of cardiovascular and anti-inflammatory effects.[59] This led to the promotion of fish oil supplements for a wide range of conditions.
5. Meanwhile, many of these early findings have been overturned by more rigorous studies,[60] and the enthusiasm for fish oil supplements has somewhat waned.
6. The current evidence is complex and contradictory but seems to suggest that fish oil supplementation might be beneficial for lowering blood pressure, normalising elevated triglyceride levels of the blood, stabilising certain heart arrhythmias, for some forms of depression, and for treating psoriasis.[61] One review also suggested that fish oil supplements *might help to reduce the symptoms of*

[59]Ponte et al. (1997).

[60]Abdelhamid et al. (2018).

[61]Pauwels and Kostkiewicz (2008).

clinical anxiety.[62] It is not necessary to take fish oil supplements to benefit from the effects of omega-3; a recent review recommended that "1–2 seafood meals per week be included to reduce the risk of congestive heart failure, coronary heart disease, ischemic stroke, and sudden cardiac death, especially when seafood replaces the intake of less healthy foods."[63] Fish oil seems to be ineffective for the prevention of Alzheimer's disease and Chron's disease.

7. Very high intake (3 g or more per day) of omega-3 fatty acids may increase the risk of bleeding and haemorrhagic stroke. Another problem is that many fish oil supplements are contaminated with mercury which is, of course, toxic.

Plausibility	👍
Efficacy	👎
Safety	👎
Cost	👍
Risk/benefit balance	👎

8.21 Garlic

(related modalities: dietary supplements, herbal medicine)

Garlic (*Alliun sativum*) is a well-known spice as well as a popular herbal remedy. It has a long history of medicinal use and was popular in many ancient cultures.

1. Garlic contains alliin which is enzymatically converted to allicin, the main active ingredient of this herbal remedy.
2. In the last three decades, garlic has been intensely investigated, and today, garlic is amongst the best-researched herbal treatments. Numerous supplements are commercially available.
3. It has been shown to have a multitude of pharmacological effects, including anti-bacterial, anti-viral, anti-fungal, anti-hypertensive, anti-thrombotic, and

---

[62]https://jamanetwork.com/journals/jamanetworkopen/fullarticle/2702216?utm_source=
fbpage&utm_medium=social_jamajno&utm_term=1773253893&utm_content=followers-article_
engagement-image_stock&utm_campaign=article_alert&linkId=56835946.

[63]Rimm et al. (2018).

anti-cancer properties. Its most thoroughly investigated effect, however, is its ability to lower elevated blood cholesterol levels.

4. The most recent meta-analysis included 14 clinical trials and concluded that garlic can reduce the level of total cholesterol, low density lipoprotein (LDL) and triglycerides, indicating its usefulness in the management of hyperlipidaemia.[64]

5. In general, the effects of garlic are small and cannot measure up to those of prescribed synthetic drugs. However, the multitude of its different effects might work in concert and add up to a significant cardiovascular benefit.

6. The evidence for garlic as a cancer preventative is much weaker and based mostly on epidemiological data. One review found 14 such investigations that "reported a beneficial role of these allium types against gastric cancer."[65]

7. Garlic consumption leads to the well-known body odour and is associated with several minor adverse effects. The most significant risk of high-dose garlic intake is that it might interact with prescribed medications, particularly with anticoagulants.[66]

Plausibility	👍
Efficacy	👍
Safety	👍
Cost	👍
Risk/benefit balance	👍

8.22 Gerson Therapy

(related modalities: alternative cancer cures, cancer diets, coffee enemas)

Gerson therapy is an 'alternative cancer cure' that is currently being recommended by entrepreneurs selling false hope to often desperate cancer patients at frequently excessive prices.

---

[64]Sun et al (2018).

[65]Guercio et al. (2014).

[66]Izzo and Ernst (2009).

1. The Gerson therapy was developed about 100 years ago by the German doctor, Max Gerson (1881–1959). He thought that the diet originally developed as a treatment for tuberculosis cured his migraines. Subsequently it was promoted for all sorts of illnesses. The 'Gerson Institute' state that "Over the past 60 years, thousands of people have used the Gerson Therapy to recover from a variety of illnesses, including: Cancer (including melanoma, breast cancer, prostate cancer, colon cancer, lymphoma and more), Diabetes, Heart disease, Arthritis, Auto-*immune disorders, and many others.*"[67] Today, the Gerson therapy is amongst the most frequently recommended 'alternative cancer cure'.[68] The Gerson clinics are situated in Mexico for the simple reason that their activities would be illegal in the US.

2. The Gerson therapy consists of ingesting raw and organically-grown vegetables and freshly-pressed vegetable juices (up to 13 large glasses/day). In addition, regular coffee enemas are administered allegedly stimulating the liver to detoxify the body. Finally, a range of supplements is usually prescribed. The treatment is normally administered in specialised hospitals, and the costs for the whole treatment package are high.

3. The Gerson therapy is often promoted by celebrities, e.g. Prince Charles. Yet, its concept flies in the face of science.

4. There is no good evidence that the Gerson therapy is effective for cancer or any other condition. A recent review stated that "no conclusions about the effectiveness of the Gerson therapy, either as an adjuvant to other cancer therapies or as a cure, can be drawn from any of the studies reported above."[69]

5. The Gerson diet is essentially a starvation diet. It deprives cancer patients of vital nutrients; in addition, it can drastically impair their quality of life. Coffee enemas remove potassium from the body and have been said to cause:

- infections
- dehydration
- fits
- salt and other mineral imbalances in the body
- heart and lung problems, even death
- constipation and inflammation of the bowel (colitis) from regular, long term use of enemas which can weaken the bowel muscle
- loss of appetite
- diarrhoea
- abdominal cramps
- aching, fever and sweating
- cold sores
- dizziness and weakness

---

[67]https://gerson.org/gerpress/.

[68]Schmidt and Ernst (2004).

[69]https://www.ncbi.nlm.nih.gov/books/NBK66029/.

6. Most patients find the diet exceedingly hard to follow, and those who fail to adhere to it are often told that it is their fault, if their cancer does not respond. Thus, they often die not merely deprived of their funds and quality of life but also feeling guilty.
7. The Gerson therapy is neither safe nor effective. Moreover, its assumed mode of action is far from plausible. It follows that its risks outweigh its benefits.

Plausibility	👎
Efficacy	👎
Safety[a]	👎
Cost	👎
Risk/benefit balance	👎

[a]Only direct risks considered

8.23   Ginkgo Biloba

(related modalities: dietary supplements, herbal medicine)

Ginkgo biloba is a tree—supposedly the oldest tree on the planet—that is native to China, Korea and Japan. It has a long history of medicinal use and has now become one of the best-selling herbal supplements of all times.

1. The ginkgo tree is today being cultivated in several parts of the world; because of its uniquely shaped leaves, it is easily recognisable.
2. Ginkgo biloba contains several families of pharmacologically active compounds.
3. Traditionally, Ginkgo biloba was used for asthma, angina, headaches, tinnitus and other conditions.
4. It is amongst the best-researched herbal remedies, and its multiple pharmacological effects are well-documented; they include an increase of microcirculatory blood flow, inhibition of platelet function and scavenging of free radicals.

5. Today ginkgo is promoted for a wide range of conditions, most frequently for dementia, circulatory problems and tinnitus.

6. The clinical evidence used to be fairly strong but has in recent years become less convincing. The most recent systematic reviews have therefore drawn equivocal conclusions:

   - "Ginkgo biloba extract has potentially beneficial effects for people with dementia when it is administered at doses greater than 200 mg/day for at least 5 months. Given the lower quality of the evidence, further rigorously-designed, multicenter-7 based, large-scale RCTs are warranted."[70]

   - "Ginkgo biloba is potentially beneficial for the improvement of cognitive function, activities of daily living, and global clinical assessment in patients with mild cognitive impairment or Alzheimer's disease. However, due to limited sample size, inconsistent findings and methodological quality of included trials, more research are warranted to confirm the effectiveness and safety of ginkgo biloba in treating mild cognitive impairment and Alzheimer's disease."[71]

   - "Ginkgo Biloba extract may have beneficial effects on patients with angina pectoris, although the low quality of existing trials makes it difficult to draw a satisfactory conclusion. More rigorous, high quality clinical trials are needed to provide conclusive evidence."[72]

   - "No confirmative conclusions on the efficacy and safety of Ginkgo biloba extract for essential hypertension could be drawn. More rigorous trials are warranted to support their clinical use."[73]

   - "Overall, there is no evidence that Ginkgo biloba has a clinically significant benefit for patients with peripheral arterial disease."[74]

7. The risks of taking ginkgo biloba extracts at the prescribed doses are generally low and relate to rare side-effects such as gastrointestinal problems, allergic reactions, and dizziness.

Plausibility	
Efficacy	

(continued)

[70]Yuan et al. (2017).

[71]Yang et al. (2016).

[72]Sun et al. (2015).

[73]Xiong et al. (2014).

[74]Nicolaï et al. (2013).

(continued)

Safety	
Cost	
Risk/benefit balance	

8.24 Glucosamine

(related modalities: chondroitin, dietary supplements)

Glucosamine is an amino sugar that is found in human cartilage. It can be produced semi-synthetically and is heavily promoted as a 'natural' dietary supplement.

1. Glucosamine is manufactured using the shells of shell-fish. Therefore, it may not be suitable for vegetarians and vegans.
2. Glucosamine is mostly used to treat osteoarthritis. Claims by manufacturers that the supplement restores lost cartilage are exaggerated and have even successfully been challenged in court.
3. It is often combined with chondroitin (see there).
4. Its pharmacological actions are similar to those of chondroitin and include anti-inflammatory, antioxidant, anti-aging, anti-fibrotic, neuroprotective and cardioprotective activities.[75]
5. Most recent systematic reviews of the clinical evidence have drawn cautious conclusions:

   - "… glucosamine has the potential to alleviate knee OA pain. Further studies are needed to evaluate the effect of glucosamine on knee function and joint preservation, as well as to evaluate the combined effect with other components, such as chondroitin."[76]
   - "Currently, there is no good evidence to support the use of glucosamine for hip or knee OA and an absence of evidence to support specific consideration of glucosamine for any clinically relevant OA subgroup according to baseline pain severity, BMI, sex, structural abnormalities or presence of inflammation."[77]

---

[75]Zahedipour et al. (2017).

[76]Ogata et al. (2018).

[77]Runhaar et al. (2017).

6. Pre-clinical research has suggested that glucosamine might have anti-cancer potential,[78] and some epidemiological studies have shown "a protective association between use of glucosamine and chondroitin and risk of colorectal cancer."[79] *But* clinical studies to confirm this notions are not yet available.
7. Glucosamine is generally considered to be safe; adverse-effects are rare and usually mild including stomach upset, constipation, diarrhoea, headache, and rash.

Plausibility	👍
Efficacy	👎
Safety	👍
Cost	👎
Risk/benefit balance	👎

8.25 Homeopathy

(related modalities: anthroposophic medicine, Bach flower remedies, homotoxicology, isopathy, Schuessler salts)

Homeopathy is popular, particularly in India, Germany, France and parts of South America. Since it has been invented about 200 years ago, it divides opinion like few other subjects in alternative medicine (Fig. 8.4).

1. Homeopathy was invented by the German physician, Samuel Hahnemann (1755–1843). At the time, our understanding of the laws of nature was woefully incomplete, and therefore Hahnemann's ideas seemed far less implausible than today. The conventional treatments of this period were often more dangerous than the disease they were supposed to cure. Consequently, homeopathy was repeatedly shown to be superior to 'allopathy' (a term coined by Hahnemann to denigrate conventional medicine) and Hahnemann's treatments were an almost instant, worldwide success.[80]

---

[78]Chou et al. (2015).

[79]Kantor et al. (2016).

[80]https://www.hive.co.uk/Product/Professor-Edzard-Ernst/Homeopathy—The-Undiluted-Facts–Including-a-Comprehensive-A-Z-Lexicon/19719982.

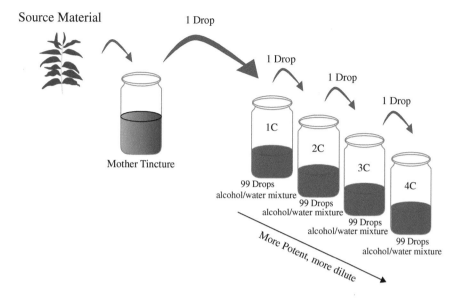

Each vial is shaken vigorously after each dilution is made.

Fig. 8.4 Potentisation. This process involves serial dilutions with succussion at each step

2. Many consumers confuse homeopathy with herbal medicine; yet the two are fundamentally different. Herbal medicines are plant extracts with potentially active ingredients. Homeopathic remedies can be based on plants or any other material and are typically so dilute that they contain not a single molecule of the substance advertised on the bottle. The most frequently used dilution (homeopaths call them 'potencies') is a 'C30'; a C30-potency has been diluted 30 times at a ratio of 1:100. This means that one drop of the staring material is dissolved in 1 000 000 000 000 000 000 000 000 000 000 000 000 000 000 000 000 000 000 000 000 drops of diluent (usually a water/alcohol mixture)—and that equates to less than one molecule of the original substance per all the molecules of the universe.

3. Homeopaths claim that their remedies work via some 'energy' or 'vital force' and that the process of preparing the homeopathic dilutions (it involves vigorous shaking the mixtures at each dilution step) transfers this 'energy' or information from one to the next dilution. They also believe that the process of diluting and agitating their remedies, which they call potentisation, renders them not less or not more potent.

4. Homeopathic remedies are usually prescribed according to the 'like cures like' principle: if, for instance, a patient suffers from runny eyes, a homeopath might prescribe a remedy made of onion, because onion make our eyes water. This and all other assumptions of homeopathy contradict the known laws of nature. In

other words, we do not fail to comprehend how homeopathy works, but we understand that it cannot work unless the known laws of nature are wrong.

5. Today, around 500 clinical trials of homeopathy have been published. The totality of this evidence fails to show that homeopathic remedies are more than placebos.[81] Numerous official statements from various countries confirm the absurdity of homeopathy, for instance:

   - "The principles of homeopathy contradict known chemical, physical and biological laws and persuasive scientific trials proving its effectiveness are not available" (**Russian Academy of Sciences, Russia**)
   - "Homeopathy should not be used to treat health conditions that are chronic, serious, or could become serious. People who choose homeopathy may put their health at risk if they reject or delay treatments for which there is good evidence for safety and effectiveness." (**National Health and Medical Research Council, Australia**)
   - "Homeopathic remedies don't meet the criteria of evidence-based medicine." (**Hungarian Academy of Sciences, Hungary**)
   - "The incorporation of anthroposophical and homeopathic products in the Swedish directive on medicinal products would run counter to several of the fundamental principles regarding medicinal products and evidence-based medicine." (**Swedish Academy of Sciences, Sweden**)
   - "There is no good-quality evidence that homeopathy is effective as a treatment for any health condition" (**National Health Service, England**)

6. Yet, many patients undeniably do get better after taking homeopathic remedies. The best evidence available today clearly shows that this improvement is unrelated to the homeopathic remedy per se. It is the result of a lengthy, empathetic, compassionate encounter with a homeopath, a placebo-response or other factors which experts often call 'context effects'.[82]

7. Whenever homeopaths advise their patients (as they often do) to forgo effective conventional treatments, they are likely to do harm. This phenomenon is best documented in relation to the advice of many homeopaths against immunisations.[83]

| Plausibility | 👎 |
| Efficacy | 👎 |

(continued)

---

[81]Ernst (2010b).

[82]Brien et al. (2011).

[83]Schmidt and Ernst (2003).

(continued)

Safety	
Cost	
Risk/benefit balance	

8.26 Homeoprophylaxis

(related modalities: homeopathy, nosodes)

Homeoprophylaxis or homeopathic immunisation is the use of homeopathic remedies as an alternative to conventional immunisations. Many homeopaths are convinced that this is an effective and safe option for protecting children and adults from infectious diseases and thus advise patients against conventional vaccinations.

1. Advice against immunisation by homeopaths and other practitioners of alternative medicine endangers public health; a recent study concluded that "children who have ever used certain Complementary and Alternative Medicine domains that may require contact with vaccine-hesitant CAM practitioners are vulnerable to lower annual uptake of influenza vaccination."[84]
2. Homeoparophylaxis normally entails the oral administration of certain homeopathic remedies, called nosodes (see there).
3. Like homeopathy, homeoprophylaxis is not biologically plausible. The remedies are so dilute that they do not contain active material is concentrations high enough for having any effect.
4. There is also no good clinical evidence to suggest that homeoprophylaxis is effective. In 2015, the Canadian Paediatric Society issued the following caution: "There is scant evidence in the medical literature for either the efficacy or safety of nosodes, which have not been well studied for the prevention of any infectious disease in humans."[85]
5. After conventional immunisations, patients develop immunity against the infection in question which can be monitored by measuring the immune response to the intervention. No such effects have been documented after homeoprophylaxis.

---

[84]Bleser et al. (2016).
[85]Rieder and Robinson (2015).

6. Despite this lack of evidence, some homeopaths—particularly those without medical training, i.e. lay-homeopaths—continue to recommend homeopathic immunisations.

7. Such promotion constitutes a serious risk for public health: once rates for conventional immunisations fall below a certain threshold, the population would lose its herd immunity. Subsequently even those individuals who were immunised are at risk of acquiring the infection. Even the UK Society of Homeopaths, the professional UK organisation for lay homeopaths, has recently stated that "… it is unethical for a homeopath to advise a patient against the use of conventional vaccines…"[86]

Plausibility	👎
Efficacy	👎
Safety	👍
Cost	👍
Risk/benefit balance	👎

8.27 Homotoxicology

(related modalities: detox, homeopathy, isopathy, nosodes)

Homotoxicolgy is a therapy developed by the German physician and homeopath Hans Reckeweg (1905–1985). It is strongly influenced by (but not identical with) homoeopathy. Proponents of homotoxicology understand it as a modern extension of homoeopathy developed partly in response to the effects of the Industrial Revolution, which imposed chemical pollutants on the human body.

1. According to the concepts of homotoxicology, any human disease is the result of toxins, which originate either from within the body or from its environment. Allegedly, each disease process runs through six specific phases and is the expression of the body's attempt to cope with these toxins. Diseases are thus viewed by proponents of homotoxicology as biologically useful defence mechanisms. Health, on the other hand, is the expression of the absence of toxins.

---

[86]https://homeopathy-soh.org/resources/position-statements/.

2. These assumptions are not based on science and bear no relationship to accepted principles of toxicology or therapeutics. Homotoxicology is therefore not plausible.
3. The therapeutic strategies of homotoxicology are essentially threefold:

   - prevention of further homotoxicological challenges,
   - elimination of homotoxins,
   - treatment of existing 'homotoxicoses'.

4. Frequently used homotoxicological remedies are fixed combinations of home-opathically prepared remedies such as nosodes, suis-organ preparations and conventional drugs. All these remedies are diluted and potentised according to the rules of homoeopathy. Proponents of homotoxicology claim that they activate what Reckeweg called the 'greater defence system'—a concerted neurological, endocrine, immunological, metabolic and connective tissue response that can give rise to symptoms and thus excretes homotoxins. Homotoxicological remedies are produced by Heel, Germany and are sold in over 60 countries.
5. The crucial difference between homotoxicology and homoeopathy is that the latter follows the 'like cures like' principle, while the former does not.
6. Numerous clinical trials of homotoxicology are available. They are usually sponsored or conducted by the manufacturer. Independent research is rare.
7. These studies are usually reviewed together with trials of homeopathic remedies which is strictly speaking not correct. A systematic review of studies of homotoxicology concluded that "the placebo-controlled, randomised clinical trials of homotoxicology fail to demonstrate the efficacy of this therapeutic approach."[87]

Plausibility	👎
Efficacy	👎
Safety	👍
Cost	👎
Risk/benefit balance	👎

---

[87]Ernst and Schmidt (2004).

8.28 Isopathy

(related modalities: homeopathy, homotoxiclogy)

Even though it fails to obey the most important assumption of homeopathy, isopathy is often considered to be a variation of homeopathy.

1. Homeopathy is characterised by following the 'like cures like' principle of Hahnemann. Isopathy does not follow this prime axiom of homeopathy and should therefore not be confused with homeopathy.
2. In isopathy, the agent that causes a disease or symptom is used to cure it.[88] It thus follows a different principle which, in analogy, could be called 'identical cures identical'.
3. A grass pollen, for instance, that causes hay-fever in a patient would be used in isopathy to cure the condition (in homeopathy, the appropriate remedy might be onion that causes similar symptoms, i.e. runny nose and watery eyes).
4. Like with homeopathy, the remedies used in isopathy are usually highly diluted and potentised. This means they do not normally contain any active ingredient at all.
5. The assumptions of isopathy are just as implausible as those of homeopathy.
6. Some of the methodologically best trials in this area are trials not of homeopathy but of isopathy. e.g.[89] Yet, the totality of the reliable evidence on isopathy fails to show that this approach id effective. In this regard, homeopathy and isopathy are comparable.
7. Most reviews and meta-analyses of clinical trials of homeopathy fail to adequately differentiate between isopathy and homeopathy. e.g.[90]

Plausibility	👎
Efficacy	👎
Safety	👍
Cost	👍
Risk/benefit balance	👎

---

[88]https://www.hive.co.uk/Product/Professor-Edzard-Ernst/Homeopathy—The-Undiluted-Facts–Including-a-Comprehensive-A-Z-Lexicon/19719982.

[89]Taylor et al. (2000).

[90]Linde et al. (1997).

8.29 Kava

(related modalities: herbal medicine)

Kava or kava kava (*Piper methysticum*) is a plant that originates from the South Pacific. The word is derived from *awa* which means bitter in Polynesian and describes the taste of the traditional Polynesian kava-beverage.

1. Kava was traditionally used by the Polynesian peoples for recreational purposes and as a remedy for conditions such as cystitis, gonorrhoea, syphilis and insomnia.
2. Kava contains several pharmacologically active constituents, for instance kavain and kavapyrone.
3. Their pharmacological activities are well-documented and include anxiolytic, relaxant and sedative effects on the central nervous system.
4. The clinical effects of kava have been extensively studied. A systematic review concluded that "the current weight of evidence supports the use of kava in treatment of anxiety with a significant result occurring in four out of six studies reviewed."[91] More recent studies support this view.[92]
5. Bases on such encouraging findings, kava became extremely popular. It is claimed that, due to the high demand during the kava-boom, poor quality products swept the markets.
6. Subsequently, Kava was associated with a number of adverse effects. The most important risk was alleged to be liver damage, the reason why it has been taken off the market in several countries.
7. It has, however, been argued that the liver-toxic effects were due to sub-optimal preparations that came on the market in the early 2000s. The above-mentioned review concluded that "safety issues should however be considered. Use of traditional water soluble extracts of the rhizome (root) of appropriate kava cultivars is advised, in addition to avoidance of use with alcohol and caution with other psychotropic medications. Avoidance of high doses if driving or operating heavy machinery should be mandatory. For regular users routine liver function tests are advised."[93]

Plausibility	👍
Efficacy	👍

(continued)

---

[91]Sarris et al. (2011).
[92]Sarris et al. (2013).
[93]Sarris et al. (2011).

(continued)

Safety	
Cost	
Risk/benefit balance	

8.30 Laetrile

(related modalities: alternative cancer cures)

Laetrile is an infamous alternative cancer cure that is relentlessly being promoted exploiting vulnerable patients and their carers.

1. Laetrile was patented 1961; it is a semisynthetic version of amygdalin which is found in the pits of apricots and many fruits, raw nuts, and plants.
2. Laetrile is usually administered by mouth as a pill or, less commonly, by injection.
3. Laetrile has been promoted since the 1950s as an alternative cancer cure, but no anticancer effects have been shown in clinical trials. The current Cochrane review concluded that "the claims that laetrile or amygdalin have beneficial effects for cancer patients are not currently supported by sound clinical data. There is a considerable risk of serious adverse effects from cyanide poisoning after laetrile or amygdalin, especially after oral ingestion. The risk-benefit balance of laetrile or amygdalin as a treatment for cancer is therefore unambiguously negative."[94]
4. Laetrile is not approved by the drug regulators of any country.
5. Laetrile is toxic and can therefore cause serious adverse effects.
6. Despite all this, Laetrile has remained popular and even some cancer charities promote it: "Laetrile is a non-toxic extract of apricot kernels. The claimed mechanism of action that is broken down by enzymes found in cancer cells. Hydrogen cyanide, one of the products of this reaction then has a local toxic effect on the cells."[95]
7. As Laetrile has no proven effectiveness and is potentially harmful, its risk benefit balance is clearly negative.

---

[94]Milazzo and Horneber (2015).

[95]http://yestolife.org.uk/all_therapies.php.

Plausibility	👎
Efficacy	👎
Safety	👎
Cost	👎
Risk/benefit balance	👎

8.31   Macrobiotic

(related modalities: cancer diets, Traditional Chinese Medicine)

Macrobiotic is a dietary regimen based on concepts that originate from Zen Buddhism; it is aimed at balancing the two assumed life forces yin and yang through diet.

1. The macrobiotic diet was popularized in the 1930s by George Ohsawa (1893–1966). (Ohsawa, his chosen name, is supposedly from the French "Oh, ça va" which means "Oh, it's fine".) He claimed to have cured his tuberculosis with his diet.
2. Michio Kushi (1916–2014) further popularised macrobiotics during the 1950s in the US and other Western countries.
3. The diet is based mainly on locally grown whole grain cereals, pulses, vegetables, seaweed, fermented soy products and fruit.
4. Nightshade vegetables (e.g. tomatoes, peppers, potatoes, eggplant), spinach, beets and avocados are used sparingly or not at all.
5. According to proponents, the crucial principle is that yin foods must be in balance with yang foods, an assumption that harps back to Traditional Chinese Medicine but lacks plausibility. Yet, some of the ideas realised in a macrobiotic diet have at least a tentative basis in science.[96]

---

[96]Harmon et al. (2015).

6. The diet is recommended for the prevention of a very wide range of conditions, most prominently cancer.[97] However, there is little good evidence that following a macrobiotic diet has positive health effects.[98]
7. Rigorous adherence to a macrobiotic diet can cause severe nutritional deficiencies and even death,[99] unless they are carefully planned. "Concerns include potential delay in conventional treatment for cancer, risks associated with nutrition deficiencies, and social limitations related to the complexities of strict adherence to this diet. Many aspects of currently popular dietary recommendations such as eating locally grown, in-season, fresh, organic foods are legacies of the macrobiotic lifestyle and diet."[100]

Plausibility	👎
Efficacy	👎
Safety	👎
Cost	👍
Risk/benefit balance	👎

8.32 Mistletoe

(related modalities: alternative cancer cures, anthroposophic medicine, herbal medicine)

Mistletoe (*Viscum album*) is a semi-parasitic plant that lives off host trees such as oak, elm, pine and apple. It has a long history of medicinal use; most recently, it has become a popular cancer remedy.

1. Its use as a caner treatment goes back to Rudolf Steiner (1861–1925) and his anthroposophical medicine.
2. Steiner considered that mistletoe lives off its host tree much like a cancer lives from a patient's body; in both cases, the end-result can be the death of the host.

---

[97]Kushi et al. (2001).
[98]Lerman (2010).
[99]Kushi et al. (2001).
[100]Kushi et al. (2001).

Following the 'like cures like' principle of homeopathy, Steiner concluded that mistletoe might be an effective cancer cure.

3. Steiner thus developed his mistletoe preparation, 'Iscador', for subcutaneous injection which is marketed by Weleda, a firm founded by a collaborator of Steiner.

4. Iscador is a fermented mistletoe extract and still the most widely used mistletoe product. Today, many other mistletoe preparations are available from various other manufacturers.

5. Some test-tube experiments suggest that ingredients of mistletoe might indeed have anti-cancer activities.[101] This is perhaps less surprising than one might think; many plants display such effects, but only rarely are they usable for treating cancer in humans.

6. The main therapeutic claims for mistletoe remedies are that they can cure cancer and improve the quality of life of cancer patients. These claims have been tested in numerous clinical trials most of which are of poor quality.

   • A systematic review concluded that "none of the methodologically stronger trials exhibited efficacy in terms of quality of life, survival or other outcome measures. Rigorous trials of mistletoe extracts fail to demonstrate efficacy of this therapy."[102]

   • Another review found that "there was no difference in survival or quality of life measures in patients who received mistletoe compared to those who did not."[103]

   • And a Cochrane review concluded that "the evidence from RCTs to support the view that the application of mistletoe extracts has impact on survival or leads to an improved ability to fight cancer or to withstand anticancer treatments is weak. Nevertheless, there is some evidence that mistletoe extracts may offer benefits on measures of QOL during chemotherapy for breast cancer, but these results need replication. Overall, more high quality, independent clinical research is needed to truly assess the safety and effectiveness of mistletoe extracts. Patients receiving mistletoe therapy should be encouraged to take part in future trails."[104]

7. Mistletoe injections are not free of adverse effects; they have been associated with soreness, inflammation at the injection sites, headache, fever, and chills.[105] Compared to conventional chemotherapy or radiotherapy, however, they cause only few and minor problems. This might explain the popularity of mistletoe for cancer patients.

---

[101]Yau et al. (2015).

[102]Ernst et al. (2003).

[103]https://www.ncbi.nlm.nih.gov/books/NBK65978/.

[104]Horneber et al. (2008).

[105]Ernst et al. (2003).

Plausibility	
Efficacy	
Safety	
Cost	
Risk/benefit balance	

8.33   Mushrooms

(related modalities: dietary supplements, herbal medicine, reishi)

The use of mushrooms for medicinal purposes has a long history in many cultures. Some mushrooms are known to be highly poisonous, some have hallucinogenic effects, and some are assumed to have pharmacological effects that can be used therapeutically.

1. Medicinal mushrooms possess properties such as anti-tumour, immunomodulating, antioxidant, cardiovascular, anti-hypercholesterolemic, anti-viral, anti-bacterial, anti-parasitic, anti-fungal, detoxification, hepatoprotective, and anti-diabetic effects.[106]
2. Several modern medicines were derived from fungi. The best-known example is penicillin; others include several cancer drugs, statins and immunosuppressants.
3. In Traditional Chinese Medicine, many herbal mixtures contain mushrooms; examples are reishi, maitake and shiitake which are all assumed to have anti-cancer properties.
4. The therapeutic claims made for mushrooms cover the whole range of conditions affecting humans and obviously depend on the type of fungus.
5. There is a paucity of clinical trials testing the effectiveness of mushrooms,[107] and most of our knowledge comes from traditional use or test-tube studies.[108,109]

---

[106]Sharma et al. (2018).

[107]https://www.ncbi.nlm.nih.gov/books/NBK401261/.

[108]Yurkiv et al. (2015).

[109]Geng et al. (2014).

6. A recent review confirmed this view by concluding that "mushrooms can be considered as useful therapeutic agents in the management and/or treatment of neurodegeneration diseases. However, this review focuses on in vitro evidence, and clinical trials with humans are needed."[110]
7. The adverse effects depend on the specific mushroom in question and, can in some instances, be serious.

Plausibility	
Efficacy	
Safety	
Cost	
Risk/benefit balance	

8.34 Nosodes

(related modalities: homeopathy, homeoprophylaxis, isopathy)

Nosodes are homeopathic remedies made from pathological materials usually originating from humans.

1. Nosodes can include diseased tissue, bodily fluids or discharges, pus, microorganisms etc.
2. They are produced as 'mother tinctures' and subsequently diluted and potentised much like all other homeopathic remedies.[111] As highly diluted nosodes no longer contain a single molecule of the original starting material, they are considered to be safe, even if they are derived from toxic or infectious materials. Caution might nonetheless be advised when the quality control procedures during manufacture are not rigorous, as has repeatedly been reported in homeopathy.[112]

---

[110]Phan et al. (2015).

[111]https://www.hive.co.uk/Product/Professor-Edzard-Ernst/Homeopathy—The-Undiluted-Facts–Including-a-Comprehensive-A-Z-Lexicon/19719982.

[112]http://www.drugnews.in/2018/08/28/hundreds-of-human-pet-homeopathy-products-recalled/.

3. Nosodes were added to the homeopathic Materia Medica only in the 1830s and are not in agreement with Hahnemann's 'like cures like' theory. Strictly speaking, treatments with nosodes are not homeopathy but isopathy (see there).
4. The treatment with nosodes lacks biological plausibility.
5. Nosodes are used for homeopathic immunisations or homeoprophylaxis. A potentised pathogenic substance is administered under the assumption that it will prevent the respective disease. This approach might seem similar to conventional immunisations; however, the crucial difference is that immunisations do contain pharmacologically active material and thus cause a immune response, while nosodes fulfil neither of these criteria.
6. There is no good clinical evidence that highly diluted nosodes have any health effects beyond placebo.
7. In 2015, the Canadian Paediatric Society issued the following caution: "There is scant evidence in the medical literature for either the efficacy or safety of nosodes, which have not been well studied for the prevention of any infectious disease in humans."[113]

Plausibility	👎
Efficacy	👎
Safety	👍
Cost	👍
Risk/benefit balance	👎

8.35 Oil Pulling

(related modalities: Ayurvedic medicine, detox, holistic dentistry)

Oil pulling is the use of oil for swishing it around your mouth for alleged health benefits.

1. Oil pulling has roots that reach back to ancient Hindu texts. Recently, it has become popular also outside India, particularly in North America.

---

[113]Rieder and Robinson (2015).

2. Coconut or sesame oils are usually employed for this therapy. The mechanism of action is poorly understood, and several theories have been put forward:

- Alkali hydrolysis of fat results in saponification or "soap making" process. Since the oils used for oil pulling contain fat, the alkali hydrolysis process emulsifies the fat into bicarbonate ions, normally found in the saliva. Soaps which are effective cleaning agents blend in the oil, hence increasing the surface area of the oil, and in turn enhancing the cleansing action.
- Another theory suggests that the viscous nature of the oil inhibits plaque accumulation and adhesion of bacteria.
- A third theory holds that the antioxidants present in the oil prevent lipid peroxidation, resulting in an antibiotic-like effect helping in the destruction of microorganisms.

3. Oil pulling is recommended to be carried out in the morning on an empty stomach. About 10 ml of oil is swished between the teeth and subsequently spat out. This should be followed by rinsing and conventional tooth brushing.
4. The practice should be repeated regularly, for acute conditions even three times per day.
5. Some studies suggest that coconut oil pulling reduces potentially dangerous bacteria in the mouth.[114] This effect has been shown to lead to a reduction in dental plaque formation,[115] halitosis (bad breath)[116] and gingivitis.[117] This collective evidence may not be strong, but it is encouraging.
6. The claimed benefits of oil pulling are not limited to the oral cavity. It is advocated also for the prevention and treatment of conditions such as headaches, migraines, thrombosis, eczema, diabetes and asthma.[118] Some proponents also claim that oil pulling is a detox therapy. None of these claims are, however, plausible or supported by good clinical evidence.
7. Provided one does not swallow the oil, there are no serious risks associated with oil pulling.

Plausibility	
Efficacy	[a]
Safety[a]	[a]

(continued)

---

[114]Peedikayil et al. (2016).
[115]Asokan et al. (2008).
[116]Asokan et al. (2011).
[117]Asokan et al. (2009).
[118]Naseem et al. (2017).

(continued)

Cost	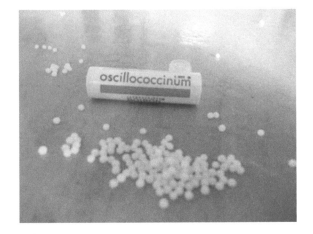
Risk/benefit balance	

^aOnly for oral conditions

8.36 Oscillococcinum

(related modalities: homeopathy, isopathy)

Oscillococcinum is the best-selling homeopathic remedy produced by Boiron, the world's largest producer of homeopathics. It is promoted as a remedy against the common cold and flu (Fig. 8.5).

1. Oscillococcinum, is made from the liver and heart of a duck. However, the duck organs are so highly diluted that no molecule of the duck is present in the final remedy. It is sold in the C200 potency which means that one part of organ extract is diluted at a ratio of 1: 10 000

Fig. 8.5 Oscillococcinum, a homeopathic preparation supposed to relieve flu symptoms. Manufactured by Boiron

000 000 000 000 000 000 000 000 000 000 000 000 000 000 000 000 000 000 000 000 000 000 000 000 000 000 000 000 000 000 000 000 000 000 000 000 000 000 000 000 000 000 000 000 000 000 000 000 000 000 000 000 000 000.

2. The reason for using duck organs is that, in the early 1920s, a French physician thought he had discovered the virus that caused the Spanish flu. It oscillated under his microscope, and he thus called it oscillococcus. Not only did it cause the flu, in the opinion of his discoverer, but it was also responsible for a whole host of other diseases, including cancer.

3. However, the virus does not exist, or at least nobody ever confirmed its existence.

4. The C200 dilution is so extreme that it corresponds to a single molecule per a multitude of universes.

5. Despite the fact that this remedy lacks any biological plausibility, several trials were initiated to test its effectiveness.

6. A Cochrane review (authored by homeopaths) has summarised these studies and concluded that "there is insufficient good evidence to enable robust conclusions to be made about Oscillococcinum($^®$) in the prevention or treatment of influenza and influenza-like illness. Our findings do not rule out the possibility that Oscillococcinum could have a clinically useful treatment effect but, given the low quality of the eligible studies, the evidence is not compelling. There was no evidence of clinically important harms due to Oscillococcinum($^®$)."[119]

7. Being so highly dilute and devoid of active molecules, Oscillococcinum cannot cause any direct adverse effects other than those to the wallet of the consumer.

Plausibility	👎
Efficacy	👎
Safety	👍
Cost	👎
Risk/benefit balance	👎

---

[119]Mathie et al. (2012).

8.37   Paleo Diet

(related modalities: none)

The paleo diet is a form of nutrition that is based on the food allegedly consumed during the paleolithic area. This period lasted for about 2.5 million years and ended about 10,000 years ago with the arrival of agriculture and the domestication of animals.

1. The Paleo diet is based on the assumption that departures from the nutrition and activity patterns of our hunter-gatherer ancestors have contributed greatly to the endemic chronic diseases of modern civilization.[120] A further assumption is that we are not well-adapted to eat grain, legumes and dairy products.
2. These assumptions are, however, not entirely plausible.
3. Critics of the Paleo diet point towards abundant evidence that

   - paleolithic humans did, in fact, eat grains and legumes,
   - humans are much more nutritionally flexible than previously thought,
   - the hypothesis that paleolithic humans were genetically adapted to specific local diets is unproven,
   - the paleolithic period was extremely long and saw a variety of forms of human settlement and subsistence in a wide variety of changing nutritional landscapes,
   - currently very little is known for certain about what paleolithic humans ate.

4. Proponents of the Paleo diet claim that it works by two fundamental principles:

   - It puts the optimal nutrition into your body.
   - It reduces or eliminates toxins.

5. The benefits claimed by proponents include:

   - Leaner, Stronger Muscles
   - Increased Energy
   - Significantly More Stamina
   - Clearer, Smoother Skin
   - Weight Loss Results
   - Better Performance and Recovery
   - Stronger Immune System
   - Enhanced Libido
   - Greater Mental Clarity
   - No More Hunger/Cravings
   - Thicker, Fuller Hair
   - Clear Eyes

---

[120]Challa and Uppaluri (2019).

6. There is little solid evidence to suggest that the paleo diet offers significant health benefits.[121] Some studies have suggested that cardiovascular risk factors can be positively influenced, for instance, in diabetics.[122] But the more specific claims, like the ones listed above, are not supported by good clinical data.
7. The safety of the paleo diet is questionable. One concern, for instance, is an adequate calcium intake, especially for those individuals at higher risk of osteoporosis.

Plausibility	👍
Efficacy	👎
Safety	👍
Cost	👍
Risk/benefit balance	👎

8.38 Placentophagy

(related modalities: dietary supplements, Traditional Chinese Medicine)

Placentophagy is the oral consumption by a woman of (usually her own) placenta after child-birth.

1. Some mammals instinctively eat their placenta after giving birth, and proponents of placentophagy argue that this habit is therefore natural and healthy also for humans.
2. Advocates of placentophagy claim it prevents post-partum bleeding, depression and other problems women may experience after child-birth.
3. A survey conducted by US anthropologists suggested that about three quarter of the women doing placentophagy claimed to benefit from it. In particular, they said they experience "improved mood", "increased energy", and "improved lactation".[123]
4. In Traditional Chinese Medicine (TCM), placenta is recommended for a range of conditions, including the management of wasting diseases, infertility and impotence. It is thus part of several TCM-mixtures.

---

[121]Tarantino et al. (2015).

[122]Jönsson et al. (2009).

[123]https://www.unlv.edu/news/article/steamed-dehydrated-or-raw-placentas-may-help-moms'-post-partum-health.

5. Instead of eating raw placenta (which few women find attractive), some proponents of placentophagy advocate drying and encapsulating the placenta which seems more acceptable and less revolting.

6. The so far only clinical trial of placentophagy was published in 2018. It concluded that "some hormones in encapsulated placenta lead to small but significant differences in hormonal profiles of women taking placenta capsules compared to those taking a placebo, although these dose-response changes were not sufficient to result in significant hormonal differences between groups. Whether modest hormonal changes due to placenta supplementation are associated with therapeutic postpartum effects, however, awaits further investigation."[124]

7. Ingesting products based on placenta that is not the patient's own carries the risk of transmitting infections.

Plausibility	👎
Efficacy	👎
Safety	👎
Cost	👍
Risk/benefit balance	👎

8.39   Reishi Mushroom

(related modalities: alternative cancer cures, dietary supplements, herbal medicine, Traditional Chinese Medicine)

Reishi (Ganoderma lucidum) is a mushroom that grows in Asia and has been used in Traditional Chinese Medicine for thousands of years, mostly for treating fatigue, asthma, cough, and liver ailments, and to promote longevity. Its Chinese name lingzhi means "herb of spiritual potency." Its Japanese name is mannentake, meaning "10,000-year-old mushroom." Reishi's use is documented in the oldest Chinese medical texts. Cultivation of reishi began only in the 1980s.

---

[124]Young et al. (2018).

1. Reishi contains polysaccharides, triterpeniods, proteins and amino acids which are claimed to be responsible for its alleged anticancer and immunostimulatory effects, its hepatoprotective action, antiviral activity, and beneficial effect on the cardiovascular system, rheumatoid arthritis, chronic fatigue syndrome, and diabetes.

2. Since several laboratory studies have shown anti-cancer and other effects in various test models, its popularity as an alternative cancer cure has been increasing. Reiki does unquestionably contain pharmacologically active constituents.

3. A plethora of dietary supplements containing reishi are currently commercially available. Their quality varies greatly.

4. A Cochrane review "did not find sufficient evidence to justify the use of G. lucidum as a first-line treatment for cancer. It remains uncertain whether G. lucidum helps prolong long-term cancer survival."[125]

5. Another Cochrane review found that "the evidence from a small number of randomised controlled trials does not support the use of G lucidum for treatment of cardiovascular risk factors in people with type 2 diabetes mellitus. Future research into the efficacy of G lucidum should be placebo-controlled and adhere to clinical trial reporting standards."[126]

6. The above-mentioned Cochrane review also stated that "reishi was generally well tolerated by most participants with only a scattered number of minor adverse events. No major toxicity was observed across the studies. Although there were few reports of harmful effect of G. lucidum, the use of its extract should be judicious, especially after thorough consideration of cost-benefit and patient preference."[127]

7. Reishi might interact with several drugs. For instance, taking reishi mushroom along with anti-hypertensives might cause the blood pressure to go too low. Similarly, it might increase the effects of anticoagulants and thus cause bleeding.

Plausibility	👍
Efficacy	👎
Safety	👍

(continued)

---

[125]https://www.cochranelibrary.com/cdsr/doi/10.1002/14651858.CD007731.pub3/full.

[126]Klupp et al. (2015).

[127]https://www.cochranelibrary.com/cdsr/doi/10.1002/14651858.CD007731.pub3/full.

(continued)

Cost	
Risk/benefit balance	

8.40   Relaxation Therapies

(related modalities: autogenic training, biofeedback, hypnotherapy, imagery, laughter therapy, meditation, progressive muscle relaxation)

Relaxation therapy is an umbrella term for treatments that rely entirely or predominantly on the relaxation response of the autonomic nervous system.

1. Many alternative treatments induce relaxation. Those that expressly rely on the relaxation response are often called relaxation therapies. These include several treatments that are listed above and discussed in separate chapters of this book.
2. The techniques common to many of these therapies include passive muscle relaxation, refocussing, control of respiration and imagery.
3. Herbert Benson (1935–) postulated that "many psychiatric and somatic stress-related diseases are but manifest variations on a theme of limbicogenic neurological hypersensitivity and resultant pathogenic arousal. The resultant stress-related diseases are, therefore, viewed as 'disorders of arousal.' From the reformulation offered … emerges a neurologically-based rationale for the clinical use of the 'relaxation response' in the treatment of stress-related diseases."[128]
4. The measurable effects of a relaxation response on the body include a decrease in measures such as:

   - heart rate,
   - oxygen consumption,
   - frequency of respiration,
   - alpha brain-wave activity.

5. Relaxation therapies are rarely curative but mostly advocated as adjunctive treatments for pain, anxiety and related disorders.
6. The clinical evidence for the specific therapies varies and is discussed in the respective chapters of this book.
7. Relaxation therapies are generally considered to be safe and experienced as agreeable or comforting.

---

[128]Everly and Benson (1989).

Plausibility	
Efficacy	See specific treatments
Safety	See specific treatments
Cost	
Risk/benefit balance	See specific treatments

8.41 Rhino Horn

(related modalities: Traditional Chinese Medicine)

Rhino horn (Xi Jiao) is one of many animal parts frequently used in Traditional Chinese Medicine (TCM).

1. *Cornu Rhinoceri Asiatici* (rhinoceros horn, RH), *Cornu Bubali* (water buffalo horn, WBH), and *Cornu Bovis grunniens* (yak horn, YH) are all ingredients of various TCM remedies. They have been used therapeutically in China for thousands of years.[129]

2. According to TCM theory, rhino horn clears the heat in the blood and de-toxifies the blood. It is also used to treat conditions causing the blood to "go the wrong way" and is recommended for conditions like boils, also causing heat. Rhino horn was once considered as one of the few life-saving drugs for people suffering from severe fever.[130] Relatively small amounts of horn are used for medicinal purposes and often mixed with the other ingredients (herbs, gypsum, or tea).

3. In 1993, the Ministry of Health of the People's Republic of China has removed rhino horn from the Chinese Medicine Pharmacopeia. However, in 2018, China's State Council reversed this ban, only to re-reverse it after wide-spread protests.[131] The Register of Chinese Herbal Medicine (RCHM) in the UK has condemned the illegal trade in endangered species.

4. Yet, the demand and prices for rhino horn and other animal parts for TCM use continue to be high.

5. Rhinos therefore continue to be threatened by the relentless poaching for the TCM-trade, and consequently their numbers are in fast decline.

---

[129]Liu et al. (2011).

[130]http://www.chineseherbshealing.com/rhinoceros-horn/.

[131]https://www.nytimes.com/2018/11/12/world/asia/china-rhino-tiger-ban.html.

6. There have been very few scientific studies of rhino horn. The few that have emerged provide no reliable evidence that rhino horn has any positive health effects in humans.[132,133]
7. The ecological damage done by the illegal trade of rhino horn (and many other animal ingredients) of TCM remedies is considerable and amounts to nothing less than a scandal.

Plausibility	👎
Efficacy	👎
Safety	👎
Cost	👎
Risk/benefit balance	👎

8.42   Shark Cartilage

(related modalities: alternative cancer cures, dietary supplements)

Shark cartilage is a dietary supplement made from the dried and powdered skeletons of sharks. Numerous products are available for sale as dietary supplements.

1. Shark cartilage is being promoted for several conditions, most notably as an alternative cancer cure.
2. The underlying assumption seems to be that sharks do not get cancer; thus, their cartilage must be a cancer cure.[134] This notion is wrong on two accounts: firstly, sharks do get cancer; and secondly is their skeleton not a cure for cancer.
3. Shark cartilage is perhaps the most widely promoted alternative cancer cure during the last 4 decades. In 1995, the annual world market for shark cartilage products exceeded US$30 million.
4. Two glycoproteins (sphyrnastatin 1 and 2) have been isolated from the cartilage of the hammerhead shark and were reported to exhibit antiangiogenic activity

---

[132]Laburn and Mitchell (1997).

[133]But et al. (1990).

[134]Ostrander et al. (2004).

inhibiting blood supply, an effect which could theoretically be helpful in human cancer therapy. However, as macromolecules are not usually absorbed by the intestinal tract, it is questionable whether, after oral administration, the sphyrnastatins ever reach the bloodstream in sufficiently high concentrations for exerting these effects.

5. Two further mechanisms of action have been suggested for shark cartilage:

   • It is claimed to kill cancer cells directly.
   • It is claimed to stimulate the immune system.

6. To date, there has been only one randomized clinical trial of cartilage as cancer treatment published in a peer-reviewed scientific journal. It compared treatment using a form of shark cartilage to treatment using a placebo, both in addition to standard care. In 83 patients having either advanced breast or advanced colon cancer, there was no difference in the quality of life or survival rate between the two groups. The authors concluded that "this trial was unable to demonstrate any suggestion of efficacy for this shark cartilage product in patients with advanced cancer."[135]

7. One review stated that "the promotion of crude shark cartilage extracts as a cure for cancer has contributed to at least two significant negative outcomes: a dramatic decline in shark populations and a diversion of patients from effective cancer treatments ... The fact that people think shark cartilage consumption can cure cancer illustrates the serious potential impacts of pseudoscience."[136]

Plausibility	
Efficacy	
Safety	
Cost	
Risk/benefit balance	

---

[135]Loprinzi et al. (2005).
[136]Ostrander et al. (2004).

8.43 St John's Wort

(related modalities: dietary supplements, herbal medicine)

St John's wort (*Hypericum perforatum*) is a plant used to produce a herbal remedy that is traditionally employed for a range of conditions (Fig. 8.6).

1. Today, St John's wort supplements are used mostly for mild to moderate depression, and many different oral preparations are commercially available as dietary supplements.

Fig. 8.6 St John's Wort (*Hypericum perforatum*). *Source* E Ernst

2. The plant has several active ingredients, including hypericin, pseudo-hypericin, and hyperforin. They seem to have a wide range of different pharmacological actions.[137]
3. Because of this fact, it has so far not been possible to produce a drug with a single constituent of this plant that is clinically effective.
4. There have been around 50 clinical trials of St John's wort for depression, many of which are of good methodological quality.
5. There results have been summarised in several reviews.

    • One review, for instance, concluded that "for patients with mild-to-moderate depression, St John's wort has comparable efficacy and safety when compared to SSRIs."[138]
    • Similarly, a meta-analysis found "significant advantage for St. John's Wort compared to placebo."[139]

6. St John's wort is considered to be safe; serious adverse effects, such as phototoxicity, have been observed but are rare. Generally, it causes less side-effects than conventional anti-depressants.[140]
7. The problem, however, is that about half of all prescription medications interact with St John's wort such that the blood level of these drugs is lowered. This includes, for instance, anticoagulants and oral contraceptives and can have serious consequences.[141] Another danger is that some commercially available remedies are substandard and contain little or no active ingredients. It is therefore advisable to purchase products only from reputable sources.

Plausibility	👍
Efficacy	👍
Safety	👍
Cost	👎
Risk/benefit balance	👍

---

[137]Müller (2003).

[138]Ng et al. (2017).

[139]Röder et al. (2004).

[140]Whiskey et al. (2001).

[141]Di Carlo et al. (2001).

8.44 Ukrain

(related modalities: alternative cancer cures, herbal medicine)

Ukrain is a semi-synthetic proprietary product derived from the common weed greater celandine (*Chelidonium majus*). It was developed and is marketed by Vasyl Novytskyi and is being promoted as an alternative cancer cure.

1. In 2012, several people including Vasyl Novytskyi, the drug's developer, were arrested in Austria for distributing the drug under suspicion of commercial fraud. Novytskyi appeared in court again in 2015 for selling Ukrain, earning an estimated 1.1 million Euros through fraud by changing labels on expired vials. In March 2015, two co-defendants of Novytskyi were exonerated for commercial fraud, while legal proceedings continued for Novytsky.
2. Ukrain has been promoted heavily, often with methods that seem unusual, to say the least. One article even claimed about Ukrain and its inventor that "It is the first medicament in the world that accumulates in the cores of cancer cells very quickly after administration and kills only cancer cells while leaving healthy cells undamaged. Its inventor and patent holder Dr. Wassil Nowicky was nominated for the Nobel Prize for this medicament in 2005 ..."[142]
3. Ukrain's main active constituents are alkaloids and thiophosphoric acid.
4. Ukrain allegedly cures not only cancer but also viral infections such as HIV.
5. The UK charity 'Yes to Life' advertises Ukrain stating that it is a "type of low toxicity chemotherapy derived from a combination of two known cytotoxic drugs that are of little use individually, as the doses required for effective anticancer action are too high to be tolerated. However the combination is effective at far lower doses, with few side effects."[143]
6. A systematic review of the clinical trials of Ukrain for cancer concluded that "the data from randomised clinical trials suggest Ukrain to have potential as an anticancer drug. However, numerous caveats prevent a positive conclusion, and independent rigorous studies are urgently needed."[144] Since then, no further convincing evidence has emerged, and Ukrain must therefore be categorised as unproven.
7. Adverse effects include injection site reactions, slight fever, fatigue, dizziness, nausea, and possibly tumour bleeding.

---

[142]http://medicdebate.org/?q=node/294.

[143]http://yestolife.org.uk/all_therapies.php.

[144]Ernst and Schmidt (2005).

Plausibility	
Efficacy	
Safety	
Cost	
Risk/benefit balance	

8.45   Urine Therapy

(related modalities: none)

Urine therapy is the use of urine for medicinal purposes.

1. Urine therapy has a long history. Records from the ancient Egyptians to Greeks, Romans and from the Middle Ages and the Renaissance testify to the practice of urine therapy.[145]
2. Some ancient texts even refer to urine as the "gold of the blood" or the "elixir of long life". The Biblical Proverb 5:15 "Drink waters out of thine own cistern and running waters out of thine own well" is interpreted by urine therapy proponents as a biblical endorsement of their treatment.
3. Urine therapy consists of drinking urine (urophagia) or massaging it into the skin or the gums. The urine is often, but not always, from the patients themselves.
4. In India, several urine preparations from cows are commercially available.[146] In Britain, auto-urine therapy, i.e. drinking one's own urine was popularized by the naturopath John W. Armstrong in early 20th century. In 1944, he published a book entitled 'The Water of Life: A treatise on urine therapy' which still is the most influential text on the subject.
5. Many extraordinary claims are being made for urine therapy. One author, for instance, claims that "multiple sclerosis, colitis, lupus, rheumatoid arthritis, cancer, hepatitis, hyperactivity, pancreatic insufficiency, psoriasis, eczema,

---

[145]Savica et al. (2011).

[146]https://www.mid-day.com/articles/cow-urine-has-become-the-booming-business-in-india-and-this-is-how/17483169.

diabetes, herpes, mononucleosis, adrenal failure, allergies and so many other ailments have been relieved through use of this therapy. After you overcome your initial gag response (I know I had one), you will realize that something big is going on, and if you are searching for health, this is an area to investigate. There are numerous reports and double blind studies which go back to the turn of the century supporting the efficacy of using urine for health."[147]

6. There are no rigorous trials of urine therapy. However, experiences with the practice of urine therapy have recently been shared in two international conferences: in 1996 in India and in 1999 in Germany.[148] In the absence of sound evidence, urine therapy must be categorised as unproven.

7. Urine therapy is generally regarded as safe. However, caution is advisable in cases where the urine is not sterile.[149]

Plausibility	👎
Efficacy	👎
Safety	👎
Cost	👍
Risk/benefit balance	👎

8.46 Veterinary Homeopathy

(related modalities: anthroposophic medicine, Bach flower remedies, homeopathy, Schuessler salts)

Veterinary homeopathy is the treatment of animals with homeopathic remedies (this book is on human health, but because of the claim that homeopathy cannot be a placebo therapy as it works in animals, veterinary homeopathy has been included).

---

[147]http://www.shirleys-wellness-cafe.com/UT/Urine.

[148]Savica et al. (2011).

[149]Ogunshe et al. (2010).

Fig. 8.7 Charles, Prince of
Wales (b. 1948), a well
known advocate of
homeopathy

1. After Hahnemann gave a lecture on the subject in the mid-1810s, homeopathy
   has been used also for treating animals. Von Boennighausen, an influential early
   homeopath, was one of the first to promote veterinary homeopathy.[150]
2. However, veterinary medical schools initially tended to reject homoeopathy, and
   the number of veterinary homeopaths remained small, even during the period
   when human homeopathy thrived. In the 1920s, veterinary homoeopathy was
   revived in Germany. Members of the "Studiengemeinschaft für tierärztliche
   Homöopathie" (Study Group for Veterinary Homoeopathy) which was founded
   in 1936 and started to investigate this approach systematically.[151]
3. Today, veterinary homeopathy has become popular not least because of the
   general boom in alternative medicine. Prominent proponents include Prince
   Charles (Fig. 8.7).

---

[150]https://www.hive.co.uk/Product/Professor-Edzard-Ernst/Homeopathy—The-Undiluted-Facts–
Including-a-Comprehensive-A-Z-Lexicon/19719982.

[151]https://www.hive.co.uk/Product/Professor-Edzard-Ernst/Homeopathy—The-Undiluted-Facts–
Including-a-Comprehensive-A-Z-Lexicon/19719982.

4. In many countries, veterinary homeopaths have their own professional organisations. In the US, for instance, homeopathic vets are organised in the Academy
   of Veterinary Homeopathy. In other countries, however, veterinarians are banned from practicing homeopathy. In the UK, only veterinarians are allowed to
   use homeopathy on animals (but anyone regardless of background can use it on
   human patients).
5. There are numerous clinical trials of veterinary homeopathy. Most of them are,
   however, of low methodological quality.
6. One review included 20 trials of which 16 had high risks of bias; the remaining
   4 had uncertain risks of bias. The authors (known proponents of homeopathy)
   concluded that "due to the poor reliability of their data, OTP-controlled trials do
   not currently provide useful insight into the effectiveness of homeopathy in
   animals."[152]
7. This means that, contrary to what is often claimed, homeopathy is not of proven
   effectiveness in animals.

Plausibility	👎
Efficacy	👎
Safety	👍
Cost	👎
Risk/benefit balance	👎

References

Abdelhamid AS, Brown TJ, Brainard JS, Biswas P, Thorpe GC, Moore HJ, Deane KH,
    AlAbdulghafoor FK, Summerbell CD, Worthington HV, Song F, Hooper L (2018) Omega-3
    fatty acids for the primary and secondary prevention of cardiovascular disease. Cochrane
    Database Syst Rev 7:CD003177
Asokan S, Rathan J, Muthu MS, Rathna PV, Emmadi P, Chamundeswari R (2008) Effect of oil
    pulling on Streptococcus mutans count in plaque and saliva using Dentocult SM Strip mutans
    test: a randomized, controlled, triple-blind study. J Indian Soc Pedod Prev Dent 26(1):12–17
Asokan S, Emmadi P, Chamundeswari R (2009) Effect of oil pulling on plaque induced gingivitis:
    a randomized, controlled, triple-blind study. Indian J Dent Res 20(1):47–51

---

[152]Mathie and Clausen (2015).

Asokan S, Kumar RS, Emmadi P, Raghuraman R, Sivakumar N (2011) Effect of oil pulling on halitosis and microorganisms causing halitosis: a randomized controlled pilot trial. J Indian Soc Pedod Prev Dent 29(2):90–94

Bamford JT, Ray S, Musekiwa A, van Gool C, Humphreys R, Ernst E (2013) Oral evening primrose oil and borage oil for eczema. Cochrane Database Syst Rev (4):CD004416

Bleser WK, Elewonibi BR, Miranda PY, BeLue R (2016) Complementary and alternative medicine and influenza vaccine uptake in US children. Pediatrics 138(5):pii: e20154664

Brien S, Lachance L, Prescott P, McDermott C, Lewith G (2011) Homeopathy has clinical benefits in rheumatoid arthritis patients that are attributable to the consultation process but not the homeopathic remedy: a randomized controlled clinical trial. Rheumatology (Oxford) 50 (6):1070–1082

But PP, Lung LC, Tam YK (1990) Ethnopharmacology of rhinoceros horn. I: antipyretic effects of rhinoceros horn and other animal horn. J Ethnopharmacol 30(2):157–168

Challa HJ, Uppaluri KR (2019) Paleolithic diet

Chou WY, Chuang KH, Sun D, Lee YH, Kao PH, Lin YY, Wang HW, Wu YL (2015) Inhibition of PKC-induced COX-2 and IL-8 expression in human breast cancer cells by glucosamine. J Cell Physiol 230(9):2240–2251

Cohen PA, Ernst E (2010) Safety of herbal supplements: a guide for cardiologists. Cardiovasc Ther 28(4):246–253

Cyranoski David (2018) Why Chinese medicine is heading for clinics around the world. Nature 561:448–450

Dat AD, Poon F, Pham KB, Doust J (2012) Aloe vera for treating acute and chronic wounds. Cochrane Database Syst Rev (2):CD008762

Di Carlo G, Borrelli F, Ernst E, Izzo AA (2001) St John's wort: prozac from the plant kingdom. Trends Pharmacol Sci 22(6):292–297

Elihu N, Anandasbapathy S, Frishman WH (1998) Chelation therapy in cardiovascular disease: ethylenediaminetetraacetic acid, deferoxamine, and dexrazoxane. J Clin Pharmacol 38(2):101–105

Ernst E (2000) Chelation therapy for coronary heart disease: an overview of all clinical investigations. Am Heart J 140(1):139–141

Ernst E (2004) Risks of herbal medicinal products. Pharmacoepidemiol Drug Saf 13(11):767–771

Ernst E (2009) Carctol: profit before patients? Breast Care (Basel) 4(1):31–33

Ernst E (2010a) Bach flower remedies: a systematic review of randomised clinical trials. Swiss Med Wkly 140:w13079

Ernst E (2010b) Homeopathy: what does the "best" evidence tell us? Med J Aust 192(8):458–460

Ernst E, Pittler MH (1998) Efficacy of homeopathic arnica: a systematic review of placebo-controlled clinical trials. Arch Surg 133(11):1187–1190

Ernst E, Schmidt K (2004) Homotoxicology—a review of randomised clinical trials. Eur J Clin Pharmacol 60(5):299–306

Ernst E, Schmidt K (2005) Ukrain—a new cancer cure? A systematic review of randomised clinical trials. BMC Cancer 5:69

Ernst E, Schmidt K, Steuer-Vogt MK (2003) Mistletoe for cancer? A systematic review of randomised clinical trials. Int J Cancer 107(2):262–267

Everly GS Jr, Benson H (1989) Disorders of arousal and the relaxation response: speculations on the nature and treatment of stress-related diseases. Int J Psychosom 36(1–4):15–21

Fenton TR, Fenton CJ (2016) Evidence does not support the alkaline diet. Osteoporos Int 27 (7):2387–2388

Fung MC, Bowen DL (1996) Silver products for medical indications: risk-benefit assessment. J Toxicol Clin Toxicol 34(1):119–126

Geng Y, Zhu S, Lu Z, Xu H, Shi JS, Xu ZH (2014) Anti-inflammatory activity of mycelial extracts from medicinal mushrooms. Int J Med Mushrooms 16(4):319–325

Grodstein F, Kang JH, Glynn RJ, Cook NR, Gaziano JM (2007) A randomized trial of beta carotene supplementation and cognitive function in men: the Physicians' Health Study II. Arch Intern Med 167(20):2184–2190

Guercio V, Galeone C, Turati F, La Vecchia C (2014) Gastric cancer and allium vegetable intake: a critical review of the experimental and epidemiologic evidence. Nutr Cancer 66(5):757–773

Guo X, Mei N (2016) Aloe vera: a review of toxicity and adverse clinical effects. J Environ Sci Health C Environ Carcinog Ecotoxicol Rev 34(2):77–96

Hadrup N, Lam HR (2014) Oral toxicity of silver ions, silver nanoparticles and colloidal silver—a review. Regul Toxicol Pharmacol 68(1):1–7

Harmon BE, Carter M, Hurley TG, Shivappa N, Teas J, Hébert JR (2015) Nutrient composition and anti-inflammatory potential of a prescribed macrobiotic diet. Nutr Cancer 67(6):933–940

Ho D, Jagdeo J, Waldorf HA (2016) Is there a role for arnica and bromelain in prevention of post-procedure ecchymosis or edema? A systematic review of the literature. Dermatol Surg 42 (4):445–463

Horneber MA, Bueschel G, Huber R, Linde K, Rostock M (2008) Mistletoe therapy in oncology. Cochrane Database Syst Rev (2):CD003297

Hudson A, Lopez E, Almalki AJ, Roe AL, Calderón AI (2018) A review of the toxicity of compounds found in herbal dietary supplements. Planta Med 84(9–10):613–626

Izzo AA, Ernst E (2009) Interactions between herbal medicines and prescribed drugs: an updated systematic review. Drugs 69(13):1777–1798

Jäger T, Scherr C, Shah D, Majewsky V, Wolf U, Betti L, Baumgartner S (2015) The use of plant-based bioassays in homeopathic basic research. Homeopathy 104(4):277–282

Jönsson T, Granfeldt Y, Ahrén B, Branell UC, Pålsson G, Hansson A, Söderström M, Lindeberg S (2009) Beneficial effects of a Paleolithic diet on cardiovascular risk factors in type 2 diabetes: a randomized cross-over pilot study. Cardiovasc Diabetol 8:35

Kantor ED, Zhang X, Wu K, Signorello LB, Chan AT, Fuchs CS, Giovannucci EL (2016) Use of glucosamine and chondroitin supplements in relation to risk of colorectal cancer: results from the Nurses' Health Study and Health Professionals follow-up study. Int J Cancer 139(9):1949–1957

Klupp NL, Chang D, Hawke F, Kiat H, Cao H, Grant SJ, Bensoussan A (2015) Ganoderma lucidum mushroom for the treatment of cardiovascular risk factors. Cochrane Database Syst Rev (2):CD007259

Korman DB (2014) Alternative means of drug therapy for cancer: antineoplastons–antitumor properties and mechanisms of action. Vopr Onkol 60(4):449–456

Kriplani P, Guarve K, Baghael US (2017) Arnica montana L—a plant of healing: review. J Pharm Pharmacol 69(8):925–945

Kushi LH, Cunningham JE, Hebert JR, Lerman RH, Bandera EV, Teas J (2001) The macrobiotic diet in cancer. J Nutr 131(11 Suppl):3056S–3064S

Laburn HP, Mitchell D (1997) Extracts of rhinoceros horn are not antipyretic in rabbits. J Basic Clin Physiol Pharmacol 8(1–2):1–11

Lamas GA, Goertz C, Boineau R, Mark DB, Rozema T, Nahin RL, Lindblad L, Lewis EF, Drisko J, Lee KL (2013) TACT Investigators Effect of disodium EDTA chelation regimen on cardiovascular events in patients with previous myocardial infarction: the TACT randomized trial. JAMA 309(12):1241–1250

Lee MS, Choi J, Posadzki P, Ernst E (2012) Aromatherapy for health care: an overview of systematic reviews. Maturitas 71(3):257–260

Lemmo W (2015) Potential interactions of prescription and over-the-counter medications having antioxidant capabilities with radiation and chemotherapy. Int J Cancer 137(11):2525–2533

Lerman RH (2010) The macrobiotic diet in chronic disease. Nutr Clin Pract 25(6):621–626

Linde K, Clausius N, Ramirez G, Melchart D, Eitel F, Hedges LV, Jonas WB (1997) Are the clinical effects of homeopathy placebo effects? A meta-analysis of placebo-controlled trials. Lancet 350(9081):834–843

Liu R, Duan JA, Wang M, Shang E, Guo J, Tang Y (2011) Analysis of active components of rhinoceros, water buffalo and yak horns using two-dimensional electrophoresis and ethnopharmacological evaluation. J Sep Sci 34(3):354–362

Loprinzi CL, Levitt R, Barton DL, Sloan JA, Atherton PJ, Smith DJ, Dakhil SR, Moore DF Jr, Krook JE, Rowland KM Jr, Mazurczak MA, Berg AR, Kim GP (2005) North Central Cancer

Treatment Group. Evaluation of shark cartilage in patients with advanced cancer: a North Central Cancer Treatment Group trial. Cancer 104(1):176–182

Mathie RT, Clausen J (2015) Veterinary homeopathy: systematic review of medical conditions studied by randomised trials controlled by other than placebo. BMC Vet Res 11:236

Mathie RT, Frye J, Fisher P (2012) Homeopathic Oscillococcinum(®) for preventing and treating influenza and influenza-like illness. Cochrane Database Syst Rev 12:CD001957

Mikami T, Kitagawa H (2013) Biosynthesis and function of chondroitin sulfate. Biochim Biophys Acta 1830(10):4719–4733

Milazzo S, Horneber M (2015) Laetrile treatment for cancer. Cochrane Database Syst Rev (4): CD005476

Morse NL, Clough PM (2006) A meta-analysis of randomized, placebo-controlled clinical trials of Efamol evening primrose oil in atopic eczema Where do we go from here in light of more recent discoveries? Curr Pharm Biotechnol 7(6):503–524

Müller WE (2003) Current St John's wort research from mode of action to clinical efficacy. Pharmacol Res 47(2):101–109

Naseem M, Khiyani MF, NaumanH Zafar MS, Shah AH, Khalil HS (2017) Oil pulling and importance of traditional medicine in oral health maintenance. Int J Health Sci (Qassim) 11 (4):65–70

Ng QX, Venkatanarayanan N, Ho CY (2017) Clinical use of Hypericum perforatum (St John's wort) in depression: a meta-analysis. J Affect Disord 210:211–221

Nicolaï SP, Kruidenier LM, Bendermacher BL, Prins MH, Stokmans RA, Broos PP, Teijink JA (2013) Ginkgo biloba for intermittent claudication. Cochrane Database Syst Rev (6): CD006888

Nortier JL, Martinez MC, Schmeiser HH, Arlt VM, Bieler CA, Petein M, Depierreux MF, De Pauw L, Abramowicz D, Vereerstraeten P, Vanherweghem JL (2000) Urothelial carcinoma associated with the use of a Chinese herb (Aristolochia fangchi). N Engl J Med 342(23):1686–1692

Ogata Y, Matono K, Tsuda H, Ushijima M, Uchida S, Akagi Y, Shirouzu K (2015) Randomized phase II study of 5-fluorouracil hepatic arterial infusion with or without antineoplastons as an adjuvant therapy after hepatectomy for liver metastases from colorectal cancer. PLoS One 10 (3):e0120064

Ogata T, Ideno Y, Akai M, Seichi A, Hagino H, Iwaya T, Doi T, Yamada K, Chen AZ, Li Y, Hayashi K (2018) Effects of glucosamine in patients with osteoarthritis of the knee: a systematic review and meta-analysis. Clin Rheumatol 37(9):2479–2487

Ogunshe AA, Fawole AO, Ajayi VA (2010) Microbial evaluation and public health implications of urine as alternative therapy in clinical pediatric cases: health implication of urine therapy. Pan Afr Med J 5:12

Ostrander GK, Cheng KC, Wolf JC, Wolfe MJ (2004) Shark cartilage, cancer and the growing threat of pseudoscience. Cancer Res 64(23):8485–8491

Pareek A, Suthar M, Rathore GS, Bansal V (2011) Feverfew (Tanacetum parthenium L.): a systematic review. Pharmacogn Rev 5(9):103–110

Pattrick M, Heptinstall S, Doherty M (1989) Feverfew in rheumatoid arthritis: a double blind, placebo controlled study. Ann Rheum Dis 48(7):547–549

Pauwels EK, Kostkiewicz M (2008) Fatty acid facts, part III: cardiovascular disease, or, a fish diet is not fishy. Drug News Perspect 21(10):552–561

Peedikayil FC, Remy V, John S, Chandru TP, Sreenivasan P, Bijapur GA (2016) Comparison of antibacterial efficacy of coconut oil and chlorhexidine on Streptococcus mutans: an in vivo study. J Int Soc Prev Commun Dent 6(5):447–452

Perry R, Terry R, Watson LK, Ernst E (2012) Is lavender an anxiolytic drug? A systematic review of randomised clinical trials. Phytomedicine 19(8–9):825–835

Phan CW, David P, Naidu M, Wong KH, Sabaratnam V (2015) Therapeutic potential of culinary-medicinal mushrooms for the management of neurodegenerative diseases: diversity, metabolite, and mechanism. Crit Rev Biotechnol 35(3):355–368

Ponte E, Cafagna D, Balbi M (1997) Cardiovascular disease and omega-3 fatty acids. Minerva Med 88(9):343–353

Posadzki P, Alotaibi A, Ernst E (2012) Adverse effects of aromatherapy: a systematic review of case reports and case series. Int J Risk Saf Med 24(3):147–161

Posadzki P, Watson L, Ernst E (2013) Contamination and adulteration of herbal medicinal products (HMPs): an overview of systematic reviews. Eur J Clin Pharmacol 69(3):295–307

Radha MH, Laxmipriya NP (2014) Evaluation of biological properties and clinical effectiveness of Aloe vera: a systematic review. J Tradit Complement Med 5(1):21–26

Rieder MJ, Robinson JL (2015) 'Nosodes' are no substitute for vaccines. Paediatr Child Health 20 (4):219–222

Rimm EB, Appel LJ, Chiuve SE, Djoussé L, Engler MB, Kris-Etherton PM, Mozaffarian D, Siscovick DS, Lichtenstein AH (2018) Seafood long-chain n-3 polyunsaturated fatty acids and cardiovascular disease: a science advisory from the American Heart Association. Circulation 138(1):e35–e47

Röder C, Schaefer M, Leucht S (2004) Meta-analysis of effectiveness and tolerability of treatment of mild to moderate depression with St. John's Wort. Fortschr Neurol Psychiatr 72(6):330–343

Runhaar J, Rozendaal RM, van Middelkoop M, Bijlsma HJW, Doherty M, Dziedzic KS, Lohmander LS, McAlindon T, Zhang W, Bierma Zeinstra S (2017) Subgroup analyses of the effectiveness of oral glucosamine for knee and hip osteoarthritis: a systematic review and individual patient data meta-analysis from the OA trial bank. Ann Rheum Dis 76(11):1862–1869

Sarris J, LaPorte E, Schweitzer I (2011) Kava: a comprehensive review of efficacy, safety, and psychopharmacology. Aust N Z J Psychiatry 45(1):27–35

Sarris J, Stough C, Bousman CA, Wahid ZT, Murray G, Teschke R, Savage KM, Dowell A, Ng C, Schweitzer I (2013) Kava in the treatment of generalized anxiety disorder: a double-blind, randomized, placebo-controlled study. J Clin Psychopharmacol 33(5):643–648

Savica V, Calò LA, Santoro D, Monardo P, Mallamace A, Bellinghieri G (2011) Urine therapy through the centuries. J Nephrol 24(Suppl 17):S123–S125

Schmidt K, Ernst E (2003) MMR vaccination advice over the Internet. Vaccine 21(11–12):1044–1047

Schmidt K, Ernst E (2004) Assessing websites on complementary and alternative medicine for cancer. Ann Oncol 15(5):733–742

Schwalfenberg GK (2012) The alkaline diet: is there evidence that an alkaline pH diet benefits health? J Environ Public Health 2012:727630

Seely DM, Wu P, Mills EJ (2005) EDTA chelation therapy for cardiovascular disease: a systematic review. BMC Cardiovasc Disord 1(5):32

Seely D, Kennedy DA, Myers SP, Cheras PA, Lin D, Li R, Cattley T, Brent PA, Mills E, Leonard BJ (2007) In vitro analysis of the herbal compound Essiac. Anticancer Res 27 (6B):3875–3882

Sharma D, Singh VP, Singh NK (2018) A review on phytochemistry and pharmacology of medicinal as well as poisonous mushrooms. Mini Rev Med Chem 18(13):1095–1109

Shrihari JS, Roy A, Prabhakaran D, Reddy KS (2006) Role of EDTA chelation therapy in cardiovascular diseases. Natl Med J India 19(1):24–26

Singh JA, Noorbaloochi S, MacDonald R, Maxwell LJ (2015) Chondroitin for osteoarthritis. Cochrane Database Syst Rev 1:CD005614

Sirtori CR, Arnoldi A, Cicero AF (2015) Nutraceuticals for blood pressure control. Ann Med 47 (6):447–456

Siti HN, Kamisah Y, Kamsiah J (2015) The role of oxidative stress, antioxidants and vascular inflammation in cardiovascular disease (a review). Vascul Pharmacol 71:40–56

Sun T, Wang X, Xu H (2015) Ginkgo Biloba extract for angina pectoris: a systematic review. Chin J Integr Med 21(7):542–550

Sun YE, Wang W, Qin J (2018) Anti-hyperlipidemia of garlic by reducing the level of total cholesterol and low-density lipoprotein: a meta-analysis. Medicine (Baltimore) 97(18):e0255

Tang JL, Zhan SY, Ernst E (1999) Review of randomised controlled trials of traditional Chinese medicine. BMJ 319(7203):160–161

Tarantino G, Citro V, Finelli C (2015) Hype or reality: should patients with metabolic syndrome-related NAFLD be on the hunter-gatherer (Paleo) diet to decrease morbidity? J Gastrointestin Liver Dis 24(3):359–368

Taylor MA, Reilly D, Llewellyn-Jones RH, McSharry C, Aitchison TC (2000) Randomised controlled trial of homoeopathy versus placebo in perennial allergic rhinitis with overview of four trial series. BMJ 321(7259):471–476

Toxicology IJO (2001) Final report on the safety assessment of Arnica montana extract and Arnica montana. Int J Toxicol 20(Suppl 2):1–11

Ulbricht C, Weissner W, Hashmi S, Rae Abrams T, Dacey C, Giese N, Hammerness P, Hackman DA, Kim J, Nealon A, Voloshin R (2009) Essiac: systematic review by the natural standard research collaboration. J Soc Integr Oncol 7(2):73–80

Whiskey E, Werneke U, Taylor D (2001) A systematic review and meta-analysis of Hypericum perforatum in depression: a comprehensive clinical review. Int Clin Psychopharmacol 16 (5):239–252

Wider B, Pittler MH, Ernst E (2015) Feverfew for preventing migraine. Cochrane Database Syst Rev 4:CD002286

Xiong XJ, Liu W, Yang XC, Feng B, Zhang YQ, Li SJ, Li XK, Wang J (2014) Ginkgo biloba extract for essential hypertension: a systemic review. Phytomedicine 21(10):1131–1136

Yang G, Wang Y, Sun J, Zhang K, Liu J (2016) Ginkgo biloba for mild cognitive impairment and alzheimer's disease: a systematic review and meta-analysis of randomized controlled trials. Curr Top Med Chem 16(5):520–528

Yau T, Dan X, Ng CC, Ng TB (2015) Lectins with potential for anti-cancer therapy. Molecules 20 (3):3791–3810

Young SM, Gryder LK, Cross C, Zava D, Kimball DW, Benyshek DC (2018) Effects of placentophagy on maternal salivary hormones: a pilot trial, part 1. Women Birth 31(4):e245–e257

Yuan Q, Wang CW, Shi J, Lin ZX (2017) Effects of Ginkgo biloba on dementia: an overview of systematic reviews. J Ethnopharmacol 4(195):1–9

Yurkiv B, Wasser SP, Nevo E, Sybirna NO (2015) Antioxidant effects of medicinal mushrooms Agaricus brasiliensis and Ganoderma lucidum (Higher Basidiomycetes): evidence from animal studies. Int J Med Mushrooms 17(10):943–955

Zahedipour F, Dalirfardouei R, Karimi G, Jamialahmadi K (2017) Molecular mechanisms of anticancer effects of glucosamine. Biomed Pharmacother 95:1051–1058

Zheng GH, Yang L, Chen HY, Chu JF, Mei L (2014) Aloe vera for prevention and treatment of infusion phlebitis. Cochrane Database Syst Rev (6):CD009162

Chapter 9
Physical Therapies

9.1 Acupressure

(related modalities: acupuncture, auriculotherapy, moxibustion, shiatsu, tui na)

Acupressure is the stimulation of specific points, called acupoints, on the body surface by pressure for therapeutic purposes. The required pressure can be applied manually of by a range of devices. Acupressure is based on the same tradition and assumptions as acupuncture. Like acupuncture, it is often promoted as a panacea, a 'cure all'.

1. Acupressure is popular, not least because patients can easily learn how and where to apply pressure manually and thus save time and money.
2. Acupressure has the advantage over acupuncture that no needles are required. Therefore, those patients who suffer from needle-phobia prefer it. Moreover, it is not burdened with the adverse effects of needling, e.g. pain, injury of a vital organ or introduction of infections.
3. One of the best-researched acupressure techniques is the application of pressure on the 'P6' acupoint which is located on the inner side of the lower arm, about three centimetres from the wrist. Some firms sell wrist bands to apply continuous pressure at this location. Early research suggested that P6 acupressure is effective against nausea and hick-ups. However, more recent studies have cast doubt on this notion. [e.g.1]
4. For clinical trials, it is possible to use a sham procedure that mimics acupressure, for instance by applying pressure on a site which is not an acupoint. Most of these sham-controlled trials suggest that acupressure is not more than a placebo therapy.[2]
5. Ear-acupressure is often advocated as a treatment to aid smoking cessation. Even though it is popular, there is no good evidence to show that it is effective

---

[1]Yilmaz Sahin et al. (2018).
[2]Li et al. (2018).

© Springer Nature Switzerland AG 2019
E. Ernst, *Alternative Medicine*,
https://doi.org/10.1007/978-3-030-12601-8_9

beyond placebo. A Cochrane review found no convincing evidence that acupressure is effective for smoking cessation.[3]

6. Several systematic reviews of the clinical trials of acupressure have been published. An overview included 9 such papers and concluded that "the effectiveness of this treatment has not been conclusively demonstrated for any condition."[4]

7. Acupressure is largely free of direct risks. As it can be taught to patients who then can apply it without supervision, it is also inexpensive.

Plausibility	👎
Efficacy	👎
Safety	👍
Cost	👍
Risk/Benefit balance	👎

9.2 Acupuncture

(related modalities: acupressure, auriculotherapy, biopuncture, moxibustion)

Acupuncture is currently one of the most popular and most thoroughly researched alternative therapy. Yet, experts are still divided in their views about it. Some accept that acupuncture works for some conditions, while many others remain unconvinced[5] (Fig. 9.1).

1. Many enthusiasts claim that acupuncture has 'stood the test of time' and that its long history proves its efficacy and safety. However, a long history of usage proves very little (think, for instance, of how long bloodletting was used, even though it killed millions).

2. There are many different forms of acupuncture. Acupuncture points can allegedly be stimulated not just by inserting needles (the most common way) but also

---

[3]https://www.cochrane.org/CD000009/TOBACCO_do-acupuncture-and-related-therapies-help-smokers-who-are-trying-to-quit.

[4]Ernst and Lee (2010).

[5]Colquhoun and Novella (2013).

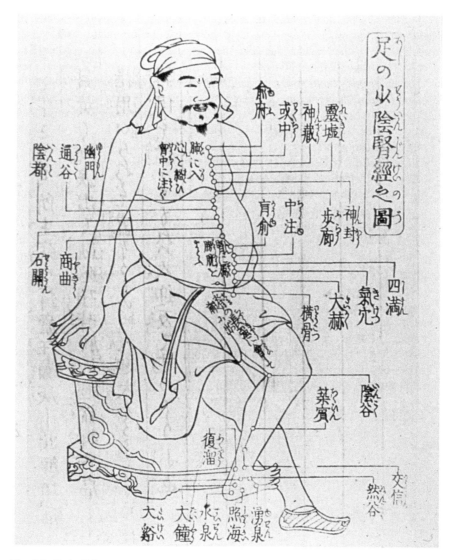

Fig. 9.1 Early Chinese depiction of acupuncture points on the human body. *Source* US National Library of Medicine

with heat, electrical currents, ultrasound, pressure, bee-stings (see apitherapy), injections (see biopuncture), light, colour, etc. Then there is body acupuncture, ear acupuncture (see auriculotherapy) and even tongue acupuncture. Some therapists employ the traditional Chinese approach, while so-called 'Western' acupuncturists adhere to the principles of conventional medicine.

3. Traditional Chinese acupuncturists have not normally studied medicine and base their practice on the Taoist philosophy of the balance between two

life-forces, 'yin and yang'. In contrast, medical acupuncturists tend to cite neurophysiological theories as to how acupuncture might work[6]; even though these may appear plausible, they are mere theories and constitute no proof for acupuncture's validity.

4. The therapeutic claims made for acupuncture are legion. According to the traditional view, acupuncture is useful for virtually every condition affecting mankind. According to 'Western' acupuncturists, acupuncture is effective for a much smaller range of conditions, mostly chronic pain. Many of the claims from both camps are based on unreliable evidence. Acupuncture is associated with a powerful placebo effect; it works better than a placebo only for very few (some say for no) conditions.[7]

5. Most of the clinical trials of acupuncture originate from China, and several investigations have shown that close to 100% of them are positive. This means that the results of these studies must be questioned.

6. Acupuncture is often promoted as being free of risks. Yet, mild to moderate side-effects of acupuncture occur in about 10% of all patients. Serious complications of acupuncture are on record as well: acupuncture needles can, for instance, injure vital organs like the lungs or the heart, and they can introduce infections into the body, e.g. hepatitis.[8] About 100 fatalities after acupuncture have been reported in the medical literature—a figure which, due to lack of a monitoring system, may disclose just the tip of an iceberg.

7. Given that, for most conditions, there is no good evidence that acupuncture works beyond a placebo effect, and that acupuncture is associated with finite risks, the risk of acupuncture usually fail to convincingly outweigh its benefits.

Plausibility	👎 [a]
Efficacy	👎 [b]
Safety	👎
Cost	👎
Risk/Benefit balance	👎

[a]Not positive for traditional concepts of acupuncture
[b]Some would argue that, for chronic pain, the evidence is positive

---

[6]Zhao (2008).

[7]Ernst (2012a).

[8]Ernst et al. (2011a).

9.3 Alexander Technique

(related modalities: Feldenkrais method, Tragerwork, zero balance)

The Alexander technique was developed by Frederick M Alexander (1869–1955), an actor who experienced vocal problems and believed he had solved them with his approach. The basic assumption is that poor habits in posture and movement can cause a range of health problems.

1. Alexander reasoned that he was inadvertently harming himself by habitually pulling his head backwards and downwards thus disrupting the normal working of his postural, breathing, and vocal processes. Retraining these functions, he seemingly resolved his recurrent voice loss problems. Subsequently, he developed an educational programme aimed at avoiding unnecessary muscular tension. Even though Alexander did not envisage his approach to become a therapy, it has in recent years become a popular alternative treatment.
2. There have only been few studies of the Alexander technique. They suggest that it is effective for chronic back pain and helpful for patients suffering from Parkinson's disease. A systematic review concluded that "strong evidence exists for the effectiveness of Alexander Technique lessons for chronic back pain and moderate evidence in Parkinson's-associated disability. Preliminary evidence suggests that Alexander Technique lessons may lead to improvements in balance skills in the elderly, in general chronic pain, posture, respiratory function and stuttering, but there is insufficient evidence to support recommendations in these areas."[9]
3. More recent studies also supported the notion that the Alexander technique might reduce the risk of falls in the elderly,[10] and alleviate neck pain.[11] However, the evidence is only tentative and not fully convincing.
4. Alexander published several books in which he created his own terminology, outlined his concepts and gave precise instructions about his methods. These volumes are largely devoid of scientific evidence.
5. The Alexander technique is taught by 'Alexander teachers' in series of 10–40 lessons lasting from 30 to 60 min. Alexander teachers closely observe their students, show them how to move with less strain and correct their posture.
6. The Alexander technique is also used by many performing artists allegedly improving their vocal functions by consciously increasing air-flow, allowing improved vocal skill and tone. The method is said to also reduce stage fright and to increase spontaneity.
7. There are few conceivable risks associated with the Alexander technique, and the costs are usually moderate.

---

[9]Woodman and Moore (2012).

[10]O'Neill et al. (2015).

[11]MacPherson et al. (2015).

Plausibility	
Efficacy	a
Safety	
Cost	
Risk/Benefit balance	a

aFor chronic low back pain

9.4   Aromatherapy

(related modalities: massage, essential oil)

Aromatherapy is currently one of the most popular of all alternative therapies.[12] It consists of the use of essential oils for medicinal purposes.

1. Aromatherapy usually involves the application of diluted essential oils via a gentle massage of the body surface. Less frequently, the essential oils are applied differently, e.g. via inhalation or a bath.
2. The chemist Rene-Maurice Gattefosse (1881–1950) coined the term 'aromatherapy' after experiencing that lavender oil helped to cure a serious burn. In 1937, he published a book on the subject: Aromathérapie: Les Huiles Essentielles, Hormones Végétales. Later, the French surgeon Jean Valnet used essential oils to help heal soldiers' wounds in World War II.
3. It seems reasonable to assume that most of the relaxing effect of aromatherapy massage is due to the gentle massage rather that caused by any specific effects of the essential oils applied. Yet, aromatherapists claim that the oils all have very specific effects that can be used to treat specific conditions (see chapter on 'essential oils').
4. A review of clinical trials of aromatherapy found some evidence for a relaxing effect but concluded that "the effects of aromatherapy are probably not strong enough for it to be considered for the treatment of anxiety. The hypothesis that it is effective for any other indication is not supported by the findings of rigorous

---

[12]Posadzki et al. (2013a).

clinical trials."[13] Another review summarised the clinical trials of aromatherapy for reducing the pain during childbirth. The authors concluded that aromatherapy is effective in reducing labor pain and duration, and generally safe to the mothers. However, due to the heterogeneity across trials in some of the outcomes, further trials with device-based pain measurements, larger sample size, and more stringent design, should be conducted before strong recommendation.[14]

5. Aromatherapy is often considered to be devoid of risks, however, this assumption is not entirely correct. A review of the potential of harm concluded that "aromatherapy has the potential to cause adverse effects some of which are serious. Their frequency remains unknown."[15]

6. The 'Tennessee Poison Center' advised consumers to observe the following rules when using aromatherapy:[16]

   - "Safely using and storing essential oils is extremely important."
   - "Use essential oil products ONLY for their intended purpose."
   - "Use only the amount stated on the label/guide."
   - "Do not swallow an essential oil unless the label says to do so."
   - "Do not use a product on the skin unless the label says to do so."
   - "Do not leave the product out (i.e. as a pesticide) unless the label says to do so."
   - "If you have bottles of essential oils at home, keep them locked up, out of sight and reach of children and pet at all times. Children act fast, so do poisons."

7. The lack of sufficiently convincing evidence regarding the effectiveness of aromatherapy combined with its potential to cause adverse effects means that its risk/benefit balance cannot be positive.

Plausibility	👍
Efficacy	👎a
Safety	👍
Cost	👍
Risk/Benefit balance	👎a

aExcept for relaxation and possibly pain during childbirth

---

[13]Cooke and Ernst (2000).

[14]Chen et al. (2018).

[15]Posadzki et al. (2012).

[16]http://wkrn.com/2016/05/10/essential-oil-exposure-doubled-over-last-4-years/.

9.5 Auriculotherapy

(related modalities: acupuncture)

Auriculotherapy is the use of an electrical, mechanical or other stimuli at specific points on the outer ear for therapeutic purposes.

1. Auriculotherapy was invented by the French neurologist Paul Nogier (1908–1996) who published his "Treatise of Auriculotherapy" in 1961.[17]
2. Auriculotherapy is based on the idea that the human outer ear is an area that reflects the entire body.
3. Proponents of auriculotherapy refer to maps where the all our inner organs and body parts are depicted on the outer ear.
4. These maps are not in line with our knowledge of anatomy and physiology. Auriculotherapy thus lacks plausibility.
5. Conditions affecting the physical, mental or emotional health of the patient are assumed to be treatable by stimulation of the surface of the outer ear.
6. Auriculotherapy is being promoted as a treatment for nearly all conceivable conditions. However, the clinical evidence that it might be effective is weak, not least because the research in this area is often of low quality and thus unreliable. One review, for instance, concluded that "because of the paucity and of the poor quality of the data, the evidence for the effectiveness of AA for the symptomatic treatment of insomnia is limited. Further, rigorously designed trials are warranted to confirm these results."[18]
7. A review of the adverse effects of auriculotherapy concluded that the most frequently reported adverse events were tenderness or pain at insertion, dizziness, local discomfort, minor bleeding and nausea, and so forth. For auricular acupressure, local skin irritation and discomfort, mild tenderness or pain, and dizziness were commonly reported. Skin irritation, local discomfort, and pain were detected in auricular electroacupuncture, and minor infection was identified in auricular bloodletting therapy. Most of these events were transient, mild, and tolerable, and no serious adverse events were identified.[19]

---

[17]https://www.amazon.co.uk/TRAITE-DAURICULOTHERAPIE-Paul-Nogier/dp/2716000107/ref=sr_1_4?s=books&ie=UTF8&qid=1536507066&sr=1-4&keywords=paul+nogier.

[18]Lee et al. (2008).

[19]Tan et al. (2014).

Plausibility	👎
Efficacy	👎
Safety	👍
Cost	👍
Risk/Benefit balance	👎

9.6 Biopuncture

(related modalities: apitherapy, acupuncture, detox)

In alternative medicine, we regularly encounter terms that have a different meaning in conventional healthcare. Biopuncture is such a term; it normally is used for puncturing bodily tissues for biopsies. In alternative medicine, the word describes a variation of acupuncture. Biopuncture is particularly popular in China and Korea.

1. Biopuncture is an acupuncture method where biological materials are injected into acupuncture points.
2. The materials used for injection range from herbal remedies such as echinacea, to homeopathic products, vitamins, non-herbal supplements, bodily fluids, bee venom or other animal products.
3. The volume that is injected is usually very small, and therefore unlikely to generate relevant therapeutic effects.
4. A frequent claim by proponents is that biopuncture is a means for detoxifying the body. Others insist that it works like acupuncture and is an effective treatment for a wide range of acute and chronic conditions.
5. There is no proof for any of these claims. Biopuncture is therefore neither a plausible nor an evidence-based treatment.
6. The best-researched form of biopuncture is 'bee-venom acupuncture' or 'apipuncture' (the use of a bee-sting or injection of bee venom at an acupoint). Yet, even for this treatment, the evidence is less than convincing.[20,21]

---

[20]Doo et al. (2015).

[21]Lim and Lee (2015).

7. Biopuncture carries similar risks as needle acupuncture; in addition, it is burdened with the risks caused by the injected material. Severe adverse effects, for instance allergic reactions, are on record.

Plausibility	👎	
Efficacy	👎	
Safety	👎	
Cost	👎	
Risk/Benefit balance	👎	

9.7   Bowen Technique

(related modalities: chiropractic, osteopathy)

The Bowen technique is a manual therapy developed by the Australian Thomas Ambrose Bowen (1916–1982). He began developing his method in the 1950s and became interested in ways to treat symptoms after noticing that certain moves of the body resulted in particular responses.

1. Bowen had no previous formal training in any modality or healthcare discipline and frequently stated that his work was 'a gift from God'. Helped by his friend and secretary, Rene Horwood, Bowen refined the technique throughout his lifetime.
2. The treatment consists of manual mobilisations called 'Bowen moves' over muscles, tendons, nerves and fascia. The therapist performs these rolling motions using the thumbs and fingers applying gentle pressure. A full treatment consists of a standardised sequence of moves. The treatment is interrupted by frequent pauses for allowing time for the body to respond. Many consumers experience this therapy as relaxing and enjoyable. The claims are that the Bowen technique works "holistically, by using the body's innate healing mechanisms. The practitioner delivers signals to the nervous system at specific locations (on muscles, tendons, ligaments or nerves), and the body does the rest, responding in its own time, as it is able."[22] These claims lack plausibility.

---

[22]http://www.bowentraining.co.uk/home/about.

3. A 2015 report by the Australian government reviewed the evidence for or against the Bowen technique and stated that "no clear evidence of effectiveness was found."[23]
4. There are no relevant clinical trials testing the efficacy of the Bowen technique for any disease or symptom. Yet proponents recommend it as a 'cure-all': "the Bowen Technique is perhaps one of the single most important tools we have to help heal the body."[24]
5. There is, however, one study that suggests that the treatment might increase the flexibility of healthy individuals.[25]
6. Claims that it improves blood flow, lymphatic drainage or emotional issues are not supported by good evidence.
7. There are no reports of serious adverse effects after Bowen therapy.

Plausibility	👎
Efficacy	👎
Safety	👍
Cost	👎
Risk/Benefit balance	👎

9.8   Chiropractic

(related modalities: applied kinesiology, craniosacral therapy, massage, osteopathy)

Chiropractic was created by DD Palmer (1845–1913), an American magnetic healer who, in 1895, manipulated the neck of a deaf janitor, Harvey Lillard, allegedly curing his deafness. It is claimed that Palmer learnt his techniques from Andrew Still, the inventor of osteopathy. Chiropractic was initially promoted as a cure-all by Palmer who claimed that 95% of diseases were due to subluxations of spinal joints (Fig. 9.2).

---

[23]www.health.gov.au/internet/main/publishing.nsf/content/0E9129B3574FCA53CA257BF0001A CD11/$File/Natural%20Therapies%20Overview%20Report%20Final%20with%20copyright%2011% 20March.pdf.

[24]https://www.bowen-technique.co.uk/how_does_work.php.

[25]Marr et al. (2011).

Founder of Chiropractic. The Creator of Chiropractic Science. The Originator of
Vertebral Adjusting. The Developer of Chiropractic Philosophy. The Foun-
tain Head of the Principles of Chiropractic, their skillful application
for the use of humanity and the reasons why and how they
Govern Life in Health and Disease. Lecturer and
Demonstrator on the Science, Art and
Philosophy of Chiropractic.

Fig. 9.2 Daniel David Palmer. *Source* US National Library of Medicine

1. Subluxations became the cornerstone of chiropractic 'philosophy'. Yet subluxations, as understood by chiropractors, do not exist.[26] Chiropractors who still believe in it diagnose subluxation in nearly 100% of the population—even in individuals who are completely symptom-free.
2. Therefore, almost all patients consulting a chiropractor receive spinal manipulations. In addition, chiropractors also employ a range of other non-drug treatments mostly borrowed from physiotherapy.
3. Today, some chiropractors focus on treating back and neck pain. So-called straight chiropractors, however, still adhere to Palmer's gospel and claim being able to treat many non-spinal conditions.
4. The evidence that chiropractic spinal manipulation is effective beyond placebo is weak for spinal problems such as back and neck pain and negative for all other conditions.[27]
5. Most chiropractors also recommend regular spinal manipulations to adjust subluxations, even in the absence of symptoms, an approach they call maintenance care. Yet, there is no good evidence to show that maintenance care is effective (except for increasing the cash-flow of chiropractors).[28]
6. Spinal manipulation causes mild to moderate adverse-effects, such as pain, in about 50% of all patients. In addition, it is associated with very serious complications, usually caused by neck manipulation damaging an artery that supplies parts of the brain resulting in a stroke and even death. Several hundred such cases have been documented in the medical literature—but, as there is no system in place to monitor such events, the true figure is almost certainly much larger.[29]
7. In view of the considerable potential for causing harm with spinal manipulations, it would be particularly important that chiropractors obtain informed consent from their patient before commencing treatment. Yet there is evidence that many chiropractors ignore this ethical imperative.[30]

Plausibility	👎
Efficacy	👎
Safety	👎

(continued)

---

[26]Mirtz et al. (2009).
[27]Ernst (2008).
[28]Ernst (2009a).
[29]Stevinson and Ernst (2002).
[30]Langworthy and Cambron (2007).

(continued)

Cost	
Risk/Benefit balance	

9.9   Craniosacral Therapy

(related modalities: chiropractic, osteopathy)

Craniosacral therapy (or craniosacral osteopathy) is a manual treatment developed by the US osteopath William Sutherland (1873–1953) and further refined by the US osteopath John Upledger (1932–2012) in the 1970s.

1. The treatment consists of gentle touch and palpation of the synarthrodial joints of the skull and sacrum.

2. Practitioners believe that these joints allow enough movement to regulate the pulsation of the cerebrospinal fluid which, in turn, improves what they call 'primary respiration'.

3. The notion of 'primary respiration' is based on the following 5 assumptions:
   - inherent motility of the central nervous system
   - fluctuation of the cerebrospinal fluid
   - mobility of the intracranial and intraspinal dural membranes
   - mobility of the cranial bones
   - involuntary motion of the sacral bones.

4. A further assumption is that palpation of the cranium can detect a rhythmic movement of the cranial bones. Gentle pressure is used by the therapist to manipulate the cranial bones to achieve a therapeutic result.

5. The degree of mobility and compliance of the cranial bones is minimal, and therefore, most of these assumptions lack plausibility.

6. The therapeutic claims made for craniosacral therapy are not supported by sound evidence. A systematic review of all 6 trials of craniosacral therapy concluded that "the notion that CST is associated with more than non-specific effects is not based on evidence from rigorous RCTs."[31] Some studies seem to indicate otherwise, but they are of lamentable methodological quality and thus not reliable.

---

[31]Ernst (2012b).

7. Being such a gentle treatment, craniosacral therapy is particularly popular for infants. But here too, the evidence fails to show effectiveness. A study concluded that "healthy preterm infants undergoing an intervention with craniosacral therapy showed no significant changes in general movements compared to preterm infants without intervention."[32]
8. The costs for craniosacral therapy are usually modest but, if the treatment is employed regularly, they can be substantial.

Plausibility	👎
Efficacy	👎
Safety	👍
Cost	👍
Risk/Benefit balance	👎

9.10   Cupping

(related modalities: detox)

Cupping is an alternative therapy that already existed in several ancient cultures. It recently became popular when US Olympic athletes displayed cupping marks on their bodies, and it was claimed that cupping is used for enhancing their physical performance.

1. There are two distinct forms: dry and wet cupping. The table below refers only to dry cupping.
2. Wet cupping involves scarring the skin with a sharp instrument and then applying a cup with a vacuum to suck blood from the wound. It can thus be seen as a form of blood-letting.
3. Dry cupping omits the scarring of the skin and merely involves placing a vacuum cup over the skin. The vacuum then creates a subcutaneous haematoma which leaves the typical cupping mark visible that remains visible for several days. Dry cupping can be understood as a form of counter-irritation. Thus, some of its alleged effects, e.g. pain control, might be plausible.

---

[32]Raith et al. (2016).

4. While dry cupping is virtually risk-free, wet cupping can lead to serious infections and permanent scarring.
5. There has been a flurry of research into the effects of (mostly dry) cupping. Most clinical trials have been seriously flawed, and thus the conclusions of systematic reviews were inconclusive, e.g.:

- No explicit recommendation for or against the use of cupping for athletes can be made. More studies are necessary for conclusive judgment on the efficacy and safety of cupping in athletes.[33]
- Cupping therapy can significantly decrease the VAS scores and ODI scores for patients with LBP compared to the control management. High heterogeneity and risk of bias existing in studies limit the authenticity of the findings.[34]
- Only weak evidence can support the hypothesis that cupping therapy can effectively improve the treatment efficacy and physical function in patients with knee osteoarthritis.[35]
- There are not enough trials to provide evidence for the effectiveness of cupping for stroke rehabilitation because most of the included trials compared the effects with unproven evidence and were not informative.[36]

6. For wet cupping, there is far less research, and some of the results that emerged from clinical trials seem less than credible.[37]
7. On balance, the risks of wet cupping do not seem to outweigh its risks, while for dry cupping the verdict is currently still uncertain.

Plausibility	👎
Efficacy	👎
Safety	👍
Cost	👍
Risk/Benefit balance	👎

---

[33]Bridgett et al. (2018).
[34]Wang et al. (2017).
[35]Li et al. (2017).
[36]Lee et al. (2010a).
[37]AlBedah et al. (2015).

9.11   Ear Candles

(related modalities: detox)

Ear candles, sometimes also called Hopi candles, are thin, long cylinders of waxed cloth that are placed into a patient's ear and lit for the purpose of achieving therapeutic effects.

1. Ear candles allegedly have a long history with the North-American Hopi tribe. This claim, however, turns out to be a marketing gimmick, as there is no evidence that the Hopis ever used such devices.
2. A burning ear candle obviously generates heat; in addition, it is claimed to produce suction.
3. The combination of both heat and suction is claimed to remove earwax as well as toxins.
4. In truth, however, ear candles neither created suction nor do they remove wax from a patient's ear, nor do they remove toxins from the body. The material sometimes found after ear-candling is simply the rest of the burnt materials.
5. Ear-candling can even lead to occlusion with candle wax in persons who previously had clean ear canals.[38] Other complications from ear candling include local burns and tympanic membrane perforations.
6. Further health claims often made for ear candling, include the alleviation of ear and sinus discomfort, rhinitis, sinusitis, glue ear, colds, flu, migraine or tinnitus. They are equally unfounded, as there is no good evidence to support them.
7. In fact, there is no sound evidence in favour ear candles at all. One review concluded that the evidence shows that its mode of action is implausible and demonstrably wrong. There are no data to suggest that it is effective for any condition. Furthermore, ear candles have been associated with ear injuries. The inescapable conclusion is that ear candles do more harm than good. Their use should be discouraged.[39]

Plausibility	👎
Efficacy	👎
Safety	👎

(continued)

---

[38]Hornibrook (2012).
[39]Ernst (2004).

(continued)

Cost	
Risk/Benefit balance	

9.12 Eurythmy

(related modalities: anthroposophical medicine)

Eurythmy is an exercise therapy which is part of anthroposophic medicine. It consists of a set of specific movements that were developed by Rudolf Steiner (1861–1925), the inventor of anthroposophic medicine, in conjunction with Marie von Sievers (1867–1948), his second wife acting as his secretary, translator, editor, and organizer.

1. Steiner stated in 1923 that eurythmy has grown up out of the soil of the Anthroposophical Movement, and the history of its origin makes it almost appear to be a gift of the forces of destiny. Steiner also wrote that it is the task of the Anthroposophical Movement to reveal to our present age that spiritual impulse which is suited to it. He claimed that, within the Anthroposophical Movement, there is a firm conviction that a spiritual impulse of this kind must enter once more into human evolution. And this spiritual impulse must perforce, among its other means of expression, embody itself in a new form of art. It will increasingly be realised that this particular form of art has been given to the world in Eurythmy.
2. Consumers learning eurythmy are taught exercises which allegedly integrate cognitive, emotional and volitional elements. Eurythmy exercises are based on speech and direct the patient's attention to their own perceived intentionality.
3. Proponent of Eurythmy believe that, through this treatment, a connection between internal and external activity can be experienced. They also make many diffuse health claims for this therapy ranging from stress management to pain control.
4. One review concluded that eurythmy seems to be a beneficial add-on in a therapeutic context that can improve the health conditions of affected persons. More methodologically sound studies are needed to substantiate this positive impression.[40]

---

[40]Lötzke et al. (2015).

5. This positive conclusion is, however, of doubtful validity. The authors of the review are from an anthroposophical university in Germany. They included studies in their review that were methodologically too weak to allow any conclusions.
6. Reliable studies of eurythmy are currently not available, and the effectiveness of the therapy must therefore be classified as unproven.
7. When learning eurythmy, there is a danger of getting drawn into the esoteric and mystical realm of the Steiner cult which is likely to undermine rational thinking not merely in the area of healthcare.

Plausibility	👎
Efficacy	👎
Safety	👍
Cost	👍
Risk/Benefit balance	👎

9.13   Feldenkrais Method

(related modalities: Alexander technique, Tragerwork)

The Feldenkrais method is an exercise therapy that allegedly integrates body and mind. It was developed by the electro-engineer Moshe Feldenkrais (1904–1984) for performing artists and as a therapeutic method.

1. The method is taught by trained instructors, often physiotherapists or alternative practitioners, in two main steps: 'functional integration' and 'awareness through movement'.
2. The instructors or teachers provide verbal and manual guidance for their patients, often called students.
3. The therapeutic aim is to improve that patient's function in daily living. Proponents of the Feldenkrais method claim that it can repair impaired connections between the motor cortex of the brain and the body, so benefiting the quality of body movement and improving wellbeing.

4. Moshe Feldenkrais stated that "behaviour is acquired and has nothing permanent about it but or belief that it is so."[41]

5. The primary reason for patients to learn the Feldenkrais method seems to be pain.[42] The therapists treats patients by directing attention to habitual movement patterns that are thought to be inefficient or strained, and attempts to teach new patterns using gentle, slow, repeated movements.

6. There have been several clinical trials testing the effectiveness of the Feldenkrais method; most were methodologically weak. A 2005 review concluded that "the evidence for the Feldenkrais method is encouraging but, due to the paucity and low quality of studies, by no means compelling."[43] More recent results show promising effects for patients suffering from back pain,[44] Parkinson's disease,[45] multiple sclerosis and loss of balance. Single studies reported significant positive effects for reduced perceived effort and increased comfort, body image perception, and dexterity.[46]

7. Overall, this evidence suggests that the Feldenkrais method is helpful in certain situations, even if the assumptions underlying it are questionable. The Feldenkrais method is generally considered to be devoid of serious adverse effects.

Plausibility	
Efficacy	
Safety	
Cost	
Risk/Benefit balance	

---

[41]Buchanan et al. (2014).

[42]Buchanan et al. (2014).

[43]https://www.thieme-connect.de/DOI/DOI?10.1055/s-2004-834763.

[44]Paolucci et al. (2017).

[45]Teixeira-Machado et al. (2015).

[46]Hillier and Worley (2015).

9.14   Flotation Therapy

(related modalities: meditation, mind-body therapies, relaxation therapies)

Flotation therapy (or flotation rest) is a treatment aimed at deep relaxation of the patient. Flotation therapy is commonly used for animals but has recently also become popular as a treatment for humans.

1. During a flotation therapy, the patient is placed in a flotation tank where she experiences complete sensory isolation, an effect that is said to 'clear the mind'.
2. According to its proponents, this experience leads to deep relaxation. In turn, relaxation is claimed to have numerous positive health effects, for instance, in the form of reducing stress, anxiety, insomnia and pain.
3. Organisations offering flotation therapy often make therapeutic claims that are neither plausible nor supported by good evidence, e.g. flotation therapy:

   - accelerates healing of injuries,
   - enhances performance,
   - rejuvenates energy levels,
   - enhances creativity,
   - improves learning capacity.

4. Flotation therapy has not often been submitted to controlled clinical trials, and the few studies that are available are limited by methodological weaknesses.
5. In one study, for instance, 65 healthy volunteers were randomized to either a wait-list control group or a flotation treatment (7 weeks flotation program with a total of twelve flotation sessions). Stress, depression, anxiety, and worst pain were significantly decreased, while optimism and sleep quality significantly increased for the flotation group.[47] Similarly encouraging findings were reported in a trial of patients suffering from generalised anxiety disorder.[48]
6. Such studies highlight a problem encountered in trials of several alternative therapies. It is often difficult or even impossible to find a placebo intervention that would allow patient-blinding. In such situations, it is not possible to be sure whether, in a clinical trial, the therapy or a placebo response was the cause of the observed outcomes.
7. There are no conceivable adverse effects of flotation therapy, except for the fact that regular flotation therapy is not cheap and that some patients might find the situation in a flotation tank more than a little claustrophobic.

---

[47]Kjellgren and Westman (2014).
[48]Jonsson and Kjellgren (2016).

Plausibility	👍
Efficacy	👍
Safety	👍
Cost	👎
Risk/Benefit balance	👍

9.15 Gua Sha

(related modalities: acupuncture, cupping, detox, Traditional Chinese Medicine)

Gua sha, sometimes referred to as "scraping", "spooning" or "coining", is a traditional Chinese treatment that has also been adopted in several other Asian countries. It has long been popular in Vietnam and is now also becoming well-known in the West.

1. The treatment consists of scraping the skin with a smooth edge placed against the pre-oiled skin surface, pressed down firmly, and then moved downwards along muscles or meridians, the assumed 'energy' channels of traditional Chinese medicine.
2. According to its proponents, gua sha stimulates the flow of the vital energy 'chi' and releases unhealthy bodily matter from blood stasis within sored, tired, stiff or injured muscle areas.
3. The technique is practised by acupuncturists, massage therapists, physical therapists, physicians, nurses and other healthcare practitioners. Proponents also claim that it stimulates blood flow to the treated areas, thus promoting cell metabolism, regeneration and healing. They furthermore assume that it has anti-inflammatory effects and stimulates the immune system. These effects are said to last for days or weeks after a single treatment.
4. The treatment causes microvascular injuries which are visible as subcutaneous bleeding and redness.
5. Gua sha practitioners make far-reaching therapeutic claims, including that the therapy alleviates pain, prevents infections, treats asthma, detoxifies the body, cures liver problems, reduces stress, and contributes to overall health. A survey

from Hong Kong showed that gua sha was most commonly used for respiratory and pain problems; other illnesses included nervousness, heat stroke, fever, infection, dizziness, diarrhoea and vomiting, oedema, and constipation.[49]

6. The assumptions that underpin gua sha are neither plausible nor backed up by sound clinical evidence. The few clinical trials of gua sha that have been published are flawed and thus less than convincing. One systematic review included 6 trials of gua sha and concluded that "preliminary evidence supported the hypothesis that Gua Sha therapy effectively improved the treatment efficacy in patients with perimenopausal syndrome. Additional studies will be required to elucidate optimal frequency and dosage of Gua Sha."[50] Because the few available studies were of poor quality, this conclusion is over-optimistic and not justified.

7. Gua sha is mildly painful, almost invariably leads to unsightly blemishes on the skin which occasionally can become infected[51] and might, on occasion, be mistaken for physical abuse.[52]

Plausibility	👎
Efficacy	👎
Safety	👍
Cost	👍
Risk/Benefit balance	👎

9.16   Hot Stone Massage

(related modalities: massage)

Hot stone massage is the application of smooth, heated stones to the body surface for therapeutic purposes. The treatment is said to have ancient roots and has become popular in recent years.

---

[49]Lam et al. (2015).
[50]Ren et al. (2018).
[51]Wiwanitkit (2017).
[52]Aprile et al. (2015).

1. Hot stone massage may consist of placing the stones on the skin of the patient; alternatively, the therapist might apply a massage oil to the skin and manually move the stones along muscles or other anatomical structures. The therapist might also employ Swedish massage techniques while the stones are in place or after they have been removed.
2. The localized heat and weight of the stones are supposed to warm and relax muscles, allowing the massage therapist to apply deeper pressure to those areas while causing less discomfort.
3. Basalt river rocks are typically used because they are naturally smooth (from the river's current) and retain heat well.
4. Patients often experience hot stone massage as comforting and relaxing. It is unlikely, however, that these effects cannot be obtained with conventional massage and other methods of applying localised heat, e.g. heat packs. Hot stone massage is often promoted via testimonials of VIPs and is a good example of what has be called a 'celebrity-based medicine'.[53]
5. The therapeutic claims made for this treatment are similar to those made for massage therapy and include, for instance, an alleviation of anxiety, depression and musculoskeletal pain.
6. There seems to be just one Medline-listed study of hot stone massage. It is a trial on healthy volunteers that concluded that "lower-limb skin temperature was altered following hot-stone stimulation applied to the abdomen, and the one-site stimulation and three-site stimulation yielded different distal foot skin-temperature reactions."[54]
7. There is no reason to assume that hot stone massage can cause serious harm (other than to the consumer's bank account), provided that the stones are applied at the correct temperature so not to cause burns.

Plausibility	👎 (sideways)
Efficacy	👎
Safety	👍
Cost	👎 (sideways)
Risk/Benefit balance	👎

---

[53]Ernst and Pittler (2006).
[54]Kuge et al. (2013).

9.17   Jin Shin Jyutsu

(related modalities: acupuncture, shiatsu, Traditional Chinese Medicine)

Jin shin jyutsu is a self-help technique based on concepts borrowed from Traditional Chinese Medicine.

1. Jin shin jyutsu is said to be an ancient healing practice re-discovered by Jiro Murai, a Japanese healer and philosopher. Apparently, Murai conducted extensive experiments on himself for over 50 years. He found that Jin Shin Jyutsu produced a depth of awareness that went beyond anything described in the ancient texts of Chinese medicine. Murai passed on his knowledge to Mary Burmeister, who returned to the US in the 1950s and devoted her life to Jin Shin Jyutsu. Thanks to her efforts, Jin Shin Jyutsu is today taught worldwide.
2. Jin shin jyutsu is supposed to work with a set of 26 points along energy pathways or meridians. Whenever such a channel gets blocked, the vital energy, chi, is said to stagnate.
3. This stagnation is seen as the cause of illness.
4. Jin shin jyutsu is aimed at de-blocking the flow of chi and restoring balance thus re-establishing good health.
5. Consequently, the body can heal itself and the patient experiences physical, mental, and spiritual harmony, according to the assumptions of proponents. Jin Shin Jyutsu is used mostly for relaxation and stress management, but some proponents make therapeutic claims that go far beyond this.
6. The method is based on notions that lack biological plausibility.
7. Only very few studies of Jin Shin Jyutsu have been published.[55,56] Their methodology is seriously flawed and therefore the effectiveness of this treatment remains entirely unproven.

Plausibility	👎
Efficacy	👎
Safety	👍
Cost	👍
Risk/Benefit balance	👎

---

[55]Lamke et al. (2014).
[56]Searls and Fawcett (2011).

9.18   Khalifa Therapy

(related modalities: massage, shiatsu)

Khalifa therapy is a manual therapy named after the Australian practitioner, Mohamed Khalifa, who invented this treatment.

1. The technique consists of on rhythmically applying manual pressure on parts of the body.
2. Mohamed Khalifa claims to be able to speed the self-healing processes of the human body. He also states that he has successfully treated many top-athletes from all over the world.
3. Khalifa therapy is a good example of how, in the realm of alternative medicine, a single person can invent a therapy and popularise it, largely due to the right sort of publicity and the gullibility of consumers who want to believe.
4. This treatment and its assumptions lack plausibility.
5. Khalifa therapy has so far only been tested in one small clinical trial. It concluded that this treatment can be helpful in the repair of anterior cruciate ligament ruptures.[57] The same trial also reported positive long-term results.[58]
6. Without an independent replication, it would be unwise to take these findings at face value.
7. The treatment seems not to be associated with significant direct risks.

Plausibility	👎
Efficacy	👎
Safety	👍
Cost	👍
Risk/Benefit balance	👎

---

[57]Ofner et al. (2014).
[58]Ofner et al. (2018).

9.19 Kinesiology Tape

(related modalities: none)

Kinesiology tape comes in the form of a self-adhesive, usually brightly coloured tape for sticking on to the skin, like a sticky plaster. It is currently being aggressively marketed and allegedly relieves all sorts of musculoskeletal problems.

1. Its proponents claim that kinesiology tape increases cutaneous stimulation, which facilitates motor unit firing, and consequently improves functional performance.
2. The product is widely sold at considerable costs and used mostly, but by no means exclusively, by athletes.
3. There have been many clinical trials of kinesiology tape.
4. Sadly, their methodology is often less than rigorous.
5. Their results are contradictory and fail to generate a clear picture about the effectiveness of kinesiology tape.
6. Recent systematic reviews arrived mostly at negative conclusions:

   - there was little quality evidence to support the use of KT over other types of elastic taping in the management or prevention of sports injuries. KT may have a small beneficial role in improving strength, range of motion in certain injured cohorts and force sense error compared with other tapes, but further studies are needed to confirm these findings. The amount of case study and anecdotal support for KT warrants well designed experimental research, particularly pertaining to sporting injuries, so that practitioners can be confident that KT is beneficial for their athletes.[59]
   - This systematic review found insufficient evidence to support the use of KT following musculoskeletal injury, although a perceived benefit cannot be discounted. There are few high-quality studies examining the use of KT following musculoskeletal injury.[60]
   - Kinesio taping is not a substitute for traditional physical therapy or exercise. Rather, KT may be most effective when used as an adjunctive therapy, perhaps by improving ROM, muscular endurance and motor control. More high quality studies that consider the multiple factors that mediate CLBP, in the short, intermediate and long term, are needed to strengthen the evidence of the effectiveness of KT on CLBP.[61]
   - The current evidence does not support the use of this intervention in these clinical populations.[62]

7. There are few significant risks other than those to the consumers' bank accounts.

---

[59]Williams et al. (2012).
[60]Mostafavifar et al. (2012).
[61]Nelson (2016).
[62]Parreira Pdo et al. (2014).

Plausibility	👎
Efficacy	👎
Safety	👍
Cost	👎
Risk/Benefit balance	👎

9.20   Lymph-Drainage

Lymph-drainage or lymphatic drainage is a gentle manual massage technique developed in the 1930s by the Danish doctor Emil Vodder (1896–1986) and his wife Estrid.

1. Lymph drainage consists of rhythmic manual movements along the lymph vessels which. This is said to push the lymph fluid through the lymphatic vessels towards the lymph-nodes and into the blood circulation. Some enthusiasts claim that this process speeds up the elimination of toxins and waste products from the body.
2. During a session of lymph-drainage, the therapist lightly moves his or her hands over the patient's skin. This often requires access to intimate regions of the body, and some patients might feel uncomfortable with such contact.
3. Most patients, however, experience the treatment as agreeable and intensely relaxing.
4. It is usually performed by massage therapists who have received special training in that method. A simplified version of the therapy can be taught to patients for regular self-treatments.
5. Lymph-drainage is being recommended for a wide range of conditions usually as an add-on therapy to complement other interventions. According to some proponents, lymph drainage can:

   - help the body fight off infection,
   - speeds up healing and recovery from illness,
   - help reduce water retention,
   - boost weight loss,
   - improve your skin texture,

- speed up healing of scar tissue,
- help to reduce cellulite.

6. There are no direct risks involved. The notion that lymph-drainage might spread cancer cells throughout the body has not been confirmed.

7. The evidence to suggest that it is effective is scant. It is best-studied as a treatment of lymphoedema, a condition that sometimes occurs after radical cancer surgery. A systematic review of 6 studies concluded that "manual lymph-drainage (MLD) is safe and may offer additional benefit to compression bandaging for swelling reduction. Compared to individuals with moderate-to-severe BCRL, those with mild-to-moderate BCRL may be the ones who benefit from adding MLD to an intensive course of treatment with compression bandaging. This finding, however, needs to be confirmed by randomized data. In trials where MLD and sleeve were compared with a non-MLD treatment and sleeve, volumetric outcomes were inconsistent within the same trial. Research is needed to identify the most clinically meaningful volumetric measurement, to incorporate newer technologies in LE assessment, and to assess other clinically relevant outcomes such as fibrotic tissue formation. Findings were contradictory for function (range of motion), and inconclusive for quality of life. For symptoms such as pain and heaviness, 60–80% of participants reported feeling better regardless of which treatment they received. One-year follow-up suggests that once swelling had been reduced, participants were likely to keep their swelling down if they continued to use a custom-made sleeve."[63]

Plausibility	👎
Efficacy	👎
Safety	👍
Cost	👍
Risk/Benefit balance	👎

---

[63]Ezzo et al. (2015).

9.21 Magnet Therapy

(related modalities: hologram gadgets)

Magnet therapy is the application of magnetic fields to the body for medicinal purposes. The type of magnet therapy that is used in alternative medicine involves wearing static magnets. (In conventional medicine, various other forms of magnetism are in used; these are, however, excluded from this discussion).

1. Static magnetic fields are applied to the body surface via a variety of devices ranging from bracelets to mattresses, insoles, belts and sticky plasters.
2. Gadgets with static magnets are currently popular medical devices and are being sold at high prices; sales figures currently exceed US$300 million per year in the US alone.
3. The magnetic fields used are too weak to penetrate deeply into the body. The treatment is thus not biologically plausible.
4. Proponents nevertheless claim that they work by increasing blood flow and oxygen supply to the underlying tissues or by affecting nerve function, tissue metabolism or regeneration.
5. Based on these assumptions, static magnets are being promoted for a wide range of conditions, often associated with pain.
6. The evidence for static magnets is less than convincing. A systematic review concluded that the evidence does not support the use of static magnets for pain relief, and therefore magnets cannot be recommended as an effective treatment. For osteoarthritis, the evidence is insufficient to exclude a clinically important benefit, which creates an opportunity for further investigation.[64]
7. As the magnetic fields are too weak to have any effects, there are also no risks in applying weak static magnets externally.

Plausibility	👎
Efficacy	👎
Safety	👍
Cost	👎
Risk/Benefit balance	👎

---

[64]Pittler et al. (2007).

9.22 Marma Massage

(related modalities: Ayurvedic medicine, massage, shiatsu)

Marma massage is a traditional form of massage therapy from India. It has its roots in Ayurvedic medicine and is now also becoming popular also outside India.

1. Ayurvedic clinicians believe that ill health is caused by obstruction of the flow of vayu (wind) through vayu carrying vessels or siras. Marma massage is claimed to increase circulation of vayu in the siras, remove tension, reduce pain and promote a deeper and more natural breathing pattern.
2. The therapy involves vigorous pressure applied by the therapist mainly on the side of the body that is affected. The pressure is applied over one or more of the 107 'Marma points' assumed to exist on our body surface. These points are located where 'flesh, veins, arteries, tendons, bones and joints meet'.[65]
3. The point-selection for any therapy is made based on the sensitivity of each point. If one location is abnormally sensitive, the therapist assumes that it needs treating until sensitivity returns to normal levels.
4. The assumptions upon which Marma massage is based are not biologically plausible.
5. The therapeutic claims made by proponents are highly diverse and wide-ranging. Most proponents view Marma massage as a panacea, a treatment that can have positive effects on almost any condition. One proponent claims that it "relaxes the muscles, nerves, bones and the whole body. It aids the digestive system by maintaining the proper balance and circulation of the body gases. It induces deep sleep, increases the appetite and generally makes life more joyful."[66]
6. The only clinical trial of Marma massage was aimed at assessing its effects in stroke patients. Its results showed that most patients believed the massage to be beneficial. Some patients found the treatment painful. However, the objective effectiveness data showed no significant advantage over usual care.[67]
7. The only known adverse effects of Marma massage are the pain experienced by patients during treatments and the dent it might leave in their savings.

Plausibility	👎
Efficacy	👎

(continued)

---

[65]Fox et al. (2006).

[66]http://www.theayurvedicclinic.com/ayurvedic-marma-massage.

[67]Fox et al. (2006).

(continued)

Safety	
Cost	
Risk/Benefit balance	

9.23 Massage

(related modalities: marma massage, lymph drainage, shiatsu)

There are many forms of massage, and several types are discussed in dedicated chapters of this book. Here we will focus on classical massage, often also called Swedish massage (Fig. 9.3).

Fig. 9.3 Illustration of the human musculoskeletal system from an early massage handbook. *Source* US National Library of Medicine

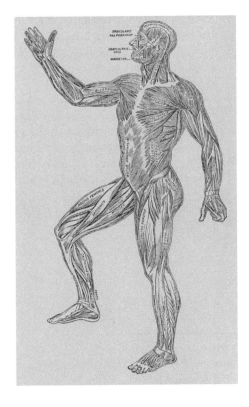

1. Most alternative types of massage are based on concepts that are out of line with our modern medical knowledge. By contrast, Swedish massage is based on the current concepts of anatomy, physiology, etc., and its mode of action is arguably more plausible than that of all other types of massage therapy.
2. It is normally performed by a trained massage therapist who would employ various techniques: effleurage (long smooth strokes), petrissage (kneading, rolling, and lifting), friction (wringing or small circular movements), tapotement (percussion), and vibration (rocking and shaking movements).
3. In most European countries, massage is considered to be part of conventional heathcare, while elsewhere it is usually viewed as an alternative therapy.[68]
4. Massage is advocated mainly to increase well-being, for relaxation and for musculoskeletal pain.
5. Rigorous clinical trials of massage therapy encounter formidable methodological, logistical and financial problems and are therefore rare.
6. Several systematic reviews of clinical trials have become available. They must be interpreted with caution, since the types of massage therapy used are often not clearly specified and differentiated. Their results vary according to the specific indication.

   - One overview identified 31 systematic reviews of massage for pain control, of which 21 were considered high-quality. The most common type of pain included in systematic reviews was neck pain (n = 6). Findings from high-quality systematic reviews describe potential benefits of massage for pain indications including labour, shoulder, neck, back, cancer, fibromyalgia, and temporomandibular disorder. However, no findings were rated as moderate- or high-strength.[69]
   - A systematic review showed that massage therapy has promise for caner palliation: massage can alleviate a wide range of symptoms: pain, nausea, anxiety, depression, anger, stress and fatigue. However, the methodological quality of the included studies was poor, a fact that prevents definitive conclusions. The evidence is, therefore, encouraging but not compelling. The subject seems to warrant further investigations which avoid the limitations of previous studies.[70]
   - Another systematic review concluded that there is currently a lack of evidence to support this assertion from RCTs that have selected participants for depression or subsyndromal symptoms of depression.[71]

---

[68]Posadzki et al. (2013a).
[69]Miake-Lye et al. (2016).
[70]Ernst (2009b).
[71]Coelho et al. (2008).

7. Adverse effects of massage are mild and infrequent; a systematic review concluded that "massage is not entirely risk free. However, serious adverse events are probably true rarities."[72]

Plausibility	👍
Efficacy	👍
Safety	👍
Cost	👎
Risk/Benefit balance	👍

9.24 Moxibustion

(related modalities: acupressure, acupuncture)

Moxibustion is a form of Traditional Chinese Medicine where acupuncture points are stimulated not by inserting needles, as in acupuncture, but by heat generated through burning sticks of dried mug-wort (or moxa) close to acupuncture points.

1. The practice lacks biological plausibility. It nevertheless has become popular, not just in China but throughout the world.
2. Moxibustion is sometimes combined with acupuncture, and the heat generated from the burning of moxa can be used for warming the acupuncture needles in situ.
3. The therapeutic claims made for moxibustion are far-reaching and similar to those made for acupuncture. Some therapists regard it as a panacea.
4. Many clinical trials have been conducted, most of which originate from China.
5. The majority of these trials are of poor quality and their results are thus not reliable.

---

[72]Ernst (2003).

6. Several systematic reviews are available, for instance:

- One systematic review concluded that there is low level of evidence based on these six trials that demonstrates the superiority of moxibustion over drug therapies in the treatment of chemotherapy-induced leukopenia. However, the number of trials, the total sample size, and the methodological quality are too low to draw firm conclusions. Future RCTs appear to be warranted.[73]
- Another systematic review failed to provide conclusive evidence for the effectiveness of moxibustion compared with drug therapy in rheumatic conditions. The total number of RCTs included in this review and their methodological quality were low. These limitations make it difficult to draw firm conclusions.[74]
- A further systematic review concluded that few RCTs are available that test the effectiveness of moxibustion in the management of pain, and most of the existing trials have a high risk of bias. Therefore, more rigorous studies are required before the effectiveness of moxibustion for the treatment of pain can be determined.[75]
- And another systematic review found that given that the methodological quality of all RCTs was poor, the results from the present review are insufficient to suggest that moxibustion is an effective treatment for constipation.[76]

7. Moxibustion is not entirely risk-free. Its adverse effects include allergic reactions, burns and infections.[77] Due to the absence of a monitoring system, the incidence of such events is currently not known.

Plausibility	👎
Efficacy	👎
Safety	👎
Cost	👍
Risk/Benefit balance	👎

---

[73]Choi et al. (2015).
[74]Choi et al. (2011).
[75]Lee et al. (2010b).
[76]Lee et al. (2010c).
[77]Park et al. (2010).

Fig. 9.4 Andrew Taylor Still. *Source* US National Library of Medicine

9.25 Osteopathy

(related modalities: chiropractic, craniosacral therapy)

Osteopathy is a form of manual therapy invented over 100 years ago by the American Andrew Taylor Still (1828–1917) (Fig. 9.4).

1. Today, US osteopaths (doctors of osteopathy or DOs) have more or less stopped practising manual therapy; they are fully recognised as medical doctors who can specialise in any medical field after their training which is similar to that of MDs. Outside the US, osteopaths practice almost exclusively manual treatments and are considered alternative practitioners. This chapter deals with the latter category of osteopaths.

2. Still defined his original osteopathy as a science which consists of such exact, exhaustive, and verifiable knowledge of the structure and function of the human mechanism, anatomical, physiological and psychological, including the chemistry and physics of its known elements, as has made discoverable certain organic laws and remedial resources, within the body itself, by which nature under the scientific treatment peculiar to osteopathic practice, apart from all ordinary methods of extraneous, artificial, or medicinal stimulation, and in harmonious accord with its own mechanical principles, molecular activities, and metabolic processes, may recover from displacements, disorganizations, derangements, and consequent disease, and regained its normal equilibrium of form and function in health and strength.[78]

3. Osteopathy is not dissimilar to chiropractic (see there). It is said that DD Palmer, the inventor of chiropractic, learnt from Still and 'adopted' many of his ideas. One important difference between the two disciplines is that osteopaths tend to use less of those techniques which are associated with serious adverse effects. This means that osteopathy tends to be less harmful than chiropractic.

4. The basic assumptions that underpin osteopathy lack biological plausibility.

5. An overview of 100 randomly selected websites of osteopaths revealed that 93% checked at least one of the criteria for pseudo-scientific claims. The author concluded that quackery is rife osteopathic practice.[79]

6. Some osteopaths consider themselves as back pain specialists, while others claim to effectively treat a much wider range of conditions.

   • For back pain, the evidence is encouraging but not conclusively positive. One review (by osteopaths) concluded that osteopathic treatment "significantly reduces low back pain. The level of pain reduction is greater than expected from placebo effects alone and persists for at least three months. Additional research is warranted to elucidate mechanistically how

---

[78]Still (1899).

[79]https://appletzara.wordpress.com/2016/04/24/osteopathy-part-2-a-review-of-100-osteopathy-websites/.

osteopathic manipulative exerts its effects, to determine if OMT benefits are long lasting, and to assess the cost-effectiveness of osteopathic manipulative treatment as a complementary treatment for low back pain."[80]

- An independent review, however, found that the data fail to produce compelling evidence for the effectiveness of osteopathy as a treatment of musculoskeletal pain.[81]
- For non-spinal conditions, the evidence is even less convincing. One review concluded, for instance, that the evidence of the effectiveness of osteopathic manipulative therapy for pediatric conditions remains unproven due to the paucity and low methodological quality of the primary studies.[82]

7. Even though adverse effects after osteopathy are less frequent than with chiropractic treatments, severe complications have been noted and "include cauda equina syndrome, lumbar disk herniation, fracture, and hematoma or hemorrhagic cyst. Contraindications … primarily involve conditions that increase bleeding risk or compromise bone, tendon, ligament, or joint integrity."[83]

Plausibility	👎
Efficacy	👍
Safety	👍
Cost	👎
Risk/Benefit balance	👍

9.26 Pilates

(related modalities: none)

Pilates is a set of physical exercises that were developed by a German of Greek decent, Joseph Pliates (1883–1967). These exercises have become popular in recent times and are said to have significant health benefits.

---

[80]Licciardone et al. (2005).

[81]Posadzki and Ernst (2011a).

[82]Posadzki et al. (2013b).

[83]Jonas (2018).

1. Pilates had been a sickly child who allegedly arrived at robust health through physical exercise. He emigrated from Germany first to England and then to the US where he and his wife Clara managed to build up a devoted following in the local dance and performing-arts community of New York.
2. He developed his specific set of exercises which he liked to call "Contrology" because they were based on the idea of muscle control. Using correct posture while doing Pilates exercises is considered to be an important step towards correcting muscle imbalances and optimising coordination.
3. Even though Pilates was not primarily developed as a therapy, countless therapeutic claims are currently made for it.
4. Pilates is often advocated for chronic low back pain. A systematic review concluded that Pilates exercise offers greater improvements in pain and functional ability compared to usual care and physical activity in the short term. Pilates exercise offers equivalent improvements to massage therapy and other forms of exercise. Future research should explore optimal Pilates exercise designs, and whether some people with CLBP may benefit from Pilates exercise more than others.[84]
5. A further systematic review found evidence of improved flexibility and dynamic balance, and of enhanced muscular endurance in healthy people in the short term. In addition, there may have been an effect on body composition in the short term.[85]
6. Pilates is particularly popular with women; a systematic review concluded that there is a paucity of evidence on Pilates for improving women's health during pregnancy or for conditions including breast cancer, obesity, or low back pain.[86]
7. While Pilates clearly might have positive health effects, it is unclear whether it is preferable to more conventional types of exercise.

Plausibility	
Efficacy	
Safety	
Cost	
Risk/Benefit balance	

[84]Wells et al. (2014).
[85]Kamioka et al. (2016).
[86]Mazzarino et al. (2015).

9.27 Polarity Therapy

(related modalities: chiropractic, energy healing, naturopathy, osteopathy, yoga)

Polarity therapy is an alternative approach that combines bodywork, diet, exercise and lifestyle counselling. It was invented by the Austrian-American chiropractor, osteopath, and naturopath Randolph Stone (1888–1981).

1. Stone aimed at an integration of Eastern and Western philosophies, principles and techniques of healing.
2. Polarity therapy is based on the assumption that our health depends on the energy flow within our body and that polarity therapy can re-adjust this flow when necessary.
3. These assumptions lack biological plausibility.
4. Polarity therapy is claimed to work for a wide range of conditions, including intoxications, HIV, stress, back pain, stomach cramps.
5. After determining the assumed source of a patient's energy imbalance, the therapist begins the first of a series of bodywork sessions designed to re-channel and release the patient's misdirected energy. This may be followed by a series of exercises called polarity yoga which include squats, stretches, rhythmic movements, deep breathing, and expression of sounds. They are assumed to be energizing and relaxing. Counselling may be included whenever appropriate as a part of a patient's highly individualised therapy regimen to promote balance.
6. According to its proponents, polarity therapy addresses many different levels: subtle energy; nervous, musculo-skeletal, cardiovascular, myofascial, respiratory and digestive systems; as well as the emotional and mental levels. It tackles many varied and different expressions of disease by unlocking the holding patterns that create the symptoms. Dr. Stone called it Polarity because it embodies the negative and positive poles and the neutrality between them. This Modality is a healing art, an anchor for a balanced lifestyle, an evolving way of being, an adjunct to other modalities.[87]
7. There have been only very few clinical trials testing the effectiveness of polarity therapy, and those that have emerges have been less than rigorous. Therefore, the effectiveness of polarity therapy is unproven.

Plausibility	👎
Efficacy	👎

(continued)

---

[87]http://www.polaritytherapy.org.uk/.

(continued)

Safety	
Cost	
Risk/Benefit balance	

9.28 Rebirthing

(related modalities: mind-body therapies)

Rebirthing or 'breath-work' is an alternative treatment invented in the 1970s by Leonard Orr (1937).

1. Orr is said to have devised rebirthing therapy after he re-lived his own birth while having a bath.
2. Rebirthing is claimed to be a spiritual approach to psychological and physical healing[88] that is supposed to build a bridge between the conscious and unconscious, between the mind and the body.
3. The 'British Rebirth Society' describes the method in glowing terms[89]: "Rebirthing is a simple, gentle yet powerful conscious breathing technique."

   - "It brings into awareness not only our unconsciously held beliefs and emotions but also the relationships we have with our bodies, ourselves, our intimates and our world. When we consciously breathe with this awareness, we make it possible to resolve, integrate and heal previously unresolved issues within ourselves. This frees up energy, bringing greater aliveness and joy and allowing us to move towards fulfillment of our potential as human beings."
   - "Rebirthing is a powerful healing method which offers you an experience of freedom and mastery in your life."
   - "Rebirthing brings expanded awareness on all levels: physical, emotional, psychological and spiritual."

4. Rebirthing is being practised by nurses, midwives and other clinicians.[90]
5. The therapeutic claims made for this therapy include:[91]

---

[88]Orr and Forman (1979).

[89]http://www.rebirthingbreathwork.co.uk/brs_what.

[90]Downe (2005).

[91]http://www.rebirthingbreathwork.co.uk/brs_what.

- "relationship difficulties or patterns that keep repeating themselves in every relationship;
- not knowing who you are and what you want;
- not living up to your potential;
- feeling trapped in a way of being, stressed out by efforts to please others;
- stress;
- job-related problems;
- depression;
- anxiety, panic attacks, phobias;
- shyness and low self-esteem, lack of confidence;
- general unhappiness with what seems like every aspect of your life;
- an inability to feel;
- abuse;
- simply wanting to get to know yourself better and enjoy life more."

4 The assumptions made for rebirthing lack plausibility, and the rebirthing scene displays many of the hallmarks of a cult.
5 There are hardly any clinical trials of rebirthing. Therefore, its effectiveness must be characterised as unproven.
6 There is little doubt that rebirthing is associated with considerable for "potential psychological and physiological harm"...[92]

Plausibility	👎
Efficacy	👎
Safety	👎
Cost	👎
Risk/Benefit balance	👎

---

[92]Heape (1984).

9.29 Reflexology

(related modalities: massage)

Reflexology (originally called 'zone therapy' by its inventor) is a manual technique where pressure is applied to the sole of the patient's foot and sometimes also other areas such as the hands or ears. It must be differentiated from a simple foot massage that is agreeable but makes no therapeutic claims beyond relaxation.

1. Reflexology is said to have its roots in ancient cultures. Its current popularity goes back to the US doctor William Fitzgerald (1872–1942) who did some research in the early 1900s and thought to have discovered that the human body is divided into 10 zones each of which is represented on the sole of the foot.[93]
2. Reflexologists thus drew maps of the sole of the foot where all the body's organs are depicted. Numerous such maps have been published and, embarrassingly, they do not all agree with each other as to the location of our organs on the sole of our feet.
3. By massaging specific zones which are assumed to be connected to specific organs, reflexologists believe to positively influence the function of these organs.
4. Reflexology is mostly used as a therapy, but some therapists also claim they can diagnose health problems through feeling tender or gritty areas on the sole of the foot which, they claim, correspond to specific organs.
5. The assumptions made by reflexologists contradict our current knowledge of anatomy and physiology and are thus not biologically plausible.
6. Reflexology has been submitted to clinical trials in several conditions, including diabetes, premenstrual syndrome, cancer patients, multiple sclerosis, symptomatic idiopathic detrusor over-activity and dementia. However, most of these studies are of poor quality. A systematic review concluded that "the best clinical evidence does not demonstrate convincingly reflexology to be an effective treatment for any medical condition."[94]
7. Reflexology can be mildly painful but usually it is experienced as pleasant and relaxing. Serious adverse effects are not expected.

Plausibility	👎
Efficacy	👎

(continued)

---

[93]http://www.reflexologyinstitute.com/reflex_fitzgerald.php.
[94]Ernst et al. (2011b).

(continued)

Safety		
Cost		
Risk/Benefit balance		

9.30 Rolfing

(related modalities: Alexander technique, chiropractic, massage therapy, osteopathy, yoga)

Rolfing is a system of bodywork invented by Ida Pauline Rolf (1896–1979) employing deep manipulation of the body's soft tissue allegedly to realign and balance the body's myofascial structures.

1. The Guild for Structural Integration describes Rolfing as "a method and a philosophy of personal growth and integrity.... The vertical line is our fundamental concept. The physical and psychological embodiment of the vertical line is a way of Being in the physical world [that] forms a basis for personal growth and integrity."[95]
2. Rolfing is being promoted as a system that reshapes the body's myofascial structure by applying pressure and energy. It is said to free the body from the effects of physical and emotional traumas. A key assumption is that fascia tightens from chronic dysfunctional movement and imbalanced muscular tension, resulting in contracture. Over time, the tightened fascia becomes shortened with disorganized collagen, constricting muscle contraction and relaxation, and consequently constricting the movements of our joints.
3. Rolf stated that Rolfers make a life study of relating bodies and their fields to the earth and its gravity field, and we so organize the body that the gravity field can reinforce the body's energy field. This is our primary concept.[96]
4. Rolfing is based on obsolete vitalistic principles and lacks scientific plausibility.
5. Proponents claim that Rolfing can bring relief from chronic back, neck, shoulder and joint pain, improve breathing, increase energy, improve self-confidence, and relieve physical and mental stress.

---

[95]https://www.rolfguild.org/mission.
[96]Rolf (1990).

6. Only very few trials of Rolfing have emerged, and none are of good quality.[97] Therefore, none of the therapeutic claims made for Rolfing are based on sound evidence.

7. Rolfing involves vigorous deep, somewhat forceful tissue manipulation and is often experienced as uncomfortable or even painful.

Plausibility	👎
Efficacy	👎
Safety	👎
Cost	👎
Risk/Benefit balance	👎

9.31   Shiatsu

(related modalities: acupressure, massage, Traditional Chinese Medicine, tui na)

Shiatsu is a (mostly) manual therapy that was popularised by Japanese Tokujiro Namikoshi (1905–2000). It developed out of the Chinese massage therapy, 'tui na'. The word shiatsu means finger pressure in Japanese; however, a range of devices is also being promoted for shiatsu.

1. In 1940, Tokujiro Namikoshi established the Japan Shiatsu College in Tokyo. He taught many practitioners, some of whom subsequently developed their own version of shiatsu.

2. Shiatsu follows the principles of Traditional Chinese Medicine based on chi, meridians, yin and yang, etc. These are philosophical concepts at best but lack scientific and biological plausibility.

3. The amount of pressure used during treatment can be considerable and therefore, Shiatsu is experienced by some patients as (mildly) painful.

4. Shiatsu is a treatment which includes not just the pressure applied by the therapist at specific points but also awareness of body posture, breathing and exercise.

---

[97]Jones (2004).

5. Similar to acupuncture, is shiatsu claimed to stimulate the body's vital energy. One observational study concluded that "clients receiving shiatsu reported improvements in symptom severity and changes in their health-related behaviour that they attributed to their treatment, suggestive of a role for shiatsu in maintaining and enhancing health."[98] A similar study observed a wide range of common, immediate and longer term effects. These included effects on initial symptoms, relaxation, sleeping, posture, and experiences of the body.[99]

6. There have been very few controlled clinical trials. A systematic review of this evidence found no convincing data to suggest that shiatsu is effective for any specific health condition.[100]

7. Even though some patients experience the treatment as painful, Shiatsu is generally considered to be a safe therapy. It is, however, not totally free of risks. One observational study found that 12–22% "of patients reported 'negative effects' after shiatsu treatment,"[101] and several case reports have associated Shiatsu also with serious complications. e.g.[102]

Plausibility	👎
Efficacy	👎
Safety	👎
Cost	👍
Risk/Benefit balance	👎

9.32 Slapping Therapy

(related modalities: detox, Traditional Chinese Medicine)

Slapping therapy is based on the notion that lapping a patient at certain points of their body has positive therapeutic effects.

---

[98]Long (2008).

[99]Long and Mackay (2003).

[100]Robinson et al. (2011).

[101]Long et al. (2009).

[102]Wada et al. (2005).

1. Hongchi Xiao, a Chinese-born investment banker, popularised this treatment which, he claims, is based on the principles of Traditional Chinese Medicine. It is also known as 'Paida'—in Chinese, this means 'to slap your body'.
2. Slapping therapy involves slapping the body surface with a view of stimulating the flow of 'chi', the vital energy postulated in Traditional Chinese Medicine. Slapping therapists believe that this ritual restores health and eliminates toxins. They also claim that the bruises which patients tend to develop after the treatment are the visible signs of toxins coming to the surface.
3. Hongchi Xiao advocates slapping as "self-healing method" that should be continued until the skin starts looking bruised. He and his follows conduct workshops and sell books teaching the public which advocate slapping therapy as a panacea, a cure-all.
4. The assumptions of slapping therapy fly in the face of science and are thus not plausible.
5. There is not a single clinical trial testing whether slapping therapy is effective. It must therefore be categorised as unproven.
6. Slapping therapy can also cause significant harm. As it costs money, it harms of course the bank accounts of patients. More importantly, it causes pain can leave unsightly bruises. Even more importantly, several fatalities have been reported where a patient was advised to give up essential conventional medicines and use slapping therapy as an alternative.[103,104]
7. Slapping therapy is unpleasant, implausible, not effective and not free of side-effects. Its risk/benefit balance is clearly negative.

Plausibility	👎
Efficacy	👎
Safety	👎
Cost	👎
Risk/Benefit balance	👎

---

[103]https://www.theguardian.com/uk-news/2016/nov/14/danielle-carr-gomm-slapping-therapy-workshop-death-three-people-arrested-wiltshire.

[104]https://www.bbc.co.uk/news/world-australia-32545732.

9.33 Spinal Manipulation

(related modalities: chiropractic, osteopathy, spinal mobilisation)

Spinal manipulation is a therapeutic technique with a long history; it is used by many manual therapists for treating back and neck pain as well as many other conditions that are unrelated to the spine (Fig. 9.5).

1. Spinal manipulation is the hallmark therapy of chiropractors. Close to 100% of all patients consulting a chiropractor will receive spinal manipulation. Many chiropractors advise to have regular spinal manipulations, even in the absence of

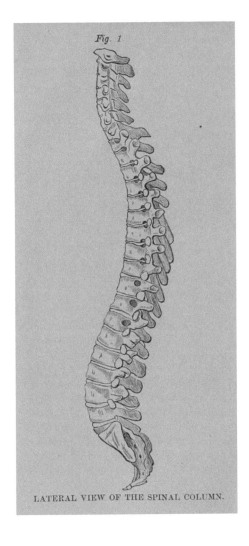

Fig. 9.5 The human spine, depiction from a 1878 book entitled 'The homoeopathic treatment of spinal curvatures'. *Source* US National Library of Medicine

LATERAL VIEW OF THE SPINAL COLUMN.

symptoms, an approach they call 'maintenance treatment'. Other healthcare professionals such as osteopaths and physiotherapists also do spinal manipulations but less regularly.

2. Most chiropractors believe that spinal manipulation can correct subluxations (a term that is also used in conventional medicine but with a different meaning) of the spine. The founding father of chiropractic, D D Palmer, postulated that 95% of all diseases are caused by subluxations.[105]

3. Yet, there is no evidence that subluxations, as postulated by chiropractors, even exist, and a sizable proportion of chiropractors are now beginning to agree that subluxations are a myth.

4. There are several techniques of spinal manipulation; some are forceful and aim at taking a spinal joint beyond its physiological range of motion. These are the techniques that have been associated most frequently with serious complications, particularly when applied to the upper spine.

5. There is little convincing evidence to show that spinal manipulations are effective.

   • A Cochrane review concluded that spinal manipulative therapy (SMT) is no more effective in participants with acute low-back pain than inert interventions, sham SMT, or when added to another intervention.[106]

   • Another Cochrane review concluded that high quality evidence suggests that there is no clinically relevant difference between SMT and other interventions for reducing pain and improving function in patients with chronic low-back pain.[107]

   • For other conditions, the evidence is even less convincing. An overview failed to demonstrate convincingly that spinal manipulation is an effective intervention for any condition.[108]

6. Spinal manipulations have been associated with serious risks. About 50% of patients experience temporary pain after such treatments, and several hundred cases of stroke, sometimes followed by death, have been reported.[109]

7. Many chiropractors, however, deny a causal relationship altogether or claim that such calamities are extremely rare. As no system has yet been implemented to monitor adverse effects of chiropractic, the true frequency of such events is unknown.

---

[105]Ernst (2008).

[106]Rubinstein et al. (2012).

[107]Rubinstein et al. (2011).

[108]Posadzki and Ernst (2011b).

[109]Stevinson and Ernst (2002).

Plausibility	
Efficacy	
Safety	
Cost	
Risk/Benefit balance	

9.34   Spinal Mobilisation

(related modalities: chiropractic, osteopathy, spinal manipulation)

Spinal mobilisation describes a set of ill-defined, usually manual techniques used by manual therapists to treat a range of conditions.

1. Osteopaths and physiotherapists use spinal mobilisation more frequently than spinal manipulation (see there). Chiropractors also employ spinal mobilisation, but often prefer manipulation.
2. Mobilisation is normally a gentler, less forceful treatment than manipulation. It often involves oscillatory, passive movements applied to a spinal region or segment.
3. As the name says, these techniques are aimed at mobilising the spinal joints to increase the range of motion of that segment or region and reduce pain. Mobilisation is rarely employed as a sole technique but usually combined with other treatments.
4. Spinal mobilisation is sometimes applied with the help of mechanical devices, such as the 'activator' or a 'drop table
5. The main indications of spinal mobilisation are back and neck pain. There is little research testing the effectiveness specifically of spinal mobilisation in isolation. One reason for this might be that it is rarely used as a sole treatment.
6. Applying less force means that spinal mobilisation is burdened with far less risks than spinal manipulation. Virtually all the serious complications that have been reported after chiropractic treatments occurred not with mobilisation but with manipulation.
7. As there is no system of monitoring adverse effects, the frequency of adverse effects after spinal mobilisation remains, however, unknown.

Plausibility	
Efficacy	
Safety	
Cost	
Risk/Benefit balance	

9.35   Tai Chi

Tai chi is an exercise therapy with a long tradition. It involves meditative movements rooted in both Traditional Chinese Medicine and the martial arts. Tai chi was originally aimed at enhancing mental and physical health; today it has become a popular alternative therapy (Fig. 9.6).

Fig. 9.6 Tai Chi became popular in the West in the 1980. *Source* US National Library of Medicine

1. Tai chi originates from China and is still much-practised there. In the West, it has recently become popular and is now advocated for a wide range of conditions.
2. A number of different styles of tai chi have emerged from the original 13 postures.
3. Tai chi should be taught in small classes in a quiet and relaxed atmosphere.
4. Tai chi is seen as a life-long endeavour and regular practice of 2–3 sessions of about 30 min per week are recommended for optimal effects.
5. The effectiveness of tai chi has been the subject of many recent studies. Several systematic reviews have become available; yet, many of them are somewhat uncritical, for instance:

   - One review concluded that the beneficial effect of tai chi on body mass density is suggested to be clinically translated to its potential for early rehabilitation and prevention of secondary osteoporosis in patients after surgical treatment of common osteoporotic fractures. The length of practicing TCC, the form and style of TCC, and the types of patient suitable for TCC are to be investigated in future studies.[110]
   - Another review found that Tai Chi for more than 8 weeks has short-term ameliorative effects on cancer related fatigue, especially among patients with breast and lung cancer. Its beneficial effects are superior to physical exercise and psychological support. It remains unclear whether there are long-term benefits, and further study is needed.[111]
   - A further review concluded that, compared to no exercise or other types of exercise with low-to-moderate intensity, Tai Chi seems a good choice for coronary disease rehabilitation in improving cardiorespiratory fitness. However, owing to the poor methodology quality, more clinical trials with large sample size, strict randomization, and clear description about detection and reporting processes are needed to further verify the evidence.[112]
   - And finally, a review of tai chi for Parkinson's disease found that Tai Chi generated better balance and one or more aspects of well-being, though mixed results were reported.[113]

---

[110]Chow et al. (2017).

[111]Song et al. (2018).

[112]Yang et al. (2018).

[113]Ćwiękała-Lewis et al. (2017).

6 Tai chi is thus being promoted over-optimistically almost like a panacea. However, a more critical assessment of the evidence rightly cautions that "many systematic reviews of t'ai chi have recently been published; however, the evidence is convincingly positive only for fall prevention and for improvement of psychological health."[114]

7 Tai chi is generally considered to be safe.

Plausibility	👎
Efficacy	👎
Safety	👍
Cost	👍
Risk/Benefit balance	👎

9.36   Tragerwork

(related modalities: mind-body therapies, massage)

Tragerwork (originally called Psychophysical Integration by its inventor) is an alternative therapy developed in the 1970s by the US doctor Milton Trager.

1. Milton Trager was a boxer who became involved in bodywork therapy when he realised that he was able to feel people's tensions in their body and relieve them with gentle movements. He then trained as a physical therapist and later even qualified as a doctor. He also learnt transcendental meditation which greatly influenced him. He opened the Trager Institute in California in 1980.
2. Tragerwork is claimed to release deleterious, so-called "holding patterns" allegedly found in muscles through gentle, rocking massage and to enhance the interaction between the body and the mind. The assumptions of Tragerwork lack plausibility.
3. Tragerwork therapists use their hands and minds to communicate feelings of lightness and freedom to their patients. Aided movements are followed by lessons in 'mentastics' (mental gymnastics) involving dance-like movements which are said to enhance a sensation of lightness.

---

[114]Lee and Ernst (2012).

4. The therapeutic claims for Tragerwork are often far-reaching[115] and include the assumptions of effectively treating asthma, autism, depression, emphysema, hypertension, low back pain, migraines, multiple sclerosis, muscular dystrophy, polio, neuromuscular diseases, pain, poor posture, sciatica, sports injuries, improvement of athletic performance, mental control, responsiveness and conservation of energy in movement.
5. There have been only very few clinical trials testing the effectiveness of Tragerwork. Those that have emerged are methodologically weak.[116]
6. None of the many therapeutic claims made by proponents of this therapy are supported by sound evidence.
7. There are few direct risks associated with Tragerwork.

Plausibility	👎
Efficacy	👎
Safety	👍
Cost	👎
Risk/Benefit balance	👎

9.37   Trigger-Point Therapy

(related modalities: massage, shiatsu)

Trigger point therapy is a manual treatment that involves applying pressure to defined points over a muscle called myofascial trigger-points.

1. Trigger points are painful spots in the muscle tissue that radiate pain to other areas of the body. They are said to be caused by some form of physiological dysfunction, such as poor posture, repetitive mechanical stress, a mechanical imbalance, or acute trauma.
2. The aim of the intervention usually is to reduce pain caused by localised muscular spasms. Other alleged benefits include an increase in the range of motion of the affected joints, and the general relaxation of mind and body.

---

[115]Russell (1994).
[116]Mehling et al. (2005).

3. The pressure is normally applied with a finger, knuckle, or elbow, for about 30 s at a time. Some therapists use laser or dry needling for trigger-point therapy.
4. The technique is usually administered by a massage therapist who is trained to identify and activate trigger points.
5. The proposed mode of action of trigger-point therapy is an increase of the supply of oxygen to the cells under conditions of hypoxia and help remove the waste products of cell metabolism, thereby breaking the vicious cycle of pain, muscle spasm and further pain.[117] An experimental study suggested that trigger-point therapy does indeed increase the pain threshold.[118]
6. The evidence for the therapeutic claims is weak, not least because of the usually low quality and paucity of the available clinical trials.[119,120,121]
7. There are few, if any, serious risks associated with trigger-point therapy.

Plausibility	👎
Efficacy	👎
Safety	👍
Cost	👍
Risk/Benefit balance	👎

9.38 Tui Na

(related modalities: massage, shiatsu, Traditional Chinese Medicine, trigger point therapy)

Tui na is a manual treatment following the assumptions of Traditional Chinese Medicine.

---

[117]Uemoto et al. (2013).
[118]Moraska et al. (2017).
[119]Espejo-Antúnez et al. (2017).
[120]Liu et al. (2015).
[121]Moraska et al. (2015).

1. Tui na has close similarities with shiatsu which is said to have evolved from tui na. Many of the techniques used in tui na resemble those of a western massage like gliding, kneading, vibration, tapping, friction, pulling, rolling, pressing and shaking.
2. Tui na involves a range of manipulations usually performed by the therapist's finger, hand, elbow, knee, or foot. They are applied to muscle or soft tissue at specific locations of the body.
3. Tui na is often used in combination with other TCM modalities, such as acupuncture or herbal medicine. Some acupuncture schools even teach tiu na to all their pupils.
4. The aim of tui na is to enhance the flow of the vital energy, chi, that is alleged to control our health. The assumptions underlying tiu na are not plausible.
5. Proponents of the therapy recommend tui na for a range of conditions, including chronic pain associated with the joints, muscles or a skeletal system, arthritis, sciatica, muscle spasms, stress, insomnia, constipation, headaches and disorders related to digestive, respiratory and reproductive systems. Tui na is claimed to be particularly suitable for the elderly and for infants.
6. Several studies and reviews of tiu na have emerged. Most of the trials and reviews are of poor quality and therefore less than reliable. One review, for instance, assessed the evidence of tui na for cervical radiculopathy. Five studies involving 448 patients were included. The analysis from the three trials indicated that tui na suggested effect on pain. None of the studies mentioned adverse effects. The authors concluded that "Tui Na alone or Tui Na plus cervical traction may be helpful to cervical radiculopathy patients, but supportive evidence seems generally weak. Future clinical studies with low risk of bias and adequate follow-up design are recommended."[122] Several serious flaws in this review render its conclusion unreliable:

- there are too few studies,
- the included RCTs lack scientific rigour,
- all trials originate from China where reliability seems to be a serious problem,
- traction is not a useful therapy for radiculopathy,
- the primary studies violate research ethics by not reporting adverse effects.

Another review concluded that "Tui Na therapy was a viable intervention that could benefit infants and young children with anorexia,"[123] and the deficits of this paper are almost identical to the previous article.

---

[122]Wei et al. (2017).
[123]Xia et al. (2014).

7. The risks of tui na are largely unknown but probably minor.

Plausibility	👎
Efficacy	👎
Safety	👍
Cost	👍
Risk/Benefit balance	👎

9.39 Visceral Osteopathy

(related modalities: chiropractic, osteopathy)

Visceral osteopathy (or visceral manipulation) is an expansion of the general principles of osteopathy and involves the manual manipulation by a therapist of internal organs, blood vessels and nerves (the viscera) from outside the body.

1. Visceral osteopathy was developed by the osteopath Jean-Piere Barral. He stated that through his clinical work with thousands of patients, he created this modality based on organ-specific fascial mobilization. And through work in a dissection lab, he was able to experiment with visceral manipulation techniques and see the internal effects of the manipulations.[124]
2. According to its proponents, visceral manipulation is based on the specific placement of soft manual forces looking to encourage the normal mobility, tone and motion of the viscera and their connective tissues. These gentle manipulations may potentially improve the functioning of individual organs, the systems the organs function within, and the structural integrity of the entire body.[125]
3. Visceral osteopathy is being practised mostly by osteopaths and less commonly chiropractors and physiotherapists.
4. Visceral osteopathy comprises of several different manual techniques firstly for diagnosing a health problem and secondly for treating it.

---

[124]https://www.barralinstitute.com/about/jean-pierre-barral.php.

[125]http://www.barralinstitute.co.uk/.

5. Several studies have assessed the diagnostic reliability of the techniques involved. The totality of this evidence fails to show that they are sufficiently reliable to be od practical use.[126]

6. Other studies have tested whether the therapeutic techniques used in visceral osteopathy are effective in curing disease or alleviating symptoms. The totality of this evidence fails to show that visceral osteopathy works for any condition.[127]

7. The treatment itself is probably safe, yet the risks of visceral osteopathy are nevertheless considerable: if a patient suffers from symptoms related to her inner organs, a visceral osteopath is likely to misdiagnose them and subsequently mistreat them. If the symptoms are due to a serious disease, this would amount to medical neglect and could, in extreme cases, cost the patient's life.

Plausibility	👎
Efficacy	👎
Safety	👍
Cost	👎
Risk/Benefit balance	👎

References

AlBedah A, Khalil M, Elolemy A, Hussein AA, AlQaed M, Al Mudaiheem A, Abutalib RA, Bazaid FM, Bafail AS, Essa A, Bakrain MY (2015) The use of wet cupping for persistent nonspecific low back pain: randomized controlled clinical trial. J Altern Complement Med 21 (8):504–508

Aprile A, Pomara C, Turillazzi E (2015) Gua Sha a traditional Chinese healing technique that could mimic physical abuse: a potential issue with forensic implications. A case study. Forensic Sci Int 249:e19–e20

Bridgett R, Klose P, Duffield R, Mydock S, Lauche R (2018) Effects of cupping therapy in amateur and professional athletes: systematic review of randomized controlled trials. J Altern Complement Med 24(3):208–219

Buchanan PA, Nelsen NL, Geletta S (2014) United States guild certified Feldenkrais Teachers®: a survey of characteristics and practice patterns. BMC Complement Altern Med 14:217

---

[126]Guillaud et al. (2018).

[127]http://www.barralinstitute.co.uk/.

Chen SF, Wang CH, Chan PT, Chiang HW, Hu TM, Tam KW, Loh EW (2018) Labor pain control by aromatherapy: a meta-analysis of randomized controlled trials. Women Birth S1871-5192 (18)30221-X

Choi TY, Kim TH, Kang JW, Lee MS, Ernst E (2011) Moxibustion for rheumatic conditions: a systematic review and meta-analysis. Clin Rheumatol 30(7):937–945

Choi TY, Lee MS, Ernst E (2015) Moxibustion for the treatment of chemotherapy-induced leukopenia: a systematic review of randomized clinical trials. Support Care Cancer 23 (6):1819–1826

Chow TH, Lee BY, Ang ABF, Cheung VYK, Ho MMC, Takemura S (2017) The effect of Chinese martial arts Tai Chi Chuan on prevention of osteoporosis: a systematic review. J Orthop Translat 12:74–84

Coelho HF, Boddy K, Ernst E (2008) Massage therapy for the treatment of depression: a systematic review. Int J Clin Pract 62(2):325–333

Colquhoun D, Novella SP (2013) Acupuncture is theatrical placebo. Anesth Analg 116(6):1360–1363

Cooke B, Ernst E (2000) Aromatherapy: a systematic review. Br J Gen Pract 50(455):493–496

Ćwiękała-Lewis KJ, Gallek M, Taylor-Piliae RE (2017) The effects of Tai Chi on physical function and well-being among persons with Parkinson's Disease: a systematic review. J Bodyw Mov Ther 21(2):414–421

Doo KH, Lee JH, Cho SY, Jung WS, Moon SK, Park JM, Ko CN, Kim H, Park HJ, Park SU (2015) A prospective open-label study of combined treatment for Idiopathic Parkinson's disease using acupuncture and bee venom acupuncture as an adjunctive treatment. J Altern Complement Med 21(10):598–603

Downe S (2005) Rebirthing midwifery. RCM Midwives 8(8):346–349

Ernst E (2003) The safety of massage therapy. Rheumatology (Oxford) 42(9):1101–1106

Ernst E (2004) Ear candles: a triumph of ignorance over science. J Laryngol Otol 118(1):1–2

Ernst E (2008) Chiropractic: a critical evaluation. J Pain Symptom Manage 35(5):544–562

Ernst E (2009a) Chiropractic maintenance treatment, a useful preventative approach? Prev Med 49 (2–3):99–100

Ernst E (2009b) Massage therapy for cancer palliation and supportive care: a systematic review of randomised clinical trials. Support Care Cancer 17(4):333–337

Ernst E (2012a) Acupuncture: what does the most reliable evidence tell us? An update. J Pain Symptom Manage 43(2):e11–e13

Ernst MD (2012b) Craniosacral therapy: a systematic review of the clinical evidence. Focus Altern Complement Ther 17(4)

Ernst E, Lee MS (2010) Acupressure: an overview of systematic reviews. J Pain Symptom Manage 40(4):e3–e7

Ernst E, Pittler MH (2006) Celebrity-based medicine. Med J Aust 185(11–12):680–681

Ernst E, Lee MS, Choi TY (2011) Acupuncture: does it alleviate pain and are there serious risks? A review of reviews. Pain 152(4):755–764

Ernst E, Posadzki P, Lee MS (2011b) Reflexology: an update of a systematic review of randomised clinical trials. Maturitas 68(2):116–120

Espejo-Antúnez L, Tejeda JF, Albornoz-Cabello M, Rodríguez-Mansilla J, de la Cruz-Torres B, Ribeiro F, Silva AG (2017) Dry needling in the management of myofascial trigger points: a systematic review of randomized controlled trials. Complement Ther Med 33:46–57

Ezzo J, Manheimer E, McNeely ML, Howell DM, Weiss R, Johansson KI, Bao T, Bily L, Tuppo CM, Williams AF, Karadibak D (2015) Manual lymphatic drainage for lymphedema following breast cancer treatment. Cochrane Database Syst Rev 5:CD003475

Fox M, Dickens A, Greaves C, Dixon M, James M (2006) Marma therapy for stroke rehabilitation —a pilot study. J Rehabil Med 38(4):268–271

Guillaud A, Darbois N, Monvoisin R, Pinsault N (2018) Reliability of diagnosis and clinical efficacy of visceral osteopathy: a systematic review. BMC Complement Altern Med 18:65

Heape SE (1984) Empyrean rebirthing: miracle or menace? J Relig Health 23(3):229–236

Hillier S, Worley A (2015) The effectiveness of the feldenkrais method: a systematic review of the evidence. Evid Based Complement Alternat Med 2015:752160

Hornibrook J (2012) Where there's smoke there's fire–ear candling in a 4-year-old girl. N Z Med J 125(1367):138–140

Jonas C (2018) Musculoskeletal therapies: osteopathic manipulative treatment. FP Essent 470:11–15

Jones TA (2004) Rolfing. Phys Med Rehabil Clin N Am 15:799–809

Jonsson K, Kjellgren A (2016) Promising effects of treatment with flotation-REST (restricted environmental stimulation technique) as an intervention for generalized anxiety disorder (GAD): a randomized controlled pilot trial. BMC Complement Altern Med 16:108

Kamioka H, Tsutani K, Katsumata Y, Yoshizaki T, Okuizumi H, Okada S, Park SJ, Kitayuguchi J, Abe T, Mutoh Y (2016) Effectiveness of pilates exercise: a quality evaluation and summary of systematic reviews based on randomized controlled trials. Complement Ther Med 25:1–19

Kjellgren A, Westman J (2014) Beneficial effects of treatment with sensory isolation in flotation-tank as a preventive health-care intervention—a randomized controlled pilot trial. BMC Complement Altern Med 14:417

Kuge H, Mori H, Tanaka TH, Hanyu K, Morisawa T (2013) Difference between the effects of one-site and three-site abdominal hot-stone stimulation on the skin-temperature changes of the lower limbs. J Integr Med 11(5):314–319

Lam CT, Tse SH, Chan ST, Tam JK, Yuen JW (2015) A survey on the prevalence and utilization characteristics of gua sha in the Hong Kong community Complement Ther Med 23(1):46–54

Lamke D, Catlin A, Mason-Chadd M (2014) "Not just a theory": the relationship between Jin Shin Jyutsu® self-care training for nurses and stress, physical health, emotional health, and caring efficacy. J Holist Nurs 32(4):278–289

Langworthy JM, Cambron J (2007) Consent: its practices and implications in United Kingdom and United States chiropractic practice. J Manipulative Physiol Ther 30(6):419–431

Lee MS, Ernst E (2012) Systematic reviews of Tai Chi: an overview. Br J Sports Med 46(10):713–718

Lee MS, Shin BC, Suen LK, Park TY, Ernst E (2008) Auricular acupuncture for insomnia: a systematic review. Int J Clin Pract 62(11):1744–1752

Lee MS, Choi TY, Shin BC, Han CH, Ernst E (2010a) Cupping for stroke rehabilitation: a systematic review. J Neurol Sci 294(1–2):70–73

Lee MS, Choi TY, Kang JW, Lee BJ, Ernst E (2010b) Moxibustion for treating pain: a systematic review. Am J Chin Med 38(5):829–838

Lee MS, Choi TY, Park JE, Ernst E (2010c) Effects of moxibustion for constipation treatment: a systematic review of randomized controlled trials. Chin Med 5:28

Li JQ, Guo W, Sun ZG, Huang QS, Lee EY, Wang Y, Yao XD (2017) Cupping therapy for treating knee osteoarthritis: the evidence from systematic review and meta-analysis. Complement Ther Clin Pract 28:152–160

Li LW, Harris RE, Tsodikov A, Struble L, Murphy SL (2018) Self-acupressure for older adults with symptomatic knee osteoarthritis: a randomized controlled trial. Arthritis Care Res (Hoboken) 70(2):221–229

Licciardone JC, Brimhall AK, King LN (2005) Osteopathic manipulative treatment for low back pain: a systematic review and meta-analysis of randomized controlled trials. BMC Musculoskelet Disord 6:43

Lim SM, Lee SH (2015) Effectiveness of bee venom acupuncture in alleviating post-stroke shoulder pain: a systematic review and meta-analysis. J Integr Med 13(4):241–247

Liu L, Huang QM, Liu QG, Ye G, Bo CZ, Chen MJ, Li P (2015) Effectiveness of dry needling for myofascial trigger points associated with neck and shoulder pain: a systematic review and meta-analysis. Arch Phys Med Rehabil 96(5):944–955

Long AF (2008) The effectiveness of shiatsu: findings from a cross-European, prospective observational study. J Altern Complement Med 14(8):921–930

Long AF, Mackay HC (2003) The effects of shiatsu: findings from a two-country exploratory study. J Altern Complement Med 9(4):539–547

Long AF, Esmonde L, Connolly S (2009) A typology of negative responses: a case study of shiatsu. Complement Ther Med 17(3):168–175

Lötzke D, Heusser P, Büssing A (2015) A systematic literature review on the effectiveness of eurythmy therapy. J Integr Med 13(4):217–230

MacPherson H, Tilbrook H, Richmond S, Woodman J, Ballard K, Atkin K, Bland M, Eldred J, Essex H, Hewitt C, Hopton A, Keding A, Lansdown H, Parrott S, Torgerson D, Wenham A, Watt I (2015) Alexander technique lessons or acupuncture sessions for persons with chronic neck pain: a randomized trial. Ann Intern Med 163(9):653–662

Marr M, Baker J, Lambon N, Perry J (2011) The effects of the Bowen technique on hamstring flexibility over time: a randomised controlled trial. J Bodyw Mov Ther 15(3):281–290

Mazzarino M1, Kerr D2, Wajswelner H3, Morris ME3 (2015) Pilates method for women's Health: systematic review of randomized controlled trials. Arch Phys Med Rehabil 96(12):2231–2242

Mehling WE, DiBlasi Z, Hecht F (2005) Bias control in trials of bodywork: a review of methodological issues. J Altern Complement Med 11(2):333–342

Miake-Lye I, Lee J, Lugar T, Taylor S, Shanman R, Beroes J, Shekelle P (2016) Massage for pain: an evidence map. VA evidence-based synthesis program reports. Washington (DC): Department of Veterans Affairs (US)

Mirtz TA, Morgan L, Wyatt LH, Greene L (2009) An epidemiological examination of the subluxation construct using Hill's criteria of causation. Chiropr Osteopat 2(17):13

Moraska AF, Stenerson L, Butryn N, Krutsch JP, Schmiege SJ, Mann JD (2015) Myofascial trigger point-focused head and neck massage for recurrent tension-type headache: a randomized, placebo-controlled clinical trial. Clin J Pain 31(2):159–168

Moraska AF, Schmiege SJ, Mann JD, Butryn N, Krutsch JP (2017) Responsiveness of myofascial trigger points to single and multiple trigger point release massages: a randomized, placebo controlled trial. Am J Phys Med Rehabil 96(9):639–645

Mostafavifar M, Wertz J, Borchers J (2012) A systematic review of the effectiveness of kinesio taping for musculoskeletal injury. Phys Sportsmed 40(4):33–40

Nelson NL (2016) Kinesio taping for chronic low back pain: a systematic review. J Bodyw Mov Ther 20(3):672–681

Ofner M, Kastner A, Wallenboeck E, Pehn R, Schneider F, Groell R, Szolar D, Walach H, Litscher G, Sandner-Kiesling A (2014) Manual khalifa therapy improves functional and morphological outcome of patients with anterior cruciate ligament rupture in the knee: a randomized controlled trial. Evid Based Complement Altern Med 2014:462840

Ofner M, Kastner A, Schwarzl G, Schwameder H, Alexander N, Strutzenberger G, Walach H (2018) RegentK and physiotherapy support knee function after anterior cruciate ligament rupture without surgery after 1 year: a randomized controlled trial. Complement Med Res 25(1):30–37

O'Neill MM, Anderson DI, Allen DD, Ross C, Hamel KA (2015) Effects of Alexander technique training experience on gait behavior in older adults. J Bodyw Mov Ther 19(3):473–481

Orr L, Forman B (1979) Rebirthing: an assertive and spiritual approach to healing. Assertive Nurse 2(1):1–3

Paolucci T, Zangrando F, Iosa M, De Angelis S, Marzoli C, Piccinini G, Saraceni VM (2017) Improved interoceptive awareness in chronic low back pain: a comparison of Back school versus Feldenkrais method. Disabil Rehabil 39(10):994–1001

Park JE, Lee SS, Lee MS, Choi SM, Ernst E (2010) Adverse events of moxibustion: a systematic review. Complement Ther Med 18(5):215–223

Parreira Pdo C, Costa Lda C, Hespanhol LC Jr, Lopes AD, Costa LO (2014) Current evidence does not support the use of Kinesio Taping in clinical practice: a systematic review. J Physiother 60(1):31–39

Pittler MH, Brown EM, Ernst E (2007) Static magnets for reducing pain: systematic review and meta-analysis of randomized trials. CMAJ 177(7):736–742

Posadzki P, Ernst E (2011a) Osteopathy for musculoskeletal pain patients: a systematic review of randomized controlled trials. Clin Rheumatol 30(2):285–291

Posadzki P, Ernst E (2011b) Spinal manipulation: an update of a systematic review of systematic reviews. N Z Med J 124(1340):55–71

Posadzki P, Alotaibi A, Ernst E (2012) Adverse effects of aromatherapy: a systematic review of case reports and case series. Int J Risk Saf Med 24(3):147–161

Posadzki P, Watson LK, Alotaibi A, Ernst E (2013a) Prevalence of use of complementary and alternative medicine (CAM) by patients/consumers in the UK: systematic review of surveys. Clin Med (Lond) 13(2):126–131

Posadzki P, Lee MS, Ernst E (2013b) Osteopathic manipulative treatment for pediatric conditions: a systematic review. Pediatrics 132(1):140–152

Raith W, Marschik PB, Sommer C, Maurer-Fellbaum U, Amhofer C, Avian A, Löwenstein E, Soral S, Müller W, Einspieler C, Urlesberger B (2016) General Movements in preterm infants undergoing craniosacral therapy: a randomised controlled pilot-trial. BMC Complement Altern Med 13(16):12

Ren Q, Yu X, Liao F, Chen X, Yan D, Nie H, Fang J, Yang M, Zhou X (2018) Effects of Gua Sha therapy on perimenopausal syndrome: a systematic review and meta-analysis of randomized controlled trials. Complement Ther Clin Pract 31:268–277

Robinson N, Lorenc A, Liao X (2011) The evidence for Shiatsu: a systematic review of Shiatsu and acupressure. BMC Complement Altern Med 7(11):88

Rolf IP (1990) Rolfing and physical reality. Inner Traditions/Bear

Rubinstein SM, van Middelkoop M, Assendelft WJ, de Boer MR, van Tulder MW (2011) Spinal manipulative therapy for chronic low-back pain. Cochrane Database Syst Rev 2:CD008112

Rubinstein SM, Terwee CB, Assendelft WJ, de Boer MR, van Tulder MW (2012) Spinal manipulative therapy for acute low-back pain. Cochrane Database Syst Rev 9:CD008880

Russell JK (1994) Bodywork–the art of touch. Nurse Pract Forum 5(2):85–90

Searls K, Fawcett J (2011) Effect of Jin Shin Jyutsu energy medicine treatments on women diagnosed with breast cancer. J Holist Nurs 29(4):270–278

Song S, Yu J, Ruan Y, Liu X, Xiu L, Yue X (2018) Ameliorative effects of Tai Chi on cancer-related fatigue: a meta-analysis of randomized controlled trials. Support Care Cancer 26 (7):2091–2102

Stevinson C, Ernst E (2002) Risks associated with spinal manipulation. Am J Med 112(7): 566–571

Still AT (1899) Philosophy of Osteopathy. Edward Brothers Inc, Ann Arbor

Tan JY, Molassiotis A, Wang T, Suen LK (2014) Adverse events of auricular therapy: a systematic review. Evid Based Complement Alternat Med 2014:506758

Teixeira-Machado L, Araújo FM, Cunha FA, Menezes M, Menezes T, Melo DeSantana J (2015) Feldenkrais method-based exercise improves quality of life in individuals with Parkinson's disease: a controlled, randomized clinical trial. Altern Ther Health Med 21(1):8–14

Uemoto L, Nascimento de Azevedo R, Almeida Alfaya T, Nunes Jardim Reis R, Depes de Gouvêa CV, Cavalcanti Garcia MA (2013) Myofascial trigger point therapy: laser therapy and dry needling. Curr Pain Headache Rep 17(9):357

Wada Y, Yanagihara C, Nishimura Y (2005) Internal jugular vein thrombosis associated with shiatsu massage of the neck. J Neurol Neurosurg Psychiatry 76(1):142–143

Wang YT, Qi Y, Tang FY, Li FM, Li QH, Xu CP, Xie GP, Sun HT (2017) The effect of cupping therapy for low back pain: a meta-analysis based on existing randomized controlled trials. J Back Musculoskelet Rehabil 30(6):1187–1195

Wei X, Wang S, Li L, Zhu L (2017) Clinical evidence of Chinese massage therapy (Tui Na) for Cervical Radiculopathy: a systematic review and meta-analysis. Evid Based Complement Altern Med 2017, Article ID 9519285:10p

Wells C, Kolt GS, Marshall P, Hill B, Bialocerkowski A (2014) The effectiveness of Pilates exercise in people with chronic low back pain: a systematic review. PLoS ONE 9(7):e100402

Williams S, Whatman C, Hume PA, Sheerin K (2012) Kinesio taping in treatment and prevention of sports injuries: a meta-analysis of the evidence for its effectiveness. Sports Med 42(2): 153–164

Wiwanitkit V (2017) Culture-bounded skin lesion—a case due to Chinese Gua Sha. Indian J Dermatol 62(4):441

Woodman JP, Moore NR (2012) Evidence for the effectiveness of Alexander Technique lessons in medical and health-related conditions: a systematic review. Int J Clin Pract 66(1):98–112

Xia QC, Feng ZX, Ping CX (2014) Evaluating the efficacy of Tui Na in treatment of childhood anorexia: a meta-analysis. Altern Ther Health Med 20(5):45–52

Yang YL, Wang YH, Wang SR, Shi PS (2018) Wang C The effect of Tai Chi on cardiorespiratory fitness for coronary disease rehabilitation: a systematic review and meta-Analysis. Front Physiol 8:1091

Yilmaz Sahin S, Iyigun E, Can MF (2018) Effect of acupressure application to the P6 acupoint before laparoscopic cholecystectomy on postoperative nausea-vomiting: a randomized controlled clinical study. Int J Nurs Stud 87:40–48

Zhao ZQ (2008) Neural mechanism underlying acupuncture analgesia. Prog Neurobiol 85(4):355–375

Chapter 10
Other Therapies

10.1 Autogenic Training

(related modalities: hypnotherapy, meditation, mind-body therapies, mindfulness, progressive muscle relaxation, transcendental meditation)

Autogenic training was developed in the 1920s by the German psychiatrist Johannes Heinrich Schultz (1884–1970). It is an auto-hypnotic relaxation technique which is very popular in Germany, but less so other countries.

1. The lack of international appreciation of autogenic training might be related to Schultz' well-documented Nazi past. In 1935, he published an essay which supported compulsory sterilization of men to eliminate hereditary illnesses. Later he was appointed deputy director of the Göring Institute in Berlin. Through this institute, he had an active role in the extermination of mentally handicapped individuals in the framework of the 'Aktion T4', the Nazi's infamous euthanasia programme.[1]
2. Autogenic training can be described as a form of self-hypnosis or auto-hypnosis. It consists of mental exercises using instructions directed at different parts of the body to control bodily perceptions, such as 'my right foot feels warm' or 'my left arm feels heavy'.
3. Patients tend to report an intense sense of relaxation during and after autogenic training.
4. Autogenic training is taught in a series of lessons by a qualified instructor. Once mastered, it should be practised regularly and does not require further supervision. It is thus an inexpensive therapy.
5. The technique is claimed to help for a range of (mostly stress-related) conditions. However, the evidence from clinical trials is scarce and, not least due to methodological problems, less than convincing.

---

[1]https://en.wikipedia.org/wiki/Johannes_Heinrich_Schultz.

© Springer Nature Switzerland AG 2019
E. Ernst, *Alternative Medicine*,
https://doi.org/10.1007/978-3-030-12601-8_10

6. A systematic review of autogenic training for the treatment of stress and anxiety found that "no firm conclusions could be drawn from this systematic review. AT, properly applied, remains to be tested in controlled trials that are appropriately planned and executed."[2]
7. Autogenic training is unlikely to cause serious adverse effects.

Plausibility	
Efficacy	
Safety	
Cost	
Risk/benefit balance	

10.2 Autologous Blood Therapy

(related modalities: none)

Autologous blood therapy (ABT) is the treatment of patients with their own blood or blood constituents.

1. In conventional medicine, autologous blood is sometimes used in elective surgery and for treating degeneration of tendons, which may occur in association with small tears.
2. In alternative medicine, ATB, or 'autohaemotherapy' as it is sometimes called, has a long tradition, particularly in Germany where many doctors of naturopathy use it. It is being promoted as a treatment of a range of conditions. This discussion is purely about the alternative form of ATB.
3. ABT involves drawing a small amount of venous blood followed by intramuscular reinjection.
4. ATB is alleged to increase the resistance to infection, enhance production of antibodies to microbial and tissue antigens and activate the cell-mediated immune defence mechanisms.[3]

---

[2]Ernst and Kanji (2000).
[3]Klemparskaya et al. (1986).

5. ATB has been reported to have beneficial effects for patients with eczema and related conditions.[4] Uncontrolled and controlled clinical trials have furthermore suggested that ATB has positive effects in patients diagnosed as having herpes zoster and chronic dermatoses such as urticaria.
6. There are only very few controlled clinical trials of ABT. One small study concluded that "ABT has beneficial effects in the treatment of atopic dermatitis, although this was not confirmed by the patient-rated assessments. The improvement in observer-rated skin condition suggested by this study needs confirmation in larger trials."[5] These results await independent replication in a larger trial.
7. As ATB uses the patient's own blood, there are few serious risks associated with the procedure, unless the rules of adequate hygiene are not observed.

Plausibility	👎
Efficacy	👎
Safety	👍
Cost	👍
Risk/benefit balance	👎

10.3 Bioresonance

(related modalities: Vega test)

Bioresonance is an alternative therapeutic and diagnostic method employing a device developed in Germany by the scientology member Franz Morell in 1977. The bioresonance machine was further developed and marketed by Morell's son in law Erich Rasche and is also known as 'MORA' therapy (MOrell + RAsche). Bioresonance is based on the notion that one can diagnose and treat illness with electromagnetic waves and that, via resonance, such waves can influence disease on a cellular level.

---

[4]Asefi and Augustin (1999).
[5]Pittler et al. (2003).

1. Even though these devices are sometimes promoted as biofeedback devices, they clearly do not belong into this category. Biofeedback is an established conventional method of gaining awareness of real physiological phenomena such as (heart rate, pain, muscle tone) using instruments that provide information on the activity of those systems, with a goal of influencing them and thus improve health outcomes.
2. Bioresonance instruments are akin to the scientologists' 'E-meter' which essentially consists of an electronic circuit measuring skin conductivity. They are neither accepted in conventional healthcare nor evidence-based.
3. The literature on bioresonance is a prime example how pseudoscientific language is being used to mislead us all: "Clarity of language is an essential element for effective communication. Using the example of bioresonance therapy, this article demonstrates how pseudo-scientific language can be used to cloud important issues. This can be seen as an attempt to present nonsense as science. Because this misleads patients and can thus endanger their health, we should find ways of minimizing this problem."[6]
4. Practitioners of bioresonance claim that they can detect and cure a range of diseases, including allergies, gastrointestinal conditions, addictions, etc. Such claims are, however, not plausible.
5. The diagnostic reliability of bioresonance has not been established.[7] In other words, the method is likely to generate false-positive and false-negative diagnoses both of which can cause serious harm.
6. The therapeutic effectiveness of bioresonance for any human condition remains unproven.[8] In other words, there is no reason to believe that bioresonance can bring about a cure of any disease or alleviate any symptom.
7. Bioresonance is dangerous in several ways. As the costs involved are considerable, it causes financial harm. As it has no diagnostic validity, it will false-negative diagnoses. This will delay or prevent effective treatments which, in extreme cases, can cost lives.

| Plausibility | |
| Efficacy | |

(continued)

---

[6]Ernst (2004).
[7]Kleine-Tebbe and Herold (2010).
[8]Schöni et al. (1997).

(continued)

Safety	👎
Cost	👎
Risk/benefit balance	👎

10.4 Coffee Enemas

(related modalities: colonic irrigation, detox, Gerson therapy)

Coffee enemas consist of the administration of warm coffee via the rectum into a patient's intestines. They have been invented by German scientists who found that this treatment increases bile flow. Coffee enemas are also part of the Gerson regimen.

1. Coffee enemas are popular with some people, not least because they cause profuse bowel movements and thus lead to immediate relief of constipation and therefore to short-lasting weight loss.
2. Coffee enemas are promoted for detox under the assumption that that the content of our colon is toxic, an obsolete theory known as 'autointoxication'. Other notions assume that coffee enemas have beneficial antioxidant effects or stimulate the liver.
3. All the theories in support of coffee enemas lack plausibility.[9]
4. Supporters of coffee enemas also claim they are effective treatments for:
   - boosting immunity
   - increasing energy
   - preventing yeast overgrowth
   - treating autoimmune diseases
   - excreting parasites from the digestive tract
   - removing heavy metals from the body
   - alleviating depression
   - treating cancer.
5. None of these therapeutic claims are backed by sound clinical evidence. Coffee enemas have not been shown to effectively treat any condition or disease.

---

[9]Teekachunhatean et al. (2012).

6. Coffee enemas can cause adverse reactions some of which can be severe and
   have even caused fatalities:[10,11,12,13]

   - electrolyte imbalances
   - rectal burns
   - nausea
   - vomiting
   - cramping
   - bloating
   - dehydration
   - bowel perforation
   - infections.

7. Coffee enemas are often recommended as a regular treatment and require the aid
   of a therapist; therefore, their costs can be considerable.

Plausibility	👎
Efficacy	👎
Safety	👎
Cost	👍
Risk/benefit balance	👎

10.5   Colonic Irrigation

(related modalities: coffee enema, detox, Gerson therapy)

Colon irrigation (also called colonic treatment, colon cleansing, rectal irrigation, colon therapy, colon hydrotherapy, colonic) is a popular alternative therapy consisting of the administration of warm water into the colon via the patient's rectum.

---

[10]Kim et al. (2012).

[11]Keum et al. (2010).

[12]Lee et al. (2008).

[13]Eisele and Reay (1980).

1. Colonic irrigation is based on the ancient and now obsolete theory of 'autoin-toxication' which holds that intestinal waste products can poison the body and are a major contributor to many, if not all diseases. In the 19th century, it was the ruling doctrine of medicine. When it became clear that its scientific rationale was wrong and colonic irrigation was not merely useless but potentially dangerous, it was exposed as quackery.[14]

2. Today, colonic irrigation made a come-back and is supported by numerous anecdotes from celebrities who usually use it for acute weight-loss.

3. It is recommended for a bewildering range of indications: alcoholism, allergies, arthritis, asthma, backache, bad breath, bloating, coated tongue, colitis, constipation, damage caused by nicotine or other environmental factors, fatigue, headache, hypercholesterolaemia, hypertension, indigestion, insomnia, joint problems, liver insufficiency, loss of concentration, mental disorders, parasite infestation, proneness to infections, rheumatoid arthritis, sinus congestion, skin problems and ulcerative colitis.

4. The treatment usually involves the administration of about 1/2 l of warm water through a proctoscope by means of an intermittent flush-out method.

5. The purpose of this procedure is to infuse the entire colon with water, in contrast to the more limited infusion of water during a conventional enema. Sometimes, ingredients such as herbal extracts are added to the water.

6. There is no sound evidence to show that any of the therapeutic claims regularly made for colonic irrigation are true. The small weight loss immediately after treatment is simply due to the evacuation of faeces and does not last longer than a few hours. A review assessed the websites of 6 professional organisations of colonic irrigation where all therapeutic claims were extracted. It concluded *that the therapeutic claims of professional organisations of colonic irrigation mislead patients.*[15]

7. Even though it is often claimed to be safe, serious adverse effects, such as perforation of the colon or depletion of vital electrolytes, are on record.[2]

Plausibility	👎
Efficacy	👎
Safety	👎

(continued)

---

[14]Ernst (1997).
[15]Ernst (2010).

(continued)

Cost	
Risk/benefit balance	

*Only direct risks considered

10.6   Colour Therapy

(related modalities: energy healing)

Colour therapy—sometimes also called 'chromotherapy'—is the use of colour for therapeutic purposes. It is distinct from light therapy which is a conventional treatment used to treat depression and other conditions.

1. It is claimed that colour therapy has ancient roots and that colour was an important element in the medicine of several ancient cultures.
2. The underlying assumption is that the energy relating to each of the seven colours of the spectrum (red, orange, yellow, green, blue, indigo and violet) resonates with the energy of each of the seven energy centres of the body.[16]
3. Specifically, it is assumed that red relates to the base chakra, orange to the sacral chakra, yellow to the solar plexus chakra, green to the heart chakra, blue to the throat chakra, indigo to the brow chakra (sometimes referred to as the third eye) and violet relates to the crown chakra.[1]
4. Proponents of this treatment believe that colour therapy affects humans on physical, emotional, spiritual, or mental levels and that it stimulated the self-healing potential of our body. It is thus promoted for most human diseased and symptoms.
5. The assumptions underpinning colour therapy fly in the face of science and are therefore not plausible.
6. The therapeutic claims made by colour therapists are not supported by sound evidence from clinical trials. In fact, rigorous clinical studies of colour therapy are currently not available.
7. The myths pertaining to colour therapy are being promoted mainly via a plethora of Internet sites and books authored by proponents of this treatment. These are invariably devoid of what one might consider reliable evidence.

---

[16]http://www.colourtherapyhealing.com/colour-therapy/what-colour-therapy.

Plausibility	👎
Efficacy	👎
Safety	👍
Cost	👍
Risk/benefit balance	👎

10.7   Crystal Healing

(related modalities: energy healing)

Crystal healing is the use of stones and crystals for medicinal purposes.

1. Various forms of crystal healing have been used in several cultures. The New Age movement has brought about the current resurgence of such treatments.
2. Crystal therapists believe that specific crystals have specific therapeutic effects and that crystals are capable of remembering both positive and negative events. They can thus be programmed and might, from time to time, need deleting unhelpful energies.[17]
3. During a treatment session, practitioners might place the crystals close to alleged energy centres of the body, or they position them in geometric patterns around the patient/client.
4. The crystals are claimed to exert their effects by emitting 'energy' to the body's energy centres and thus stimulate the self-healing properties of our body.
5. None of the assumptions that underpin crystal healing are rational or scientifically plausible.
6. Many therapists make specific claims about the health benefits of crystal healing.[18] For instance:

---

[17]https://www.holisticshop.co.uk/articles/introduction-guide-crystals.

[18]https://www.britishacademyofcrystalhealing.co.uk/how-to-use-crystals.

- Rose quartz is considered to be the stone of love—in this case, love of the self, in the form of self-esteem and self-worth. Rose quartz is simply brimming with happiness and is a very positive stone that can help bring out forgiveness, compassion, and tolerance in users.
- Fluorite is of mental order and clarity, and can be used to help alleviate instability, paving the way for a more balanced view of life. Fluorite is also the stone of learning, and can improve concentration and focus, while simultaneously reducing the anxiety that can sometimes make retaining information difficult.
- Lapis lazuli is thought to be beneficial to the throat, vocal cords, and larynx, and can help to regulate endocrine and thyroid issues. This is one of the most effective stones to meditate with, as lapis lazuli is the stone of higher awareness, able to bring information to the mind in images rather than words.

However, none of these claims are supported by evidence. In fact, there are no rigorous trials testing the therapeutic value of crystal healing.

7. Many entrepreneurs nevertheless sell 'healing crystals' to consumers, often at inflated prices

Plausibility	👎
Efficacy	👎
Safety	👍
Cost	👎
Risk/benefit balance	👎

10.8 Distant Healing

(related modalities: energy healing)

Distant healing is a form of 'energy healing' where the healer operates at a distance from the patient. This distance can be considerable; proponents of distant healing see no obstacle in healing even over very large distances.

1. The term 'energy' must be put in inverted commas, because the underlying concepts have nothing in common with the energy defined in physics. Real energy is measurable and quantifiable.
2. 'Energy' as used in alternative medicine describes a nebulous concept of a life-force that originates from the obsolete notions of vitalism. This type of 'energy' is neither measurable nor quantifiable.
3. In distant healing, the healer, who often works for free, sends 'healing energy' across space in the belief that it is received by the patient and thus stimulates her self-healing potential. This process does not require the physical presence of the patient.
4. Proponents of distant healing offer various modes of action for their treatment; some claim, for instance, that quantum physics provides a scientific explanation as to how it works.
5. The assumptions that underpin distant healing are not biologically plausible.
6. There has been some research testing whether distant healing is effective. Most of the studies available to date have serious methodological flaws. One review of 8 clinical trials showed that "the majority of the rigorous trials do not to support the hypothesis that distant healing has specific therapeutic effects. The results of two studies furthermore suggest that distant healing can be associated with adverse effects."[19] And another review concluded that "the evidence to date does not yet provide confidence in its clinical efficacy."[20]
7. Reading the literature published by proponents of distant healing, one cannot help but being impressed by the amount of pseudo-scientific language that is being employed to mislead the reader.

Plausibility	👎
Efficacy	👎

(continued)

[19]Ernst (2003).
[20]Radin et al. (2015).

(continued)

Safety	
Cost	
Risk/benefit balance	

10.9   Faith Healing

(related modalities: spiritual healing, energy healing)

Faith healing is the attempt to bring about healing through divine intervention. It is a form of paranormal or energy healing. Contrary to a frequently voiced view, its effectiveness as a therapy can be assessed scientifically.

1. The Bible and other religious texts provide numerous examples of divine healing, and believers see this as a proof that faith healing is possible.
2. There are also numerous reports of people suffering from severe diseases, including cancer and AIDS, who were allegedly healed by divine intervention.
3. Faith healing often takes the form of laying on hands where the preacher channels the divine energy via his hands into the patient's body. Some places of pilgrimage, such as Lourdes in France, specialise in faith healing and produce seemingly impressive statistics which, however, do not withstand scientific scrutiny. A review of the 'cures' recorded in Lourdes showed that "no cure has been certified from 1976 through 2006."[21]
4. Faith healing has no basis in science, is biologically not plausible and its effectiveness lacks scientific proof.
5. There are several explanations for the cases that have allegedly been healed by divine intervention, for instance, spontaneous remission or placebo response.
6. Another explanation is fraud. For instance, the famous German faith healer, Peter Popoff, was exposed in 1986 for using an earpiece to receive radio messages from his wife giving him the home addresses and ailments of audience members which he purported had come from God during these faith healing rallies.

---

[21]François et al. (2014).

7. Faith healing may per se be safe, but it can nevertheless do untold indirect harm, and even fatalities are on record: "Faith healing, when added as an adjuvant or alternative aid to medical science, will not necessarily be confined to mere arguments and debates but may also give rise to series of complications, medical emergencies and even result in death."[22]

Plausibility	👎
Efficacy	👎
Safety	👍
Cost	👍
Risk/benefit balance	👎

10.10   Hologram Gadgets

(related modalities: energy healing, magnet therapy)

Hologram bracelets are wristbands that include a hologram that allegedly exerts positive effects on the health of its wearer. Hologram gadgets are also available as necklaces, insoles etc. They became popular after several celebrities were seen wearing them. Numerous manufacturers now offer these devices for sale.

1. Proponents claim that the hologram is programmed to regulate the energy flow through the body which allegedly stimulates the self-healing abilities of our body and, in turn, leads to positive health effects.
2. One manufacturer, who has been selling such bracelets since 2007, claims that the programming "mimics Eastern philosophies".
3. The assumptions underpinning hologram gadgets lack any plausibility. The assumption that they affect the wearer's health is thus not plausible.
4. The therapeutic claims made for these devices usually focus on improved physical and mental performance.

---

[22]Wasti et al. (2015).

5. The claims for such gadgets rely entirely on testimonials, often those by celebrities.
6. Several informal attempts to verify their actions objectively have failed to produce any positive results. In other words, there is no reliable evidence to back up any of the health claims made for these devices.
7. The costs for these devices can be considerable and are not justified.

Plausibility	👎
Efficacy	👎
Safety	👍
Cost	👎
Risk/benefit balance	👎

10.11   Hypnotherapy

(related modalities: autogenic training, meditation, mind-body therapy, relaxation therapy)

Hypnotherapy is the use of a trance-like state (hypnosis) for therapeutic purposes. It can be traced back to ancient cultures, but more recently Anton Mesmer (1734–1815) introduced hypnotherapy into medicine. Initially Mesmer was highly successful—until a Royal Commission investigated his method of 'animal magnetism' and concluded its effects were entirely due to imagination (Fig. 10.1).

1. Hypnotherapy induces in many but not all individuals a state of deep relaxation that is potentially helpful in a range of conditions.
2. Today, there are different schools of hypnotherapy, e.g. Ericksonian hypnotherapy, cognitive behavioural hypnotherapy, curative hypnotherapy.
3. Various healthcare professionals practise hypnotherapy, including doctors, dentists, psychologists and nurses.
4. Hypnotherapy is used to treat many conditions or symptoms, from pain and stress control to irritable bowel syndrome and drug dependency.

Fig. 10.1 Anton Mesmer. *Source* US National Library of Medicine

5. The evidence from clinical trials is mixed. Most systematic reviews emphasise the often poor-quality of the primary studies:

- "Hypnosis reduces pain intensity and anxiety ratings in adults undergoing burn wound care. However, because of the limitations discussed, clinical recommendations are still premature."[23]
- "Due to exploratory designs and high risk of bias, the effectiveness of hypnosis or hypnotherapy in stress reduction remains still unclear."[24]
- "There are still only a relatively small number of studies assessing the use of hypnosis for labour and childbirth. Hypnosis may reduce the overall use of analgesia during labour, but not epidural use. No clear differences were

[23]Provençal et al. (2018).
[24]Fisch et al. (2017).

found between women in the hypnosis group and those in the control groups for satisfaction with pain relief, sense of coping with labour or spontaneous vaginal birth. Not enough evidence currently exists regarding satisfaction with pain relief or sense of coping with labour and we would encourage any future research to prioritise the measurement of these outcomes. The evidence for the main comparison was assessed using GRADE as being of low quality for all the primary outcomes with downgrading decisions due to concerns regarding inconsistency of the evidence, limitations in design and imprecision."[25]

- "We have not shown that hypnotherapy has a greater effect on six month quit rates than other interventions or no treatment. The effects of hypnotherapy on smoking cessation claimed by uncontrolled studies were not confirmed by analysis of randomised controlled trials."[26]

6. Contrary to what is often claimed, hypnotherapy is not free of adverse effects. It has been associated with the 'false memory syndrome' where unpleasant recollections that have never occurred are implanted into the patient's brain. Hypnotherapy should not be used by patients who suffer from psychoses or personality disorders.

7. Hypnotherapy is considered to be a conventional treatment by most experts, but some alternative practitioners disagree.

Plausibility	👍
Efficacy	👍
Safety	👍
Cost	👍
Risk/benefit balance	👍

---

[25]Madden et al. (2016).
[26]Abbot et al. (1998).

10.12   Imagery

(related modalities: mind-body therapy)

Imagery (also called guided imagery or visualisation) is an alternative therapy where the patient is taught by a trained practitioner to evoke certain mental images, sounds, tastes, smells or other sensations associated with certain therapeutic aims in the hope to facilitate reaching these aims.

1. Imagery is a mind-body therapy which is often recommended as a symptomatic therapy for a range of conditions and normally used in addition to other treatments.
2. It is easy to use and can be learnt quickly and economically, for instance, in groups or via a video.
3. Imagery is said to alleviate symptoms such as pain, stress, anxiety, and low mood.
4. Some research suggests that guided imagery might enhance the body's immune function.
5. Several systematic reviews of guided imagery for various conditions have been published and most report encouraging results, e.g.:

   - "Guided imagery appears to be beneficial for adults with arthritis and other rheumatic diseases."[27]
   - "Guided motor imagery and mirror therapy alone may be effective, although this conclusion is based on limited evidence."[28]
   - "The evidence that guided imagery alleviates non-musculoskeletal pain is encouraging but remains inconclusive."[29]
   - "Evidence could be identified on the use of guided imagery associated with relaxation therapy as a complementary approach to drug analgesia in post-operative pain control..."[30]
   - "Guided imagery is a promising patient-centered approach for the improvement of a number of patients' outcomes that merits further investigation in critical care."[31]

6. Proponents of guided imagery also claim that this technique can improve general health, creativity and mental as well as physical performance.
7. Imagery is normally a safe therapy. Yet, in some people, guided imagery can exacerbate or aggravate mental and physical conditions; for instance, it can worsen the symptoms of post-traumatic stress disorder, phobias and other mental problems.

---

[27]Giacobbi et al. (2015).
[28]Bowering et al. (2013).
[29]Posadzki et al. (2012).
[30]Felix et al. (2019).
[31]Hadjibalassi et al. (2018).

Plausibility	👍	
Efficacy	👍	
Safety	👍	
Cost	👍	
Risk/benefit balance	👍	

10.13   Johrei Healing

(related modalities: energy healing)

Johrei healing is a form of paranormal healing popular in Japan; it has recently been promoted also in Europe and the US.

1. In Japanese, Johrei means "purification of the spirit". Johrei healing has been called "a non-invasive approach to treating chronic diseases based on assessing and adjusting an individual's physiological and emotional responses through their bio-energetic field. Reconnective Healing™ (RH) is defined as: '…not just energy healing, but instead a more comprehensive spectrum of healing composed of energy, light, and information.'"[32]
2. According to its proponents, the aim is the "channelling of a spiritual energy or Divine Light to purify one's spiritual body and awaken our divine nature."[33] "Its main purpose is to awaken the soul to the power of the Divine Light, which can change self-centred lives into God-centred ones."[34]
3. After some basic training, anyone can allegedly administer Johrei healing. It is thus an economical form of therapy.
4. Like all variations of paranormal healing, Johrei lacks biological plausibility.
5. Johrei healing has several of the characteristics that are typical for a cult.

---

[32]Baldwin and Trent (2017).

[33]http://johreicentreuk.blogspot.com/.

[34]Baldwin and Trent (2017).

6. A few pre-clinical or in vitro studies have been sponsored by Japanese funders. They all seem to report positive results; however, their relevance for human health is questionable.
7. There have been hardly any clinical trials testing the effectiveness of Johrei healing in the management of medical conditions. The few studies that have emerged fail to show that this treatment is superior to placebo.,[35,36]

Plausibility	👎
Efficacy	👎
Safety	👍
Cost	👍
Risk/benefit balance	👎

10.14   Laughter Therapy

(related modalities: relaxation therapy)

Laughter or humour therapy is the use of laughter for therapeutic purposes.

1. Laughter therapy is mostly practised as a group therapy. In some hospitals, clowns are also employed for laughter therapy of children.
2. The contagious nature of laughter is used to make participants laugh.
3. Consequently, they relax which can have positive effects on health.
4. Laughter is said to decrease blood levels of cortisol, epinephrine, growth hormone, and 3,4-dihydrophenylacetic acid (a major dopamine catabolite), indicating a reversal of the stress response.[37]

---

[35]Gasiorowska et al. (2009).
[36]Canter et al. (2006).
[37]Yim (2016).

5. Laughter therapy is claimed to provide physical benefits, such as helping to:

   - Relax muscles throughout the body
   - Trigger the release of endorphins (the body's natural painkillers)
   - Relieve pain
   - Improve mental functions (i.e., alertness, memory, creativity)
   - Improve overall attitude and well-being
   - Reduce stress/tension
   - Improve sleep
   - Strengthen social bonds and relationships.

6. Many of these outcomes are, however, not as well-documented as claimed by proponents.

7. A systematic review concluded that "trials with clown doctors in pediatric population have shown conflicting results in allaying anxiety amongst children undergoing either hospitalization or invasive procedures."[38] Another assessment was more positive: "the meta-analysis confirmed the effectiveness of pre-operative clown therapy on reducing psychological distress in children and parents."[39] And a third review concluded that "there exists sufficient evidence to suggest that laughter has some positive, quantifiable effects on certain aspects of health."[40]

Plausibility	👍
Efficacy	👍
Safety	👍
Cost	👍
Risk/benefit balance	👍

[38]Sridharan and Sivaramakrishnan (2016).

[39]Zhang et al. (2017).

[40]Mora-Ripoll (2010).

10.15   Leech Therapy

(related modalities: cupping)

Leech therapy is the application of blood-sucking leeches to the skin of a patient for therapeutic purposes.

1. The treatment with leeches (*Hirudo medicinalis*) goes back to ancient Egypt. It had its hay-day during the middle ages when it was used as a form of blood-letting. In conventional medicine, it is today sometimes employed after plastic surgery for improving outcomes of skin grafts.
2. The underlying assumption was that all diseases are due to an imbalance of the four humours: blood, phlegm, black and yellow bile, and that leeching can re-balance such imbalances.
3. The leech is equipped with suckers and three jaws each with about 100 tiny teeth. This enables the animal to pierce the skin and suck blood.
4. The leech employs three different ingredients to enable blood-sucking:

   - an anaesthetic renders the bite painless,
   - a vasodilator secures sufficient blood-flow from the patient to the leech,
   - and an anticoagulant prevents the blood from clotting.

5. Leech therapy is currently experiencing a renaissance as a form of alternative medicine.
6. Several studies have suggested that, applied locally at the site of the problem, leech therapy alleviates the pain of osteoarthritis. A systematic review found "moderate to strong evidence for the reduction of pain, functional impairment, and joint stiffness after medical leech therapy in patients with osteoarthritis of the knee."[41] Because there are only few rigorous trials, because the studies fail to adequately control for a placebo effect, and because they originate all from the same research group, this evidence is not as convincing as one would hope.
7. Leech therapy is generally considered to be safe. However, in rare cases, it can cause allergic reactions[42] or infections.[43]

Plausibility	👍
Efficacy	👎

(continued)

---

[41]Lauche et al. (2014).

[42]Çakmak et al. (2018).

[43]Bykowski et al. (2018).

(continued)

Safety	
Cost	
Risk/benefit balance	

10.16   Meditation

(related modalities: hypnotherapy, mind-body therapies)

Meditation is the term used for techniques that focus someone's mind on a particular object and are aimed at temporarily achieving a mentally clear and emotionally calm state. While specific forms of meditation are discussed in separate chapters, the following deals with meditation in more general terms.

1. Meditation has ancient roots and has been part of most religions, most notably Buddhism and Hinduism.
2. As a religious practice, it was originally supposed to bring you closer to the deity you are worshiping.
3. As an alternative therapy, meditation is supposed to induce deep relaxation which, in turn, is said to have positive effects on a wide range of conditions.
4. There are numerous techniques of meditation and different schedules; in most cases, it is recommended to practice meditation daily. Most forms of meditation do not exist as solitary practices but are part of a more complex set of rules, life-styles and behaviours.
5. Some forms of meditation employ aids such as music, physical postures, certain activities or mantras.
6. Even though there are many clinical studies and several reviews of meditation, the evidence demonstrating that meditation has meaningful health effects is far from strong, not least because of the methodological problems encountered and the frequently poor quality of these trials.

   - One systematic review, for instance, concluded that "there is some evidence that meditation is beneficial in improving quality of life in asthma patients. As two out of four studies in our review were of poor quality, further trials with better methodological quality are needed to support or refute this finding."[44]

---

[44]Paudyal et al. (2018).

- Another systematic review found that "at present there is not enough information available on the effects of meditation in haematologically-diseased patients to draw any conclusion."[45]
- A further review concluded that "Meditation programs… reduce multiple negative dimensions of psychological stress. Stronger study designs are needed to determine the effects of meditation programs in improving the positive dimensions of mental health as well as stress-related behavioral outcomes."[46]
- Another review found that, "as a result of the limited number of included studies, the small sample sizes and the high risk of bias, we are unable to draw any conclusions regarding the effectiveness of meditation therapy for ADHD. The adverse effects of meditation have not been reported. More trials are needed."[47]
- And further review found that "meditation interventions for older adults are feasible, and preliminary evidence suggests that meditation can offset age-related cognitive decline."[48]

7. There are only few, relatively minor risks of meditation. One concern can be that, via meditation classes, consumers can be (and often are) recruited to some form of cult or sect.

Plausibility	👎
Efficacy	👎
Safety	👍
Cost	👍
Risk/benefit balance	👎

---

[45]Salhofer et al. (2016).
[46]Goyal et al. (2014).
[47]Krisanaprakornkit et al. (2010).
[48]Gard et al. (2014).

10.17   Mindfulness

(related modalities: mind-body therapies)

Mindfulness is a form of meditation which involves bringing one's attention to experiences occurring in the present moment while sitting silently and paying attention to thoughts, sounds, the sensations of breathing or parts of the body.

1. Many experts do not consider mindfulness to be an alternative therapy but see it as a set of psychological methods that have long become well-accepted, conventional treatments.
2. There are several forms of mindfulness meditation; one of the best-known and most thoroughly researched is Mindfulness-Based Stress Reduction developed by Jon Kabat-Zinn (1944–). It uses a combination of mindfulness meditation, body awareness, and yoga to help people become more mindful.
3. Mindfulness programs are currently popular and have been widely adopted in schools, hospitals, and other settings. They are also being applied to initiatives such as for healthy aging, weight management, athletic performance enhancement, for children with special needs, and as a help during the perinatal period.
4. Novices are advised to start with short periods of about 10 min of meditation practice per day. With regular practice, it becomes easier to keep the attention focused and the length of time spent practising can be extended.
5. There has been much research interest in mindfulness, and many studies are now available. However, the quality of these trials is often poor which is one reason why the evidence is less clear than one would hope.
6. Several systematic reviews have assessed mindfulness for various medical conditions, e.g.:

   - A systematic review of mindfulness for chronic headaches concluded that, "due to the low number, small scale and often high or unclear risk of bias of included randomized controlled trials, the results are imprecise; this may be consistent with either an important or negligible effect. Therefore, more rigorous trials with larger sample sizes are needed."[49]
   - A systematic review of mindfulness for addictions found "support for the effectiveness of the mindfulness-based interventions."[50]
   - An overview included "26 reviews and found a substantially consistent picture... Improvements in depressive disorders, particularly recurrent major depression, were strongly supported. Evidence for other psychological conditions was limited by lack of data. In populations with physical conditions, the evidence for significant improvements in psychological well-being was clear, regardless of population or specific mindfulness

---

[49]Anheyer et al. (2018).
[50]Sancho et al. (2018).

intervention. Changes in physical health measures were inconclusive; however, pain acceptance and coping were improved."[51]

7. Some reports have linked mindfulness to increasing fear and anxiety panic or "meltdowns" after treatments. However, these seem to be rare events; in general, mindfulness is considered to be a safe therapy.

Plausibility	👍
Efficacy	👍
Safety	👍
Cost	👍
Risk/benefit balance	👍

10.18 Music Therapy

(related modalities: relaxation therapies)

Music therapy is the use of music for therapeutic purposes, usually supervised by a trained therapist who has completed an approved music therapy programme.

1. Several forms of music therapy exist. They can consist of a patient passively listening to live or recorded music, or of patients actively participating in performing music. Music therapy often takes place at the bedside of a patient during a hospital stay.
2. Proponents claim to make use of all aspects of music, physical, emotional, mental, social, aesthetic, and spiritual.
3. Music therapy is always employed to complement other treatments; it is never a curative or causal approach and usually aimed at inducing relaxation and enhancing physical and emotional well-being or at promoting motor and communication skills.

---

[51]Long et al. (2017).

4. The aim of the therapist frequently is to help people whose lives have been affected by injury, illness or disability through supporting their psychological, emotional, cognitive, physical, communicative and social needs.[52]

5. There is a paucity of rigorous studies assessing the effectiveness of music therapy for specific condition, not least due to methodological obstacles and funding issues.

6. Several systematic reviews of clinical studies have nevertheless emerged.

   • One review of music therapy for Alzheimer's disease, for example, concluded that, "despite the positive outcome of this review, the available evidence remains inconsistent due to the small number of randomized controlled trials."[53]

   • Another review found that "music interventions may be beneficial for gait, the timing of upper extremity function, communication outcomes, and quality of life after stroke. These results are encouraging, but more high-quality randomised controlled trials are needed on all outcomes before recommendations can be made for clinical practice."[54]

   • A further review showed that "providing people with dementia with at least five sessions of a music-based therapeutic intervention probably reduces depressive symptoms but has little or no effect on agitation or aggression. There may also be little or no effect on emotional well-being or quality of life, overall behavioural problems and cognition. We are uncertain about effects on anxiety or social behaviour, and about any long-term effects."[55]

   • And another review concluded that "music interventions may have beneficial effects on anxiety, pain, fatigue and quality of life in people with cancer. Furthermore, music may have a small effect on heart rate, respiratory rate and blood pressure. Most trials were at high risk of bias and, therefore, these results need to be interpreted with caution."[56]

7. There are no serious risks associated with any form of music therapy.

Plausibility	👍
Efficacy	👎
Safety	👍

(continued)

---

[52]https://www.bamt.org/.

[53]Moreira et al. (2018).

[54]Magee et al. (2017).

[55]van der Steen et al. (2017).

[56]Bradt et al. (2016).

(continued)

Cost	
Risk/benefit balance	

10.19   Neural Therapy

(related modalities: biopuncture)

Neural therapy was invented in 1925 by the German doctor Ferdinand Huneke (?–1938) and his brother Walter. They believed to have discovered that the injection of a small dose of a local anaesthetic at specific sites has instant health effects at locations remote from the injection site.

1. Neural therapy consists of (mostly) sub-cutaneous injections of the local anaesthetic Novocain into reflex or interference-zones which Huneke called 'Stoerfelder' (areas of disturbance). They are claimed to be "manifestations of cell membrane instability and typically trigger abnormal autonomic nervous system responses. Interference fields may be found in scars, autonomic ganglia, teeth, internal organs or other locations where local tissue irritation exists."[57]
2. The causes of these phenomena can be diverse:

   - infections,
   - emotional trauma,
   - physical trauma for instance from any type of surgery, accidents, deep cuts, biopsies, childbirth, dental procedures, vaccinations, burns, tattoos, etc.

3. A single injection is often supposed to inactivate the zone and thus have an immediate effect on a remote part of the body which Hunecke called the 'Sekundenphaenomen' (phenomenon within seconds).
4. Proponents of neural therapy claim to be able to treat "any symptom related to bodily functions controlled by the autonomic nervous system, such as palpitations, brochospasm, indigestion, constipation, sexual dysfunction, dysmenorrhea or even cold hands or feet, may be partially or totally caused by an interference field."[58]
5. The response to neural therapy can, according to proponents, be permanent or just temporary. In the latter case, a further therapy is recommended. "Each time

---

[57]http://www.neuraltherapybook.com/NTdefined.php.

[58]http://www.neuraltherapybook.com/NTdefined.php.

an interference field is treated, there should be a longer response. Treatment is then repeated until it is no longer required."[59]

6. There are only very few studies of neural therapy. A review of the available data concluded that "neither the rationale nor the individual mechanisms, nor its therapeutic efficacy have been investigated scientifically."[60]

7. The few risks of neural therapy include puncturing vital organs with the needle, infections and allergic reactions to the local anaesthetic, all of which seem to be rare events.

Plausibility	👎
Efficacy	👎
Safety	👎
Cost	👍
Risk/benefit balance	👎

10.20 Pranic Healing

(related modalities: energy healing, faith healing)

Pranic healing has ancient roots; more recently, it was popularised by Choa Kok Sui (1954–2007). It is a form of paranormal or energy healing that purports to stimulate the self-healing properties of our body.

1. In Hinduism, prana is assumed to be the vital force that permeates the universe on all levels. Prana is believed to be the type of energy that is responsible for the body's health and maintenance. Proponents believe that prana is essential for the body to function.

2. Pranic healing bears several of the hallmarks of a cult. For 20 years, Choa Kok Sui travelled the world instructing students in over 60 countries. He authored 25 books which have been published in more than 30 languages. He is said to have helped establish more than 100 'Pranic Healing Centres' in over 90 countries.

---

[59]Rajagopal et al. (2018).
[60]Ernst and Fialka (1994).

3. Pranic healing is allegedly a type of healing that creates and maintains health by restoring the energy of the chakras. "During a pranic healing session, the healers pray to the almighty before, during and after the healing session, which facilitates the presence of divine energy in healing."[61]
4. None of the assumptions of pranic healing are based on verifiable facts or good science; they are therefore not plausible.
5. Pranic healing is said to be a holistic approach as it assumes a person in its complexity and does not separate the body and the mind. Such assumptions, which are made in most forms of alternative medicine, are fallacious in that they ignore that all good medicine is holistic (see entry on holistic medicine).
6. The therapeutic claims are far-reaching; essentially, pranic healing is considered to be a panacea, a cure-all.
7. There have been very few clinical trials of pranic healing.[62] Their results do not justify a positive recommendation to use this treatment for any condition.

Plausibility	👎
Efficacy	👎
Safety	👍
Cost	👆
Risk/benefit balance	👎

10.21 Prayer

(related modalities: energy healing, faith healing)

Prayer is one of the oldest and most widespread interventions used with the intention of alleviating illness and promoting good health. It is used by believers throughout the world regardless of the religion they belong to.

1. Prayer can be defined as the solemn request or thanksgiving to God or other object of worship.
2. Intercessory prayer is practised by people of all faiths and involves a person or group setting aside time for petitioning god on behalf of another person who is

---

[61]https://bodyspirithealth.com/2015/08/02/what-happens-during-a-pranic-healing-session/.
[62]Rajagopal et al. (2018).

in need. Intercessory prayer is organised, regular, and committed. Those who practise it usually do not ask for payments because they hold a committed belief.

3. The mechanisms by which prayer might work therapeutically are unknown, and hypotheses about its mode of action will depend to a large extent on the religious beliefs in question. People who believe in the possibility that prayers might improve their health assume that god could intervene on their behalf by blessing them with healing energy.

4. These assumptions lack scientific plausibility.

5. Numerous clinical trials have been conducted. Most of them fail to adequately control for bias, and their findings are not uniform.

6. A systematic review of all these studies is available. It included 10 trials with a total of 7646 patients. The authors concluded that the "findings are equivocal and, although some of the results of individual studies suggest a positive effect of intercessory prayer, the majority do not and the evidence does not support a recommendation either in favour or against the use of intercessory prayer. We are not convinced that further trials of this intervention should be undertaken and would prefer to see any resources available for such a trial used to investigate other questions in health care."[63]

Plausibility	👎
Efficacy	👎
Safety	👍
Cost	👍
Risk/benefit balance	👎

10.22   Progressive Muscle Relaxation

(related modalities: meditation, relaxation therapies)

Progressive muscle relaxation (PMR) is a therapy developed in the 1930s by the US physician Edmund Jacobson (1888–1983). It has repeatedly been modified by others; consequently, several different variations of PMR currently exist.

---

[63]Roberts et al. (2009).

1. The basic concept is that patients learn how to relax voluntary muscles. Once they have mustered this task, involuntary muscles follow automatically. Eventually, a 'relaxation response'[64] with deep relaxation of both the body and the mind is said to ensue.
2. The technique can be taught by first actively tensing voluntary muscles and then relaxing them. Many experts would probably argue that PMR is a well-accepted conventional and no longer an alternative treatment.
3. PMR allegedly causes a host of measurable physiological changes such as a reduction of stress hormones, a decrease of blood pressure, a slowing of heart frequency and respiratory rate.
4. The method is used as a stress management technique and as an adjuvant treatment of a wide range of conditions that are associated with stress.
5. There have been numerous clinical trials of PMR as an adjunctive therapy for several conditions. In general, the results have been encouraging. However, the often-poor quality of the studies limits the conclusiveness of the evidence.
6. One systematic review, for instance, found that "there is evidence that PMR might have a few benefits for patients undergoing chemotherapy. Still, the small number of studies included and their poor quality limit the significance of our results."[65] And another systematic review concluded that "PMR might be a useful add-on treatment to reduce state anxiety and psychological distress and improve subjective well-being in persons with schizophrenia."[66]
7. Normally, PMR is not associated with serious adverse effects; however, patients with psychoses might experience an aggravation of their condition.

Plausibility	👍
Efficacy	👍
Safety	👍
Cost	👍
Risk/benefit balance	👍

---

[64]https://en.wikipedia.org/wiki/The_Relaxation_Response.
[65]Pelekasis et al. (2017).
[66]Vancampfort et al. (2013).

10.23 Qigong

(related modalities: energy healing, meditation, mind-body therapies, tai chi, Traditional Chinese Medicine)

Qigong is a branch of Traditional Chinese Medicine using meditation, exercise, deep breathing and other techniques with a view of strengthening the assumed life force 'qi' and thus improving health and prolong life. Qigong has ancient roots in China and has recently also become popular in other countries.

1. There are several distinct forms of qigong which can be categorized into two main groups, internal qigong and external qigong. Internal qigong refers to a physical and mental training method for the cultivation of oneself to achieve optimal health in both mind and body. Internal qigong is not dissimilar to tai chi but it also employs the coordination of different breathing patterns and meditation. External qigong refers to a treatment where qigong practitioners direct their qi-energy to the patient with the intention to clear qi-blockages or balance the flow of qi within that patient.
2. According to Taoist and Buddhist beliefs, qigong allows access to higher realms of awareness.
3. The assumptions of qigong are not scientifically plausible.
4. Proponents of qigong recommend it for the treatment and prevention of a wide range of conditions, symptoms and situations, including stress management, hypertension, chronic pain, depression, insomnia, cardiac rehabilitation, immune function and for enhancing the quality of life of cancer patients.
5. Despite the absence of a scientific basis, qigong has been submitted to numerous clinical trials and several systematic reviews of these data have recently been published.
6. One overview of systematic reviews of clinical trials testing the effectiveness of qigong included 10 systematic reviews. They related to a wide range of conditions. The primary studies and several of the reviews were associated with a high risk of bias. Five reviews concluded that qigong is effective and five reviews failed to reach this conclusion. The authors (which included a qigong master) concluded that "the effectiveness of qigong is based mostly on poor quality research. Therefore, it would be unwise to draw firm conclusions at this stage."[67]
7. While qigong is generally considered to be safe, there are isolated reports that suggest that it might trigger latent psychoses.

---

[67]Lee et al. (2011).

Plausibility	
Efficacy	
Safety	
Cost	
Risk/benefit balance	

10.24   Reiki

(related modalities: energy healing)

Reiki is a form of paranormal or energy healing popularised by Japanese Mikao Usui (1865–1926). Rei means universal spirit (sometimes thought of as a supreme being) and ki is the assumed universal life energy.

1. Reiki is based on the assumptions of Traditional Chinese Medicine and the existence of 'chi', the life-force that determines our health.
2. Reiki practitioners believe that, with their hands-on healing method, they can transfer 'healing energy' to a patient which, in turn, stimulates the self-healing properties of the body. They assume that the therapeutic effects of this technique are obtained from a 'universal life energy' that provides strength, harmony, and balance to the body and mind.
3. There is no scientific basis for such notions, and reiki is therefore not plausible.
4. Reiki is used for a number of conditions, including the relief of stress, tension and pain.
5. There have been several clinical trials testing the effectiveness of reiki. Unfortunately, their methodological quality is usually poor.
6. A systematic review summarising this evidence concluded that "the evidence is insufficient to suggest that reiki is an effective treatment for any condition. Therefore, the value of reiki remains unproven."[68] And a Cochrane review found that "there is insufficient evidence to say whether or not Reiki is useful for people over 16 years of age with anxiety or depression or both."[69]

---

[68]Lee et al. (2008).

[69]Joyce and Herbison (2015).

7. Reiki appears to be generally safe, and serious adverse effects have not been reported. Some practitioners advise caution about using reiki in people with psychiatric illnesses because of the risk of bringing out underlying psychopathology.

Plausibility	👎
Efficacy	👎
Safety	👍
Cost	👍
Risk/benefit balance	👎

10.25   Spiritual Healing

(related modalities: energy healing)

Spiritual healing is a form of paranormal or energy healing. It is similar to faith healing (see there), except that there is no need for the patient or the healer to believe in any deity. Spiritual healing is distinct from the act of providing spiritual support to patients.

1. Spiritual healing has been defined as the direct interaction between one individual (the healer) and a patient, with the intention of improving the patient's condition or curing the illness.
2. Treatment can occur through personal, direct contact between healer and patient or at a (sometimes large) distance.
3. Spiritual healers, who are usually not medically qualified, believe that the therapeutic effect results from the channelling of 'energy' from an undefined source via the healer to the patient.
4. The main problem with this concept is that there is no evidence that this energy actually exists. Therefore, the assumptions on which spiritual healing is based lack plausibility.
5. The central claim of healers is that they promote or facilitate self-healing and wellbeing, both of which could be relevant to patients with any type of condition. An article by enthusiasts of spiritual healing explains: "All conditions can be treated by spiritual healing—but not all people. Some people are more

receptive than others to this treatment, due to a number of factors such as karma and mental outlook. As such the results of healing can vary a great deal. If the patient has faith in the technique and the healer, this will of course aid the healing process, but is not necessary; this is not faith healing as practiced in some religions—it is based instead on spiritual energy. This being the case, it is possible for a skeptic to receive healing and benefit from it."[70]

6. The evidence from clinical trials of spiritual healing is contradictory. Many studies have serious flaws, and the most reliable trials fail to show effects beyond placebo. Research papers often fail to differentiate between different types of paranormal healing. One Cochrane, for instance, review "found inconclusive evidence that interventions with spiritual or religious components for adults in the terminal phase of a disease may or may not enhance well-being. Such interventions are under-evaluated. All five studies identified were undertaken in the same country, and in the multi-disciplinary palliative care interventions it is unclear if all participants received support from a chaplain or a spiritual counsellor. Moreover, it is unclear in all the studies whether the participants in the comparative groups received spiritual or religious support, or both, as part of routine care or from elsewhere. The paucity of quality research indicates a need for more rigorous studies."[71]

7. As long as it is not used as an alternative to effective therapies, spiritual healing cannot cause harm to patients. However, like all forms of paranormal healing, it may undermine rational thought by making consumers believe in myths.

Plausibility	👎
Efficacy	👎
Safety	👍
Cost	👍
Risk/benefit balance	👎

---

[70]https://www.aetherius.org/healing-yourself-and-others/.
[71]Candy et al. (2012).

10.26   Therapeutic Touch

(related modalities: energy healing)

Therapeutic touch (TT) is a form of paranormal or energy healing developed by Dora Kunz (1904–1999), a psychic and alternative practitioner, in collaboration with Dolores Krieger, a professor of nursing.

1. According to Kunz, TT has its origins in ancient Yogic texts.
2. TT is popular and practised predominantly by US nurses; it is currently being taught in more than 80 colleges and universities in the U.S., and in more than seventy countries.
3. According to one TT-organisation, "TT is a holistic, evidence-based therapy that incorporates the intentional and compassionate use of universal energy to promote balance and well-being. It is a consciously directed process of energy exchange during which the practitioner uses the hands as a focus to facilitate the process."[72]
4. The assumptions that form the basis for TT are not biologically plausible.
5. Several trials and reviews of TT have emerged. However, many of them are by ardent proponents of TT, seriously flawed, and thus less than reliable. e.g.,[73,74]
6. One rigorous pre-clinical study, co-designed by a 9-year-old girl, found that "experienced TT practitioners were unable to detect the investigator's 'energy field.' Their failure to substantiate TT's most fundamental claim is unrefuted evidence that the claims of TT are groundless and that further professional use is unjustified."[75]
7. There are no reasons to assume that TT causes direct harm. One could, however, argue that, like all forms of paranormal healing, it undermines rational thinking.

Plausibility	👎
Efficacy	👎
Safety	👍

(continued)

---

[72]http://therapeutictouch.org/what-is-tt/.

[73]Monroe (2009).

[74]Tabatabaee et al. (2016).

[75]Rosa et al. (1998).

(continued)

Cost	
Risk/benefit balance	

10.27   Transcendental Meditation

(related modalities: mind-body therapies)

Transcendental meditation (TM) is a meditation technique developed in the 1950 s by the Indian guru Maharishi Mahesh Yogi (1918–2008).

1. TM employs silent mantras, a word that has to be repeated in one's mind for 15–20 min twice per day while sitting with the eyes closed to aid the meditation process. An individualized mantra is chosen by the teacher using an undisclosed procedure and the novice meditator is instructed to keep it secret. Consumers pay to learn the technique and are typically recruited via public promotional lectures.
2. Maharishi made several world tours and enthused numerous celebrities, not least the Beatles. He is said to have trained over 40,000 TM teachers who, in turn, taught allegedly more that 5 million people the technique of TM.
3. The TM movement has hallmarks of a cult. It operates a worldwide network of TM teaching centres. The organization is alleged to have a membership of about 900,000 an estimated net worth of $US 3.5 billion.
4. The health claims made for TM are numerous and often far-reaching. TM is claimed to be helpful for most medical conditions as well as for improving performance of school children and other healthy people. The benefits claimed for TM include positive effects on personal development, mental health, physical health, education and society more generally.
5. The TM movement has sponsored many studies of TM which invariably report positive effects on human health.
6. These studies are often of deplorable quality, and independent replications frequently cannot confirm their findings.

   - For instance, our own review of TM for hypertension concluded that "all the randomized clinical trials of TM for the control of blood pressure published to date have important methodological weaknesses and are potentially biased by the affiliation of authors to the TM organization. There is at present insufficient good-quality evidence to conclude whether or not TM has a cumulative positive effect on blood pressure."[76]

- Similarly, a Cochrane review concluded that "currently, there are few trials with limited evidence to date, we could draw no conclusions as to the effectiveness of TM for the primary prevention of CVD. There was considerable heterogeneity between trials and the included studies were small, short term and at overall serious risk of bias. More and larger long-term, high-quality trials are needed."[77]

7. Reports of adverse events of TM are rare, but include exacerbation of pre-existing depression and anxiety, depersonalization, attempted suicide and precipitation of schizophrenic episodes. This suggests that people with pre-existing mental health problems should take up meditation only under the supervision of a qualified psychiatrist or psychotherapist experienced in the use of such techniques in a therapeutic context.[78] In addition, there is the risk of getting drawn into a cult-like movement.

Plausibility	👎
Efficacy	👎
Safety	👎
Cost	👎
Risk/benefit balance	👎

10.28   Zero Balance

(related modalities: energy healing, massage, mind-body therapies)

Zero balance is a mind-body therapy developed by the medical doctor Fritz Smith in the early 1970s.

---

[76]Canter and Ernst (2004).

[77]https://www.cochranelibrary.com/cdsr/doi/10.1002/14651858.CD010359.pub2/full.

[78]Canter and Ernst (2004).

1. Zero Balancing (ZB) has been defined as "the art and skill of balancing body energy with body structure through the use of conscious touch. ZB is unique as a therapeutic tool, as its aim is to work with energy and structure simultaneously. ZB bridges the gap between energetic therapies and structural therapies, maximizing the potential of both and creating a new world of possibilities for health-care professionals."[79]

2. One enthusiast describes zero balancing as "a powerful body-mind therapy that uses skilled touch to address the relationship between energy and structures of the body. Following a protocol that typically lasts 30 to 45 min, the practitioner uses finger pressure and gentle traction on areas of tension in the bones, joints and soft tissue to create fulcrums, or points of balance, around which the body can relax and reorganize. Zero Balancing focuses primarily on key joints of our skeleton that conduct and balance forces of gravity, posture and movement. By addressing the deepest and densest tissues of the body along with soft tissue and energy fields, Zero Balancing helps to clear blocks in the body's energy flow, amplify vitality and contribute to better postural alignment. A Zero Balancing session leaves you with a wonderful feeling of inner harmony and organization."[80]

3. The claims frequently made for zero balancing include the notions that the treatment:

   - Increases feelings of health and well-being
   - Releases stress and improves the flow of energy in our bodies
   - Reduces pain and discomfort
   - Enhances stability, balance and freedom
   - Amplifies the sense of connection, peace and happiness
   - Releases mental, emotional and physical tension
   - Supports us through transitions and transformations
   - Improves quality of life and increases capacity for enjoyment.

4. The theoretical assumptions of, and the clinical claims for zero balancing lack plausibility.

5. The texts on zero balancing tend to be prime examples of pseudoscience using pseudoscientific language. One example must suffice: "The topic of energy therapies is prompted by the increasing attention of healthcare practitioners and consumers to Eastern philosophies and ancient healing practices. This article includes a conceptual framework of quantum physics principles providing the basis of interpretation of energetic phenomena, along with the exploration of theoretical concepts involving energy as a communicational network. An overview of the contemplative tradition of meditation indicates its necessity as a requisite element of energy therapies, the practice combining a knowledge base of the core scientific precepts with the experience of restorative strategies. The

---

[79]Ralston (1998).

[80]https://www.zerobalancing.com/about.

relevance of energy therapies as a path to self-transcendence along with the application of a specific touch technique, Zero Balancing, is highlighted."[81]

6. As no clinical trials have been published, there is no evidence that zero balancing has any health effects and the therapy must be classified as unproven.
7. Zero balancing is unlikely to cause any direct adverse effects.

Plausibility	👎
Efficacy	👎
Safety	👍
Cost	👎
Risk/benefit balance	👎

References

Abbot NC, Stead LF, White AR, Barnes J, Ernst E (2000) Hypnotherapy for smoking cessation. Cochrane Database Syst Rev 2:CD001008

Anheyer D, Leach MJ, Klose P, Dobos G, Cramer H (2018) Mindfulness-based stress reduction for treating chronic headache: a systematic review and meta-analysis. Cephalalgia 1:333102418781795

Asefi M, Augustin M (1999) Regulative therapy: treatment with nonspecific stimulants in dermatology in traditional and modern perspectives. Forsch Komplementarmed 6(Suppl 2):9–13

Baldwin AL, Trent NL (2017) An integrative review of scientific evidence for reconnective healing. J Altern Complement Med 23(8):590–598

Bowering KJ, O'Connell NE, Tabor A, Catley MJ, Leake HB, Moseley GL, Stanton TR (2013) The effects of graded motor imagery and its components on chronic pain: a systematic review and meta-analysis. J Pain 14(1):3–13

Bradt J, Dileo C, Magill L, Teague A (2016) Music interventions for improving psychological and physical outcomes in cancer patients. Cochrane Database Syst Rev 8:CD006911

Bykowski MR, Zhu X, Diaz-Garcia R (2018) Ceftriaxone-resistant aeromonas hydrophila infection following leech therapy: a new resistant strain. Ann Plast Surg 81(3):327–328

Çakmak T, Çaltekin İ, Gökçen E, Savrun A, Yaşar E (2018) Kounis syndrome due to hirudotherapy (leech therapy) in emergency department; a case report. Turk J Emerg Med 18 (2):85–87

---

[81]Denner (2009).

Candy B, Jones L, Varagunam M, Speck P, Tookman A, King M, Spiritual and religious interventions for well-being of adults in the terminal phase of disease, Cochrane Database Syst Rev. 2012 16;(5):CD007544

Canter PH, Ernst E (2004) Insufficient evidence to conclude whether or not transcendental meditation decreases blood pressure: results of a systematic review of randomized clinical trials. J Hypertens 22(11):2049–2054

Canter PH, Brown LB, Greaves C, Ernst E (2006) Johrei family healing: a pilot study. Evid Based Complement Alternat Med 3(4):533–540

Denner SS (2009) The science of energy therapies and contemplative practice: a conceptual review and the application of zero balancing. Holist Nurs Pract 23(6):315–334

Eisele JW, Reay DT (1980) Deaths related to coffee enemas. JAMA 244(14):1608–1609

Ernst E (1997) Colonic irrigation and the theory of autointoxication: a triumph of ignorance over science. J Clin Gastroenterol 24(4):196–198

Ernst E (2003) Distant healing—an "update" of a systematic review. Wien Klin Wochenschr 115 (7–8):241–245

Ernst E (2004) Bioresonance, a study of pseudo-scientific language. Forsch Komplementarmed Klass Naturheilkd 11(3):171–173

Ernst E (2010) Colonic irrigation: therapeutic claims by professional organisations, a review. Int J Clin Pract 64(4):429–431

Ernst E, Fialka V (1994) Neural therapy in the light of recent data. Fortschr Med 112(31):433–434

Ernst E, Kanji N (2000) Autogenic training for stress and anxiety: a systematic review. Complement Ther Med 8(2):106–110

Felix MMDS, Ferreira MBG, da Cruz LF, Barbosa MH (2019) Relaxation therapy with guided imagery for postoperative pain management: an integrative review. Pain Manag Nurs 20(1):3–9

Fisch S, Brinkhaus B, Teut M (2017) Hypnosis in patients with perceived stress—a systematic review. BMC Complement Altern Med 17(1):323

François B, Sternberg EM, Fee E (2014) The Lourdes medical cures revisited. J Hist Med Allied Sci 69(1):135–162

Gard T, Hölzel BK, Lazar SW (2014) The potential effects of meditation on age-related cognitive decline: a systematic review. Ann N Y Acad Sci 1307:89–103

Gasiorowska A, Navarro-Rodriguez T, Dickman R, Wendel C, Moty B, Powers J, Willis MR, Koenig K, Ibuki Y, Thai H, Fass R (2009) Clinical trial: the effect of Johrei on symptoms of patients with functional chest pain. Aliment Pharmacol Ther 29(1):126–134

Giacobbi PR Jr, Stabler ME, Stewart J, Jaeschke AM, Siebert JL, Kelley GA (2015) Guided imagery for arthritis and other rheumatic diseases: a systematic review of randomized controlled trials. Pain Manag Nurs. 16(5):792–803

Goyal M, Singh S, Sibinga EMS, Gould NF, Rowland-Seymour A, Sharma R, Berger Z, Sleicher D, Maron DD, Shihab HM, Ranasinghe PD, Linn S, Saha S, Bass EB, Haythornthwaite JA (2014) Meditation programs for psychological stress and well-being [Internet]

Hadjibalassi M, Lambrinou E, Papastavrou E, Papathanassoglou E (2018) The effect of guided imagery on physiological and psychological outcomes of adult ICU patients: a systematic literature review and methodological implications. Aust Crit Care 31(2):73–86

Joyce J, Herbison GP (2015) Reiki for depression and anxiety. Cochrane Database Syst Rev 4: CD006833

Keum B, Jeen YT, Park SC, Seo YS, Kim YS, Chun HJ, Um SH, Kim CD, Ryu HS (2010) Proctocolitis caused by coffee enemas. Am J Gastroenterol 105(1):229–230

Kim S, Cha JM, Lee CH, Shin HP, Park JJ, Joo KR, Lee JI, Jeun JW, Lim K, Lim JU, Choi JH (2012) Rectal perforation due to benign stricture caused by rectal burns associated with hot coffee enemas. Endoscopy 44(Suppl):2

Kleine-Tebbe J, Herold DA (2010) Inappropriate test methods in allergy. Hautarzt 61(11):961–966

Klemparskaya NN, Shalnova GA, Ulanova AM, Kuzmina TD, Chuhrov AD (1986) Immunomodulating effect of autohaemotherapy (a literature review). J Hyg Epidemiol Microbiol Immunol 30(3):331–336

Krisanaprakornkit T, Ngamjarus C, Witoonchart C, Piyavhatkul N (2010) Meditation therapies for attention-deficit/hyperactivity disorder (ADHD). Cochrane Database Syst Rev 6:CD006507

Lauche R, Cramer H, Langhorst J, Dobos G (2014) A systematic review and meta-analysis of medical leech therapy for osteoarthritis of the knee. Clin J Pain 30(1):63–72

Lee CJ, Song SK, Jeon JH, Sung MK, Cheung DY, Kim JI, Kim JK, Lee YS (2008a) Coffee enema induced acute colitis. Korean J Gastroenterol 52(4):251–254

Lee MS, Pittler MH, Ernst E (2008b) Effects of reiki in clinical practice: a systematic review of randomised clinical trials. Int J Clin Pract 62(6):947–954

Lee MS, Oh B, Ernst E (2011) Qigong for healthcare: an overview of systematic reviews. JRSM Short Rep 2(2):7

Long J, Briggs M, Astin F (2017) Overview of systematic reviews of mindfulness meditation-based interventions for people with long-term conditions. Adv Mind Body Med 31(4):26–36

Madden K, Middleton P, Cyna AM, Matthewson M, Jones L (2016) Hypnosis for pain management during labour and childbirth. Cochrane Database Syst Rev 5:CD009356

Magee WL, Clark I, Tamplin J, Bradt J (2017) Music interventions for acquired brain injury. Cochrane Database Syst Rev 1:CD006787

Monroe CM (2009) The effects of therapeutic touch on pain. J Holist Nurs 27(2):85–92

Mora-Ripoll R (2010) The therapeutic value of laughter in medicine. Altern Ther Health Med 16 (6):56–64

Moreira SV, Justi FRDR, Moreira M (2018) Can musical intervention improve memory in Alzheimer's patients? Evidence from a systematic review. Dement Neuropsychol. 12(2):133–142

Paudyal P, Jones C, Grindey C, Dawood R, Smith H (2018) Meditation for asthma: systematic review and meta-analysis. J Asthma 55(7):771–778

Pelekasis P, Matsouka I, Koumarianou A (2017) Progressive muscle relaxation as a supportive intervention for cancer patients undergoing chemotherapy: a systematic review. Palliat Support Care 15(4):465–473

Pittler MH, Armstrong NC, Cox A, Collier PM, Hart A, Ernst E (2003) Randomized, double-blind, placebo-controlled trial of autologous blood therapy for atopic dermatitis. Br J Dermatol 148 (2):307–313

Posadzki P, Lewandowski W, Terry R, Ernst E, Stearns A (2012) Guided imagery for non-musculoskeletal pain: a systematic review of randomized clinical trials. J Pain Symptom Manage 44(1):95–104

Provençal SC, Bond S, Rizkallah E, El-Baalbaki G (2018) Hypnosis for burn wound care pain and anxiety: a systematic review and meta-analysis. Burns. 44(8):1870–1881

Radin D, Schlitz M, Baur C (2015) Distant Healing Intention Therapies: an Overview of the Scientific Evidence. Glob Adv Health Med. 4(Suppl):67–71

Rajagopal R, Jois SN, Mallikarjuna Majgi S, Anil Kumar MN, Shashidhar HB (2018) Amelioration of mild and moderate depression through Pranic Healing as adjuvant therapy: randomised double-blind controlled trial. Australas Psychiatry 26(1):82–87

Ralston AL (1998) Zero balancing: information on a therapy. Complement Ther Nurs Midwifery 4 (2):47–49

Roberts L, Ahmed I, Hall S, Davison A (2009) Intercessory prayer for the alleviation of ill health. Cochrane Database Syst Rev 2:CD000368

Rosa L, Rosa E, Sarner L, Barrett S (1998) A close look at therapeutic touch. JAMA 279 (13):1005–1010

Salhofer I, Will A, Monsef I, Skoetz N (2016) Meditation for adults with haematological malignancies. Cochrane Database Syst Rev 2:CD011157

Sancho M, De Gracia M, Rodríguez RC, Mallorquí-Bagué N, Sánchez-González J, Trujols J, Sánchez I, Jiménez-Murcia S, Menchón JM (2018) Mindfulness-based interventions for the treatment of substance and behavioral addictions: a systematic review. Front Psychiatry 29 (9):95

Schöni MH, Nikolaizik WH, Schöni-Affolter F (1997) Efficacy trial of bioresonance in children with atopic dermatitis. Int Arch Allergy Immunol 112(3):238–246

Sridharan K, Sivaramakrishnan G (2016) Therapeutic clowns in pediatrics: a systematic review and meta-analysis of randomized controlled trials. Eur J Pediatr 175(10):1353–1360

Tabatabaee A, Tafreshi MZ, Rassouli M, Aledavood SA, AlaviMajd H, Farahmand SK (2016) Effect of therapeutic touch in patients with cancer: a literature review. Med Arch 70(2):142–147

Teekachunhatean S, Tosri N, Sangdee C, Wongpoomchai R, Ruangyuttikarn W, Puaninta C, Srichairatanakool S (2012) Antioxidant effects after coffee enema or oral coffee consumption in healthy Thai male volunteers. Hum Exp Toxicol 31(7):643–651

van der Steen JT, van Soest-Poortvliet MC, van der Wouden JC, Bruinsma MS, Scholten RJ, Vink AC (2017) Music-based therapeutic interventions for people with dementia. Cochrane Database Syst Rev 5:CD003477

Vancampfort D, Correll CU, Scheewe TW, Probst M, De Herdt A, Knapen J, De Hert M (2013) Progressive muscle relaxation in persons with schizophrenia: a systematic review of randomized controlled trials. Clin Rehabil 27(4):291–298

Wasti H, Kanchan T, Acharya J (2015) Faith healers, myths and deaths. Med Leg J 83(3):136–138

Yim J (2016) Therapeutic benefits of laughter in mental health: a theoretical review. Tohoku J Exp Med 239(3):243–249

Zhang Y, Yang Y, Lau WY, Garg S, Lao J (2017) Effectiveness of pre-operative clown intervention on psychological distress: a systematic review and meta-analysis. J Paediatr Child Health 53(3):237–245

Chapter 11
Umbrella Terms

11.1 Alternative Cancer Cures

(related modalities: Antineoblastons, cancer diets, Carctol, coffee enemas, Essiac, Gerson therapy, Laetrile, mistletoe, New German Medicine, shark cartilage, Ukrain)

There are uncounted so-called 'alternative cancer cures', and the most important ones can be found as separate entries in this book. The treatments in question are very diverse but they nevertheless have certain features in common:

1. Most 'alternative cancer cures' originate from the ideas developed by a single, often charismatic individual who claims to have found the answer to all forms of cancer (as cancer is an umbrella term for a range of different diseases, it is highly unlikely that one single cure for all of them will ever exist).
2. Alternative cancer cures are often promoted by celebrities, hyped by the press and marketed via books or the Internet,[1] but they are never supported by published studies in the peer-reviewed medical literature.
3. They target the most desperate cancer patients who understandably tend to cling to every straw they can find.
4. Proponents of alternative cancer cures tend to be entrepreneurs who, using scientific-sounding terminology, exploit patients by selling them false hope at high, often exceedingly high prices.
5. Alternative cancer cures are invariably fake: they are neither biologically plausible nor clinically effective. Thus, they do not cure any type of cancer, let alone all cancers.

---

[1]Schmidt and Ernst (2014).

© Springer Nature Switzerland AG 2019
E. Ernst, *Alternative Medicine*,
https://doi.org/10.1007/978-3-030-12601-8_11

6. If a therapy, for instance a plant extract, shows real promise as a cancer treatment, it is rapidly scrutinised by researchers and, if effective, adopted by oncologists. The notion of an alternative cancer cure presupposes that conventional oncologists shun a potentially valuable treatment simply because it emerged from the realm of alternative medicine. The notion that the pharmaceutical industry or other organisations are suppressing alternative cancer cures is a classical conspiracy theory with no basis in reality.[2]

7. Alternative cancer cures are extremely dangerous. There are many examples of people who died needlessly early because they used some bogus therapy as an alternative to conventional oncology (Steve Jobs is a prime example). Several studies have shown that patients who fall for the notion of an alternative cancer cure shorten their survival time by 50% or more[3]

Plausibility	👎
Efficacy	👎
Safety	👎
Cost	👎
Risk/benefit balance	👎

11.2 Anthroposophic Medicine

(related modalities: homeopathy, mistletoe)

Anthroposophic medicine is a form of healthcare developed in the 1920s by Rudolf Steiner (1861–1925) in collaboration with the physician Ita Wegman (1876–1943). It is based on Steiner's mystical ideas of anthroposophy (Fig. 11.1).

---

[2]https://jamanetwork.com/journals/jamainternalmedicine/fullarticle/1835348.

[3]edzardernst.com/2017/08/use-of-alternative-medicine-hastens-death-of-cancer-patients/.

Fig. 11.1 Rudolf Steiner
(1861–1925), founder of
anthroposophic medicine

1. Steiner had developed his 'philosophy' of anthroposophy from personal experiences, occult notions and mystical concepts.
2. Ita Wegman studied medicine after having met Steiner in 1902. She pioneered an 'alternative cancer treatment' with a fermented mistletoe extract, according to Steiner's ideas. Together, Wegman and Steiner wrote Steiner's last book entitled 'Extending Practical Medicine' which was meant as a theoretical basis for their anthroposophical medicine. Wegman was also a co-founder of the pharmaceutical firm 'Weleda' which became the biggest producer of anthroposophical remedies.
3. Proponents of anthroposophic medicine make several irrational assumptions, for instance, they claim that our past lives influence our present health, or that the course of an illness is determined by our 'karmic' destiny.

4. Practitioners of anthroposophic medicine are usually medically trained; they employ a variety of treatments including massage, exercise, counselling, and a range of remedies (more than 1300 different anthroposophic medicinal products are currently on the market). Most of the remedies are, like homeopathic remedies, highly diluted but they are not normally prescribed according to the 'like cures like' principle and are therefore distinct from homeopathy.

5. The most widely used anthroposophic remedy is the fermented mistletoe extract promoted for cancer sold by Weleda under the trade-name of 'Iscador'. Steiner argued that the mistletoe plant grows parasitically on a tree and eventually kills it—just like a malignant tumour grows in a body and may thus kill it. Based on this analogy, he reckoned Iscador was a cure for cancer. Yet, the evidence for mistletoe extracts fails to be positive; a 2017 systematic review concluded that "The use of mistletoe as a treatment for people with cancer has been investigated in clinical studies. Reports of improved survival and/or quality of life have been common, but nearly all of the studies had major weaknesses that raise doubts about the reliability of the findings. At present, the use of mistletoe cannot be recommended outside the context of well-designed clinical trials…"[4]

6. Most other anthroposophic remedies are also not supported by sound evidence.[5]

7. Practitioners of anthroposophic medicine may cause serious harm. For instance, they tend to advise against immunizations which, of course, can have detrimental effects both on an individual as well as societal level.

Plausibility	👎
Efficacy	👎
Safety	👍 a
Cost	👎
Risk/benefit balance	👎

[a]Depends on the exact nature of the treatment in question

---

[4]https://www.ncbi.nlm.nih.gov/books/NBK66054/.

[5]Hamre et al. (2017).

11.3 Anti-aging Remedies

(related modalities: colonic irrigation, detox, dietary supplements, yoga)

Aging is a natural process; it might be influenced or delayed by a healthy life-style, but it cannot be halted by using this or that alternative therapy. "Anti-aging" practitioners promise their clients to look, feel and act like they did many years ago.

1. Anti-aging treatments are cleverly marketed and widely promoted in self-help books, the popular media, and by celebrities.
2. Thus, the anti-aging industry has grown largely unchecked into a multi-billion-dollar business.[6] For example, in the US the industry that promotes the use of hormones as a treatment for slowing or reversing the aging process generated about $50 billion of revenue in 2009.[7]
3. The nature of the anti-aging treatments on offer varies; examples are detox, herbal remedies, hormonal treatments and stem cell therapy.
4. The claims that are being made are equally diverse, for example:

   - Feeling of vitality and rejuvenation
   - Looking younger
   - Better concentration and mental capacity
   - Longer life
   - Improved quality of life
   - Improved capacity for physical activities
   - Improved quality of hair
   - Increased libido.

5. Life extension research is, of course, a serious branch of science; yet, it is largely unrelated to the current boom of anti-aging business promoting bogus treatments for quick profit.
6. A systematic review of herbal anti-aging skin products included 11 clinical trials. Some of them suggested positive results in terms of reduced skin-wrinkling, but the trials were methodologically weak, lacked independent replications, and suggested only small, short-lasting effects of little or no clinical relevance.[8]
7. The risks of anti-aging treatments depend on the nature of the therapy. Contrary to what is usually claimed, most options are not devoid of risks, and some can cause even serious harm. As most anti-ageing treatments are expensive, some exceedingly so, the harm to the consumers' bank account should also be considered.

---

[6]Fishman et al. (2015).

[7]http://articles.chicagotribune.com/2009-06-15/news/0906140132_1_anti-aging-hormones-ama-council.

[8]Hunt et al. (2010).

Plausibility	👎
Efficacy	👎
Safety	👍
Cost	👎
Risk/benefit balance	👎

11.4 Apitherapy

(related modalities: acupuncture)

Apitherapy is the use of products from the honeybee hive for medicinal purposes. It is thus an umbrella term for a diverse range of different treatments.

1. The bee-related products can be derived from honey, bee pollen, propolis, royal jelly or bee venom.[9]
2. They can be administered orally, topically or via direct bee-sting. The latter technique is sometimes used over acupuncture points and called apipuncture or bee venom acupuncture.[10]
3. References to medical properties of bee products can be found in Chinese, Korean, Russian, Egyptian and Greek traditional medicines.
4. Proponents of apitherapy recommend it for a wide range of conditions. Some of the most common therapeutic claims include:

   - Bee venom stimulates a healthy immune response
   - Bee venom reduces pain and inflammation in the joints caused by conditions such as arthritis
   - Royal jelly and propolis treat burns
   - Propolis has antibacterial and antifungal properties
   - Honey is an antibacterial agent

---

[9]Fratellone et al. (2016).
[10]Cherniack and Govorushko (2018).

5. There is some preliminary evidence that the topical application of honey and related products might have benefits for would healing.[11]
6. One review concluded that "propolis has been reported to have various health benefits related to gastrointestinal disorders, allergies, and gynecological, oral, and dermatological problems. Royal jelly is well known for its protective effects on reproductive health, neurodegenerative disorders, wound healing, and aging. Nevertheless, the exact mechanisms of action of honey, propolis, and royal jelly on the abovementioned diseases and activities have not been not fully elucidated, and further research is warranted to explain their exact contributions."[12] The evidence for these and other types of apitherapy is, however, weak.
7. The risks of apitherapy depend on the nature of the therapy in question. Some forms of apitherapy can cause serious harm. For instance, bee-stings may cause severe allergic reactions, including anaphylactic shock.

Plausibility	👎
Efficacy	👎
Safety	👎
Cost	👎
Risk/benefit balance	👎

11.5 Ayurveda

(related modalities: herbal medicine, massage, meditation, yoga)

Ayurveda is a system of healthcare developed in India around the mid-first millennium BCE. Ayurvedic medicine involves a range of techniques, including meditation, physical exercises, nutrition, relaxation, massage and medication. This discussion is focussed on the latter.

1. Ayurvedic medicine thrives for balance and claims that the suppression of natural urges leads to illness. Emphasis is placed on moderation.
2. Up to 80% of people in India use some form of traditional medicine, a category which includes Ayurveda. During recent decades, Ayurvedic medicine has become popular also in many Western countries.

---

[11]Vandamme et al. (2013).
[12]Pasupuleti et al. (2017).

3. Ayurvedic medicines are extremely varied. They usually are mixtures of multiple ingredients and can consist of plants, animal products and minerals.
4. They often also contain toxic substances, such as heavy metals which are deliberately added in the ancient belief that they can have positive health effects. The truth, however, is that they can cause serious adverse effects.[13]
5. Relatively few studies of Ayurvedic remedies exist and most are methodologically weak. A Cochrane review, for instance, concluded that, "although there were significant glucose-lowering effects with the use of some herbal mixtures, due to methodological deficiencies and small sample sizes we are unable to draw any definite conclusions regarding their efficacy. Though no significant adverse events were reported, there is insufficient evidence at present to recommend the use of these interventions in routine clinical practice and further studies are needed."[14]
6. The efficacy of Ayurvedic remedies depends on the exact nature of the ingredients. Generalisations are therefore problematic. Promising findings exist for a relatively small number of ingredients, including Boswellia, Turmeric,[15] Frankincense,[16] Andographis paniculata.[17]
7. The risk/benefit balance for Ayurvedic remedies varies according to the nature of the ingredients. In many cases, it fails to be positive.

Plausibility	
Efficacy	
Safety	
Cost	
Risk/benefit balance	

---

[13]Ernst (2002).
[14]Sridharan et al. (2011).
[15]Bannuru et al. (2018).
[16]Ernst (2008).
[17]Coon and Ernst (2004).

11.6 Buteyko Technique

(related modalities: yoga)

The Buteyko technique (known in Russia as 'Voluntary Elimination of Deep Breathing') is a method to control respiration developed by the Russian Konstantin Buteyko (1923–2003).

1. Inspired by the methods of respiratory control in yoga, the Buteyko technique is specifically aimed at easing the symptoms of respiratory conditions, particularly asthma.
2. Konstantin Buteyko postulated that there is a connection between hyperventilation and asthma and that it should be possible to reduce asthma symptoms by deliberate breath control.
3. The Eucapnic Buteyko method is an adaptation of Buteyko's original technique which was first introduced in Australia and is now used worldwide. It includes the same focus on ventilation control, but the approach has been re-designed with the aim of achieving better patient-compliance.
4. Both Buteyko methods depend crucially on the cooperation of the patient who has to attend long sessions of learning the technique and must follow the somewhat tedious programme rigorously.
5. A Cochrane review of Buteyko and similar breathing techniques concluded that "there is no credible evidence regarding the effectiveness of breathing exercises for the clinical symptoms of dysfunctional breathing/hyperventilation syndrome. It is currently unknown whether these interventions offer any added value in this patient group or whether specific types of breathing exercise demonstrate superiority over others."[18]
6. Specifically for asthma, the evidence is a little more encouraging but also far from being conclusively positive.[19,20]
7. There are few serious risks associated with the Buteyko technique, unless it is employed as a replacement for effective asthma therapies.

Plausibility	
Efficacy	
Safety	

(continued)

---

[18]Jones et al. (2013).
[19]Austin (2013).
[20]Cooper et al. (2003).

(continued)

| Cost | |
| Risk/benefit balance | |

11.7 Cancer Diets

(related modalities: alternative cancer cures, Gerson therapy)

Many diets are currently promoted for the treatment of cancer. Often the claims or implications are that cancer can be cured by eating certain foods and avoiding others. The media are guilty of promoting such nonsensical notions. Even though there is plenty of research into diet and cancer—Medline lists almost 45,000 articles on the subject—dietary cancer cures have not been identified.

1. There are undeniable associations between diet and cancer. They indicate that some foods might increase the risks of some cancers, while other nutrients might reduce the risks.[21] One meta-analysis, for instance, concluded that a high intake of dietary fiber could significantly reduce the risk of ovarian cancer compared with a low fiber intake.[22]
2. The numerous diets currently promoted as cancer cures differ vastly and include vegan diets, vegetarianism, raw food, whole food, juicing, paleo diet, ketogenic diet, sugar-free diet, alkaline diet, etc. Some cancer diets are named after their inventor, such as Budwig, Gerson, Moerman, Kelly, Breuss, Henderson and Young.
3. The proponents of these diets often promote nebulous, unscientific notions about the nature and causes of cancer. Frequently cancer is said to be one uniform condition, while in fact it is an umbrella term for a range of diseases with different causes that require different treatments.
4. Cancer diets have in common that they lack plausibility as well as sound clinical evidence. In other words, none of these diets are effectives cures for any cancer.[23,24]

---

[21]Wang et al. (2017).
[22]Huang et al. (2018).
[23]Maisch et al. (2018).
[24]Huebner et al. (2014).

5. Some of these diets fail to supply sufficient calories and can, if followed rigorously, lead to or aggravate the malnutrition than many cancer patients suffer from. They are thus not merely ineffective but also potentially harmful.
6. The costs of following such diets can be high, at times even excessive.
7. In view of the lack of effectiveness and their considerable potential for causing harm, the risk/benefit balance of such cancer diets is clearly negative.

Plausibility	👎
Efficacy	👎
Safety	👎
Cost	👎
Risk/benefit balance	👎

11.8   Detox

(related modalities: colonic irrigation, dietary supplements, homotoxicology, naturopathy)

Detox is short for 'detoxification'. In conventional medicine, the term is used for treatments that wean drug-dependent patients off their drugs. In alternative medicine, detox has become an umbrella term for a wide range of treatments that allegedly rid our bodies of toxins. Here we only discuss the latter form of detox.

1. The belief that our body is full of toxins which threaten our good health is extremely wide-spread across all areas of alternative medicine.
2. These toxins can allegedly originate from our body's own metabolism, from the environment, from prescribed drugs, or from the food we consume.
3. Proponents of detox claim that their treatments help the body get rid of these toxins and thus restore health. In truth, they not only fail to be effective, but many are also seriously dangerous.

4. The nature of the toxins in question is rarely defined by proponents of detox. Thus, we cannot easily determine whether the treatments are successful or not in eliminating them from the body.
5. The nature of the therapies used for detox varies greatly. It would be hard to find one alternative treatment for which some proponents do not believe that it detoxes the body. Proponents also claim all sorts of health benefits of detox:

   - More energy and wellbeing
   - Stronger immunity
   - Faster fat burning
   - Fewer allergies and other conditions
   - Fewer aches and pains
   - Healthier skin, hair and nails.

6. The assumption that some toxins can accumulate in our body is, of course, correct. However, it is usually exaggerated beyond all proportions by proponents of detox.
7. The assumption that any of the alternative detox treatments effectively eliminate toxins from our body lacks sound evidence. Our body has powerful mechanism to achieve this aim on its own, and there is no good evidence that herbal, homeopathic, energetic, colonic irrigation, the Narconon programme of scientology, or other alternative treatments aid these processes. One review of the literature concluded that "the promotion of alternative detox treatments provides income for some entrepreneurs but has the potential to cause harm to patients and consumers."[25]

Plausibility	👎
Efficacy	👎
Safety	👎
Cost	👎👎
Risk/benefit balance	👎👎

---

[25]Ernst (2012b).

11.9 Energy Healing

(related modalities: distant healing, faith healing, Johrei healing, pranic healing, prayer, Qigong, Reiki, spiritual healing, Therapeutic Touch)

Energy healing is an umbrella term for a range of paranormal healing practices. Their common denominator is the belief in a mystical 'energy' that can be used for therapeutic purposes.

1. Forms of energy healing have existed in many ancient cultures. The 'New Age' movement has brought about a revival of these ideas, and today energy healing systems are amongst the most popular alternative therapies in the US as well as in many other countries. Popular forms of energy healing include those listed above. Each of these are discussed and referenced in separate chapters of this book.
2. Energy healing relies on the esoteric belief in some form of 'energy' which is distinct from the concept of energy understood in physics and refers to some life force such as chi in Traditional Chinese Medicine, or prana in Ayurvedic medicine.
3. Some proponents employ terminology from quantum physics and other 'cutting-edge' science to give their treatments a scientific flair which, upon closer scrutiny, turns out to be but a veneer of pseudo-science.
4. The 'energy' that energy healers refer to is not measurable and lacks biological plausibility.
5. Considering its implausibility, energy healing has attracted a surprisingly high level of research activity. Its findings are discussed in the respective chapters of each of the specific forms of energy healing.
6. Generally speaking, the methodologically best trials of energy healing fail to demonstrate that it generates effects beyond placebo.
7. Even though energy healing is *per se* harmless, it can do untold damage, not least because it significantly undermines rational thought in our societies.

Plausibility	👎
Efficacy	👎
Safety	👍
Cost	👎
Risk/benefit balance	👎

11.10 Halotherapy

(related modalities: none)

Halotherapy is the use of salt for medicinal purposes. There are different types of halotherapy ranging from drinking salty spring water to swimming in salt water or inhaling salt solutions. In continental Europe, these treatments are traditionally considered to be part of physical medicine. In the realm of alternative medicine, halotherapy usually means exposing the body to salty air. It is this type of halotherapy that this chapter is mainly referring to.

1. Halotherapy is by no means a new invention; in fact, in some European regions, it was already practised in the middle ages.
2. Exposing the body to salty air was traditionally achieved by sitting patients for some time in a salt mine. This tradition continues to the present day.
3. Halotherapy is said to have anti-inflammatory, draining, mucolytic, immunomodulatory, and sanogenetic actions.[26]
4. Proponents claim that this alleviates respiratory conditions such as asthma, bronchitis, smoking-related symptoms, depression, anxiety, as well as skin conditions like psoriasis, eczema and acne.
5. Halotherapy has so far not been extensively tested in clinical trials. Most of the few studies that have emerged originate from Russia and are of poor or very poor methodological quality. Their findings are thus less than reliable.
6. There is thus very little sound evidence to suggest that halotherapy is clinically effective. A pilot study testing the effects of salt inhalation in asthmatic children concluded that this might have some positive symptomatic effects.[27] A review concluded that the inclusion of halotherapy as a therapy for chronic obstructive pulmonary disease cannot be made at this point and there is a need for high quality studies to determine the effectiveness of this therapy.[28]
7. The side-effects are usually short-term and include coughing, wheezing, shortness of breath and headache.

---

[26]Khan et al. (2016).

[27]Bar-Yoseph et al. (2017).

[28]Rashleigh et al. (2014).

Plausibility	
Efficacy	
Safety	
Cost	
Risk/benefit balance	

11.11 Heilpraktiker

A Heilpraktiker (verbal translation: healing practitioner) is a practitioner of alternative medicine who has legal status in Germany. As this profession is often portrayed by proponents of alternative medicine as an ideal solution,[29] it is briefly discussed here.

1. The Heilpraktiker was created during the Third Reich. Some of the top Nazis like Hess and Himmler were very much in favour of alternative medicine. They decreed that all the many lay-practitioners of the era became recognised in law as Heilpraktiker.
2. This new profession was not allowed to train new clinicians and thus was meant become extinct within one generation. By this time, the Nazis expected that alternative medicine would have been fully integrated into conventional medicine.
3. After the war, the Heilpraktiker challenged this decree in court and won their case. Thus, the Heilpraktiker were able to continue to the present day. Currently, about 35,000 Heilpraktiker are licensed in Germany.[30]
4. The Heilpraktiker has no medical education to speak of, is nevertheless a fully recognised healthcare professional, is licensed to carry out a wide range of diagnostic and therapeutic procedures and may treat almost any type of condition or disease. A recent survey showed that Heilpraktiker commonly treat general and unspecified conditions (68%), followed by psychological illnesses (64%) and musculoskeletal complaints (53%).[31] Typically, a Heilpraktiker

---

[29]Ernst (1996).
[30]Ernst (2001).
[31]Kattge et al. (2017).

practises not one or two different alternative therapies but employs a wide range of such treatments, including acupuncture, homeopathy, herbal medicine, neural therapy, reflexology and various detox treatments, etc.

5. This situation has effectively created a two-tier system of German healthcare with medically competent doctors on one side and medically incompetent Heilpraktiker on the other. Many healthcare experts find this double standard unacceptable and want to change it for the protection of the public.[32]

6. Due to powerful lobbying, such change has so far been averted. Some German health insurances even reimburse the costs of consulting Heilpraktiker.

7. Therefore, patients remain at risk of being misdiagnosed or treated with ineffective interventions. Reports of patients coming to serious harm are being published with tragic regularity.

Plausibility	👎
Efficacy	👎
Safety	👎
Cost	👎
Risk/benefit balance	👎

11.12   Herbal Medicine (Rational)

(related modalities: dietary supplements)

When discussing herbal medicine, it is useful to differentiate between rational and traditional herbal treatments. Rational herbal medicine (sometimes also called rational phytotherapy) means the use of one herbal remedy for one defined condition, for example St John's wort for depression (traditional herbal medicine is the subject of the next chapter). Thus, rational herbal medicine is akin to conventional pharmacotherapy, except that it employs herbal extracts instead of synthetic drugs.

---

[32]https://de.wikipedia.org/wiki/Münsteraner_Kreis.

1. Many of our modern drugs were originally derived from plants. Such drugs (e. g. Aspirin, Taxol, morphine, etc.) contain one single, well-defined, extensively researched active constituent. Herbal remedies are based on entire plants and typically contain a multitude of pharmacologically active ingredients. It can thus be difficult or impossible to define which ingredient is responsible for which pharmacological activity.

2. Even though national regulations differ greatly, herbal remedies generally do not have to be supported by evidence for efficacy to be legally available. Therefore, a given remedy might or might not have been tested in clinical trials to determine whether it works for the condition advertised. In fact, only very few (less than 30) herbal remedies are supported by sound evidence for efficacy, while thousands do not meet this criterion.

3. The popular notion that herbal remedies are natural and therefore safe is little more than an advertising gimmick. As plants contain active chemicals, they might be therapeutic, but they also might be toxic (some of the most powerful poisons originate from the plant kingdom; think of hemlock, poison ivy etc.). One review, for instance, concluded that "serious adverse effects were noted only for four HMs: Herbae pulvis standardisatus, Larrea tridentate, Piper methysticum and Cassia senna. The most severe adverse effects were liver or kidney damage, colon perforation, carcinoma, coma and death. Moderately severe adverse effects were noted for 15 HMs: Pelargonium sidoides, Perna canaliculus, Aloe vera, Mentha piperita, Medicago sativa, Cimicifuga racemosa, Caulophyllum thalictroides, Serenoa repens, Taraxacum officinale, Camellia sinensis, Commifora mukul, Hoodia gordonii, Viscum album, Trifolium pratense and Stevia rebaudiana. Minor adverse effects were noted for 31 HMs: Thymus vulgaris, Lavandula angustifolia Miller, Boswellia serrata, Calendula officinalis, Harpagophytum procumbens, Panax ginseng, Vitex agnus-castus, Crataegus spp., Cinnamomum spp., Petasites hybridus, Agave americana, Hypericum perforatum, Echinacea spp., Silybum marianum, Capsicum spp., Genus phyllanthus, Ginkgo biloba, Valeriana officinalis, Hippocastanaceae, Melissa officinalis, Trigonella foenum-graecum, Lagerstroemia speciosa, Cnicus benedictus, Salvia hispanica, Vaccinium myrtillus, Mentha spicata, Rosmarinus officinalis, Crocus sativus, Gymnema sylvestre, Morinda citrifolia and Curcuma longa."[33]

4. Herbal remedies can also interact with prescribed medicines. For instance, St John's wort (one of the best-studied herbal remedies in this regard) powerfully interacts with about half of all prescription drugs—it lowers their level in the blood which means that a patient on anti-coagulants, for example, would lose her anti-coagulant protection and might suffer from a (potentially fatal) blood clot. One review concluded that "serious herb-drug interactions were

---

[33]Posadzki et al. (2013a).

noted for Hypericum perforatum and Viscum album. The most severe interactions resulted in transplant rejection, delayed emergence from anaesthesia, cardiovascular collapse, renal and liver toxicity, cardiotoxicity, bradycardia, hypovolaemic shock, inflammatory reactions with organ fibrosis and death. Moderately severe interactions were noted for Ginkgo biloba, Panax ginseng, Piper methysticum, Serenoa repens and Camellia sinensis. The most commonly interacting drugs were antiplatelet agents and anticoagulants."[34]

5. In many countries, including the US, the regulation of herbal remedies is so lax, that there is no guarantee that an herbal remedy which is being legally sold is safe. The regulators are only allowed to intervene once there are reports of adverse effects.

6. Several investigations in the US have shown that the dose of the herbal ingredient printed on the label of a commercial product can range virtually from 0–100%. Similarly, there is little safe-guard that the ingredients listed on the label correspond to the ones in the preparation. It is therefore advisable to purchase not just well-researched herbal remedies but also those marketed by trustworthy manufacturers via respectable outlets.[35]

7. There are thousands of different herbal remedies, and it is impossible to generalise across all of them. Some are well-researched, while others are not; some are efficacious, while others are not; some are safe, while others are not.[36]

Plausibility	👍
Efficacy	👍 (sideways)
Safety	👍 (sideways)
Cost	👍 (sideways)
Risk/benefit balance	👍 (sideways)

[34]Posadzki et al. (2013b).

[35]Zhang et al. (2012).

[36]Ernst (2005).

11.13   Herbal Medicine (Traditional)

(related modalities: naturopathy)

Traditional herbal medicine typically involves consulting herbal practitioner. Herbalists come in numerous guises depending what tradition they belong to: Chinese herbalists, traditional European herbalists, Ayurvedic practitioners, Kampo practitioners etc. Their treatments are fundamentally different from the rational herbal medicine, the topic discussed in the previous chapter (Fig. 11.2).

1. Traditional herbal therapy is by far the most common form of herbal medicine. Herbalists, who often have no medical training to speak of, claim to be able to treat most medical conditions without referring their patients to practitioners of conventional medicine.[37]
2. Herbalists frequently employ their very own diagnostic methods (e. g. 'tongue and pulse diagnoses' used by Chinese herbalists) and are normally neither trained nor qualified to use conventional diagnostic methods. The traditional diagnostic techniques of herbalists have either not been validated at all or they have been tested and found to be not valid.
3. Herbalists usually do not recognise conventional disease categories. Instead, they arrive at a diagnosis according to their specific philosophies which have no basis in reality (for instance, Taoism in traditional Chinese herbalism).
4. Herbalists individualise their treatments, meaning that 10 patients suffering from depression, for instance, might receive 10 different, tailor-made herbal mixtures according to their individual characteristics; and none of the 10 patients might receive St John's wort, the only herbal remedy proven to work for depression. Typically, such prescriptions contain not one herbal ingredient, but are complex mixtures of many—up to 10 to 20—herbs or herbal extracts.
5. Even though the efficacy of the individualised herbal approach can be tested in rigorous trials, and even though about a dozen such studies is available today, there is currently no good evidence to show that it is effective. The only systematic review of such studies concluded that there is no convincing evidence to support the use of individualised herbal medicine in any indication.[38]
6. The risk of harm through individualised herbal mixtures can be considerable: the more ingredients, the higher the likelihood that one of them has toxic effects, or that one interacts with a prescription drug taken concurrently.
7. Essentially, this means that there is no good evidence that individualised herbal treatments as used by herbal practitioners across the globe generate more good than harm.

---

[37]Fisher et al. (2008).
[38]Guo et al. (2007).

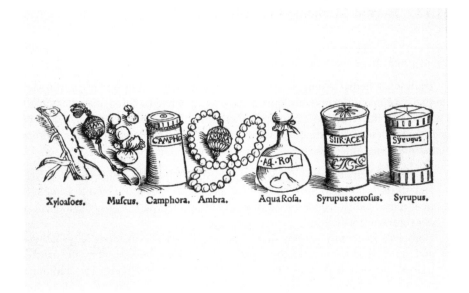

Fig. 11.2 Early depiction of herbal medicine

Plausibility	👎
Efficacy	👎
Safety	👎
Cost	👎
Risk/benefit balance	👎

11.14   Holistic Dentistry

(related modalities: integrative medicine)

Holistic or biological dentistry is not a well-defined term. Holistic dentists say they want to look after their patients' total well-being by integrating various alternative therapies into their routine care. In the USA, there is a Holistic Dental Association, while in the UK, holistic dentists might be members of the British Society for Mercury-free Dentistry, the British Society of Dental Acupuncture or the British Homeopathic Dental Association.

1. Holistic dentistry is popular in many countries. One survey from Germany concluded that alternative treatments are recommended by German dentists and requested by their patients, but the scientific evidence for these treatments are often low or unclear.[39] Holistic dentistry is not a specialty of the dental profession; according to its proponents, it is a philosophy of practice.
2. The type of alternative therapies holistic dentists employ varies greatly. Examples include acupuncture, homeopathy (e. g. homeopathic arnica after operative procedures), nutritional advice, dietary supplements, hypnotherapy.
3. Holistic dentists tend to be more concerned about amalgam fillings than their conventional colleagues and often recommend removing them (an exercise which demonstrably increases blood mercury levels).
4. Many of them also are against the fluoridisation of our drinking water claiming that this is poisonous.
5. Holistic dentists also tend to be critical of the routine use of systemic antibiotics.
6. Holistic dentists frequently make specific therapeutic claims; for instance, the British Society of Dental Acupuncture claim on their website[40] that the typical conditions that may be helped by a dentist using acupuncture are:

- TMJ (jaw joint) problems
- Facial pain
- Muscle spasm in the head and neck
- Stress headaches and Migraine
- Rhinitis and sinusitis
- Gagging
- Dry mouth problems
- Post-operative pain
- Dental anxiety.

Similarly, the British Homeopathic Dental Association claim on their website[41] that studies have shown that the use of homeopathy improves bone healing around implants and reduces healing time with ulcers.

7. Most of the statements and claims made by holistic dentists are either nonsensical, or not based on sound evidence, or both, and can be easily disclosed as marketing gimmicks aimed at increasing the cash-flow of the dentist.

---

[39]Baatsch et al. (2017).

[40]http://www.dental-acupuncture.org/how-can-acupuncture-help/.

[41]http://www.bhda.co.uk/.

Plausibility	👎
Efficacy	👎
Safety	👎
Cost	👎
Risk/benefit balance	👎

11.15   Holistic Medicine

(related modalities: integrative medicine)

Holistic medicine is healthcare of the whole person, considering mental and social factors, rather than just the physical symptoms of a disease.

1. Holism is a label that many alternative practitioners like to attribute to themselves. They tend to use it for distancing themselves from the alleged reductionism of modern biomedicine.[42]
2. Yet, all good clinical medicine is and always has been holistic. Micheal Baum and many other observers have pointed out that true "holism in medicine is an open-ended and exquisitely complex understanding of human biology that over time has led to spectacular improvements in the length and quality of life of patients with cancer and that this approach encourages us to consider the transcendental as much as the cell and molecular biology of the human organism. 'Alternative' versions of holism are arid and closed belief systems, locked in a time warp, incapable of making progress yet quick to deny it in the field of scientific medicine."[43]
3. Proponents of alternative medicine frequently pretend or imply to be the only clinicians who practice holistically.
4. This notion has created a most effective straw man whereby conventional medicine is attacked for not being holistic or even inhuman.[44]

---

[42]Givati (2015).
[43]Baum (2010).
[44]Barrett et al. (2003).

5. The typical alternative approach to holism tends to consist of a series of bogus alternative treatments some of which may be directly harmful, while others are just useless but nevertheless detrimental because they replace effective therapies that would alleviate patients' suffering.
6. It has been pointed out that *not every aspect of alternative medicine can be seen as holistic*.[45] Some of the modalities discussed in this book are amongst the least holistic in all healthcare; examples include

   - Colonic irrigation
   - Dowsing
   - Ear candles
   - Iridology
   - Neural therapy
   - Reflexology.

7. Holistic medicine therefore turns out to be a concept that is valuable in every respect. However, it is not a concept of alternative medicine but one of all healthcare.

Plausibility	
Efficacy	
Safety	
Cost	
Risk/benefit balance	

11.16   Integrative Medicine

(related modalities: holistic dentistry)

Integrative (or integrated) medicine (or healthcare) is the attempt to add alternative therapies to the treatments used in routine care. Even though integrative

---

[45]Saks (1997).

medicine has become popular and politically correct term, there is much to criticise about its assumptions and practice.

1. According to its proponents, integrated medicine (IM) is based mainly on two concepts. The first is that of "whole person care", and the second is often called "the best of both worlds".

2. The principle of the "best" of the world of alternative medicine combined with the "best" of conventional healthcare seems commendable at first glance but, at closer inspection, serious doubts emerge.[46,47]

3. Best should signify "the most effective" or more precisely "being associated with the most convincingly positive risk/benefit balance". If we understand "the best of both worlds" in this way, the concept becomes synonymous with the concept of evidence-based medicine (EBM; according to the principles of EBM, treatments must be shown to be safe as well as effective. When treating their patients, doctors should, according to EBM-principles, combine the best external evidence with their own experience as well as with the preferences of their patients).

4. If "the best of both worlds" is synonymous with EBM, we don't need this confusing duplicity of concepts; it would only distract from the auspicious efforts of EBM to continuously improve healthcare.

5. As to the principle of "whole person care", it should be stressed that all good medicine is, was, and always will be holistic: today's GPs, for instance, should care for their patients as whole individuals dealing the best they can with physical problems as well as social and spiritual issues. If some doctors neglect the holistic aspect of care, they are, by definition, not good doctors. And, if the deficit is wide-spread, we should reform conventional healthcare. But delegating holism to practitioners of integrative medicine would be tantamount to abandoning an essential element of good healthcare.

6. It follows that the promotion of IM under the banner of holism makes no sense. Either it is superfluous because it misleads patients into believing holism is an exclusive feature of integrative medicine, while, in fact, it is a hallmark of any good healthcare. Or, if holism is neglected or absent in conventional medicine, it detracts us from the important task to remedy this deficit.

7. In practice, integrative medicine is often synonymous with the use of unproven or disproven treatments in clinical routine.[48] This cannot be in the best interest of the patient.

---

[46]Ernst (2016).

[47]Maizes et al. (2009).

[48]Ernst (2012b).

Plausibility	
Efficacy	
Safety	
Cost	
Risk/benefit balance	

11.17   Kampo

(related modalities: herbal medicine, Traditional Chinese Medicine)

Kampo (or Kampo medicine) is the Japanese form of traditional herbal medicine that is still very popular in Japan. Kampo means 'Chinese style' in Japanese (Fig. 11.3).

1. Kampo developed out of traditional Chinese herbal medicine after it was introduced into Japan in the 7th century. In the early 20th century, Kampo was further influenced by modern Western medicine and science.
2. The Kampo system is a pragmatic and simplified version of Chinese herbal medicine. Kampo medicines are standardised and not individualised as in Chinese herbal medicine. They are based on the current symptoms of the patient, interpreted in the philosophy of Kampo. Kampo diagnostics consider hypofunction and hyperfunction, heat and cold, superficies and interior, and yin and yang.
3. Today, Kampō is fully integrated into the Japanese national health care system, and numerous Kampo preparations are registered in Japan and reimbursable from public funds.
4. These standardised formulas contain mixtures of herbal ingredients. They are manufactured under proper quality control. The most commonly used plants include liquorice, ginger and Chinese peony root.
5. Most Japanese doctors routinely prescribe Kampo medicines, and most patients combine Kampo with Western medicine. Since 2002, the teaching of Kampo has been included in Japanese curricula of medical and pharmacy education.

Fig. 11.3 Early 19th century
textbook of Kampo Medicine.
Source US National Library
of Medicine

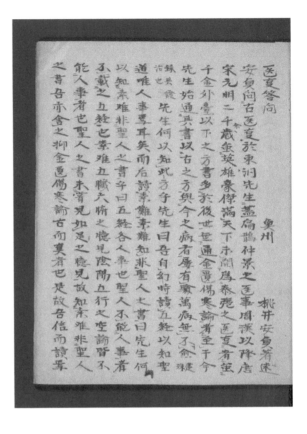

6. The efficacy of Kampo medicines is often less solidly documented than one
   would hope or expect. There is a remarkable shortage of high-quality clinical
   trials.[49]
7. As Kampo medicines contain pharmacologically active ingredients, they can
   also cause adverse effects and might interact with synthetic drugs. Yet, the risks
   of Kampo are currently woefully under-investigated.[50,51]

---

[49]Motoo et al. (2014).

[50]Ikegami et al. (2003).

[51]Borchers et al. (2000).

Plausibility	👍
Efficacy[a]	
Safety[a]	
Cost[a]	
Risk/benefit balance[a]	

[a]Depends on the nature of the specific preparation

11.18 Kneipp Therapy

Kneipp therapy is the umbrella term for an array of naturopathic treatments popularised in Germany by father Kneipp about 150 years ago.

1. Sebastian Kneipp (1821–1897) was a Bavarian priest; he is considered to be one of the forefathers of German naturopathy and provides an important link between the European nature cure movement of the 19th century and American naturopathy.[52]
2. Kneipp promoted various types of water cures, exercise, herbal treatments, nutrition and 'mental hygiene' to strengthen the body's health and resistance. He is credited with introducing a more holistic view into the healthcare of his time which included mental, social, and spiritual aspects.
3. The central element in Kneipp's regimen is the application of water. Based on the concepts of Preissnitz, Kneipp developed a range of treatments (pourning, wrapings, compresses, rinsing off, total-baths and partial-baths) using cold and hot water. Most of these treatments are suitable for self-treatment.
4. As a young man, Kneipp had allegedly cured his own tuberculosis with the help of such treatments. Later he authored several popular books about his methods and experiences.
5. As a catholic priest, Kneipp believed that the most effective remedies against diseases are those naturally provided by God.

---

[52]Locher and Pforr (2014).

6. Kneipp cures became (and still are) very popular in Germany. Even today, entire spa towns live on Kneipp's ideas and reputation. A firm marketing a wide range of natural Kneipp products has grown into a thriving business. Today, there are 600 organizations that are a part of Kneipp Worldwide, and there are approximately 1000 members of the International Society of Kneipp Physicians.
7. While many of Kneipp's concepts seem to make some common sense, there are hardly any clinical trials to demonstrate that the Kneipp cure is clinically effective in the treatment or prevention of any condition.[53,54,55]

Plausibility	
Efficacy	
Safety	
Cost	
Risk/benefit balance	

11.19 Mind-Body Therapies

(related modalities: autogenic training, imagery, laughter therapy, mindfulness, progressive muscle relaxation, relaxation therapy, transcendental meditation, yoga)

Mind-body therapies include a range of treatments that claim to exert a positive influence on health via the mind. This category includes several therapies discussed in separate chapters as listed above (Fig. 11.4).

1. Some proponents of mind-body therapies seem to suggest that, conventional clinicians are unaware that the mind can influence they and claim that they adhere to the long obsolete division between the mind and the body.

---

[53]Schencking et al. (2013).

[54]Diehm and Diehm (2002).

[55]Doering et al. (2001).

Fig. 11.4 Julia Anderson Root, from her 1886 book entitled 'Healing power of mind. A treatise of mind cure'. *Source* US National Library of Medicine

2. The mind, emotions and attention play important roles in the experience of many symptoms, for instance, pain. Conventional medicine does not only account for this fact but also exploits it in numerous ways.
3. Most mind-body therapies are supposed to induce a degree of relaxation which, in turn, can lead to a reduction of symptoms. One review, for instance, suggested that "mind-body therapies deal with common experiences that cause distress around cancer diagnosis, treatment, and survivorship including loss of control, uncertainty about the future, fears of recurrence, and a range of physical and psychological symptoms including depression, anxiety, insomnia, and fatigue."[56]
4. Mind-body therapies are usually not curative but symptomatic treatments.
5. Thus, they are rarely used as sole therapies but employed in conjunction with further treatments which often makes it difficult or impossible to know their relative contribution to the clinical outcome.

---

[56]Carlson (2017).

6. Most mind-body therapies can be delivered to groups of patients which, for a range of reasons, can be preferable to individual therapy.
7. For several mind-body therapies, the evidence is encouraging but rarely compelling. This is usually due to

- a paucity of studies,
- the methodological problems encountered when conducting such clinical trials,
- the low quality of the existing trials,
- and the lack of research funds in this area.

Plausibility	👎
Efficacy	👎
Safety	👍
Cost	👍
Risk/benefit balance	👎

11.20   Naturopathy

(related modalities: detox, herbal medicine, massage)

Naturopathy can be defined as an eclectic system of health care that uses elements of alternative and conventional medicine to support and enhance self-healing processes. Naturopaths employ treatments based on therapeutic options that are thought of as natural, e. g. naturally occurring substances such as herbs, as well as water, exercise, diet, fresh air, pressure, heat and cold—but occasionally also acupuncture, homeopathy and manual therapies.

1. In many countries, naturopathy is not a protected title; this means your naturopaths may have some training, but this might not be obligatory. Medical doctors can, of course, also practice naturopathy. Some countries allow the titles 'doctors of naturopathy' or 'naturopathic physicians'; these practitioners tend to

see themselves as primary care physicians even though they have not been to medical school.[57,58]

2. Naturopathy is steeped in the obsolete concept of vitalism which is the belief that living organisms are fundamentally different from non-living entities because they contain some non-physical element or are governed by different principles than are inanimate things. Naturopaths claim that they are "guided by a unique set of principles that recognize the body's innate healing capacity, emphasize disease prevention, and encourage individual responsibility to obtain optimal health."[59]

3. Naturopathic treatment modalities include diet and clinical nutrition, behavioral change, hydrotherapy, homeopathy, botanical medicine, physical medicine, pharmaceuticals, and minor surgery.[60] There is some evidence to suggest that some of the treatments used by naturopaths are effective (for instance, herbal medicine or relaxation; these are discussed in separate chapters of this book) for treating some conditions. This is, however, not the case for all the treatments in question (for instance detox or applied kinesiology; these are also discussed in separate chapters of this book). There is little good evidence to suggest that naturopathy as a whole is effective, a fact which led to the discontinuation of its reimbursement in countries such as Australia.[61]

4. Naturopathy is implicitly based on the assumption that natural means safe. This notion is demonstrably wrong and misleading: not all the treatments used by naturopaths are natural, and hardly any are totally free of risks.

5. Many naturopaths advise their patients against conventional treatments such as vaccines and thus endanger public health.

6. Naturopaths tend to believe they can cure or at least alleviate the symptoms of all diseases. Consequently, many of the therapeutic claims for naturopathy found on the Internet and elsewhere are dangerously over-stated.

7. The direct risks of naturopathy depend, of course, on the therapy in question; some of the risks are considerable. One critic of naturopaths concluded that "an examination of their literature … reveals that it is replete with pseudoscientific, ineffective, unethical, and potentially dangerous practices."[62]

---

[57]Smith and Logan (2002).

[58]Atwood (2003).

[59]Fleming and Gutknecht (2010).

[60]Smith and Logan (2002).

[61]Ooi et al. (2018).

[62]Atwood (2003).

Plausibility	
Efficacy	
Safety	
Cost	
Risk/benefit balance	

11.21   New German Medicine

(related modalities: alternative cancer cures, naturopathy)

New German Medicine (GNM) is the creation of Ryke Geerd Hamer (1935–2017), a German doctor. The name is reminiscent of the 'Neue Deutsche Heilkunde' created by the Nazis during the Third Reich.[63]

1. Hamer received his medical licence in 1963 but was later struck off because of malpractice. He then continued his practice as a 'Heilpraktiker' (see there).
2. According to proponents, "GNM Therapy is a spoken therapy based on the findings and research of the Germanic New Medicine of Dr.Hamer. On the understanding that every disease is triggered by an isolating and shocking event, GNM Therapy assists in finding the DHS (shocking moment) in our lives that preceded the dis-ease and in turn allowing our bodies to complete its natural healing cycle back to full health."[64]
3. Hamer believed to have discovered the '5 laws of nature':

   - The Iron Rule of Cancer
   - The two-phased development of disease
   - Ontogenetic system of tumours and cancer equivalent diseases
   - Ontogenetic system of microbes
   - Natures biological meaning of a disease.

4. Hamer also postulated that:

   - All diseases are caused by psychological conflicts.

---

[63]Ernst (2001).

[64]http://www.gnmtherapy.co.uk/about-the-gnm/.

- Conventional medicine is a conspiracy of Jews to decimate the non-Jewish population.
- Microbes do not cause diseases.
- AIDS is just an allergy.
- Cancer is the result of a mental shock.

5. None of Hamer's 'discoveries' and assumptions are plausible or based on facts.
6. There is no sound evidence that GNM is effective for any condition.
7. Several deaths have been associated with Hamer's approach. e.g.[65]

Plausibility	👎
Efficacy	👎
Safety	👎
Cost	👎
Risk/benefit balance	👎

11.22 Orthomolecular Medicine

(related modalities: dietary supplements)

Orthomolecular medicine is the term for a form of mega-vitamin therapy coined in the 1960s by Linus Pauling (1901–1994).[66]

1. Pauling had two Nobel prizes to his name and was once called "one of the 20 greatest scientists of all time."[67]
2. In 1968, he published a paper stating that "the functioning of the brain is affected by the molecular concentrations of many substances that are normally

---

[65]https://derstandard.at/2000043742380/18-Jaehrige-starbEltern-verweigerten-krebskranker-Tochter-Therapie.

[66]Weiss (2017).

[67]https://en.wikipedia.org/wiki/Linus_Pauling.

present in the brain. The optimum concentrations of these substances for a person may differ greatly from the concentrations provided by his normal diet and genetic machinery. Biochemical and genetic arguments support the idea that orthomolecular therapy, the provision for the individual person of the optimum concentrations of important normal constituents of the brain, may be the preferred treatment for many mentally ill patients."[68] It was the start of his (and the world's) obsession with mega-doses of vitamins.

3. Orthomolecular medicine assumes that an optimum nutritional environment in the body is a precondition for good health and suggests that diseases reflect nutritional deficiencies.

4. Treatment for disease, according to this view, involves the correction of imbalances or deficiencies based on individual biochemistry by use of high doses of vitamins, minerals, amino acids, trace elements and fatty acids.

5. The assumptions of orthomolecular medicine lack biological plausibility.

6. Although there are some encouraging reviews e.g.[69] no compelling evidence exists that orthomolecular treatments are clinically effective for patients who do not suffer from nutritional deficiencies.

7. Pauling's foray into alternative medicine is a telling example how even the smartest people can get it wrong when they leave their area of expertise.

Plausibility	👎
Efficacy	👎
Safety	👎
Cost	👎
Risk/benefit balance	👎

---

[68]Pauling (1968).
[69]Janson (2006).

11.23   Ozone Therapy

(related modalities: alternative cancer cures, holistic dentistry)

Ozone therapy is the use of ozone for medicinal purposes. Ozone is a toxic gas that can be used at high concentrations to sterilise equipment or external wounds.[70] These conventional methods of employing ozone are excluded from the discussion below.

1. Ozone (O_3) is a gas with three atoms of oxygen (O) linked in a cyclic structure. It is a by-product of water purification, bleaching and any process generating a spark or electric arc in the presence of oxygen. It is also found in the atmosphere, with higher altitudes containing higher levels of ozone.
2. In alternative medicine, ozone is advocated for several serious conditions, including AIDS, cancer and multiple sclerosis as well as less serious problems such as musculoskeletal disorders. A systematic review found that "the use of ozone therapy in musculoskeletal diseases is based on poor quality studies. Currently, data supporting an adequate risk/benefit ratio for ozone therapy in rheumatic diseases is lacking."[71]
3. In dentistry, ozone therapy is sometimes used to treat caries. A systematic review concluded that "the clinical evidence for the use of ozone in treatment of caries is not compelling."[72]
4. Another form of ozone therapy involves taking a sample of blood from a patient's vein, saturating it with ozone, and then re-injecting it into the patient's vein.
5. There is no good evidence to suggest that ozone therapy is effective for cancer[73] or any other condition.
6. The risks of ozone therapy are usually played down by its proponents. Yet, numerous reports of serious complications, including hepatitis and several fatalities have been reported.
7. Unless positive evidence emerges, the risk/benefit balance of ozone therapy for any condition fails to be positive.

---

[70]Fitzpatrick et al. (2018).
[71]Carmona (2006).
[72]Burke (2012).
[73]Clavo et al. (2018).

Plausibility	👎
Efficacy	👎
Safety	👎
Cost	👎
Risk/benefit balance	👎

11.24   Placebo

(related modalities: none)

A placebo is a treatment that does *per se* not have any health effects, but generates effects because of the context in which it is administered. One of the many formal definitions of a placebo is 'a medicine or procedure prescribed for the psychological benefit to the patient rather than for any physiological effect'.

1. In clinical research, placebos are often given to patients in the control group of a clinical trial. Put simply, this allows the investigators to tell what proportion of the outcome is due to the specific effect of the treatment tested and what part of the outcome is due to the placebo effect.
2. In clinical routine, the placebo effect is a phenomenon that accompanies every treatment of a conscious patient. In other words, it is part of nearly every response to any therapy, and we do not need to administer a placebo for a patient to benefit from a placebo response.[74]
3. For clinicians, it is not possible to tell how much of a patient's response to a treatment was due to the prescribed therapy *per se* and how much of it was caused by a placebo effect.
4. The placebo effect operates mostly via unconscious conditioning of the patient —much like classical conditioning of Pavlov's dogs—and via conscious expectation of the patient and the clinician.[75]

---

[74]Ernst (2007).
[75]Ernst (2007).

5. Many alternative therapies seem to rely mostly or entirely on the placebo effect. Some enthusiasts argue that this is fine: it does not matter how a therapy works; even if it works via a placebo effect, it is bound to help a patient. Thus, they believe, even an ineffective (not better than a placebo) therapy has its legitimate place in healthcare. Yet, this view is questionable, not least because (as pointed out above) even effective treatments generate a placebo effect in addition to their specific effect. This means that only generating a placebo response by administering an ineffective alternative therapy cannot be in the best interest of the patient.

6. Placebo effects are just one of several non-specific or context effects. Other phenomena that are often erroneously subsumed under the placebo umbrella are, for instance, the natural history of the condition (the fact that most conditions get better over time, even without any intervention) and the regression towards the mean (the phenomenon that extreme values tend to return to the average).[76]

7. Placebo effects are usually beneficial, but they can also have unwanted consequences; these are called nocebo effects and refer, for instance, to adverse effects of drugs which a patient might experience while receiving a placebo and assuming it is the active drug.

Plausibility	👍
Efficacy	👎
Safety	👍
Cost	👎
Risk/benefit balance	👎

11.25 Slimming Aids

Slimming aids are treatments promoted for the purpose of losing body weight. These therapies are heavily advertised, for instance, via the Internet, and often promoted by celebrities.

---

[76]Ernst and Resch (1995).

1. Obesity has long been recognised as a serious health problem. It has now reached epidemic proportions, and many entrepreneurs are currently trying to exploit the wish of many consumers to lose weight by marketing bogus treatments for body weight reduction. The market for such treatments has grown rapidly and slimming aids are now a multi-billion business.
2. Numerous alternative therapies are claimed to be effective and safe for body weight reduction.
3. Many clinical trials have become available. Their quality is often poor, and their results are usually unconvincing.
4. Several systematic reviews have summarised this evidence for specific slimming aids such as guar gum, ephedra, phaseolus vulgaris, supplements containing conjugated linoleic acid, green tea, garcinia extracts, calcium supplements, chromium, and chitosan.
5. One overview of systematic reviews concluded "that the existing systematic reviews of clinical trials testing the efficacy of food supplements in reducing body weight fail to provide good evidence that any of these preparations generate clinically relevant weight loss without undue risks."[77]
6. Many alternative slimming aids are associated with side-effects which, in some cases, are serious and can even include death.[78]
7. Another risk of such slimming aids is adulteration with effective but potentially harmful medicines. One investigation from the US concluded that "the FDA has taken action to remove some weight loss supplements from the market that contain banned ingredients. Unfortunately, based on the findings of this study, it is evident that products containing these ingredients remain on the market today."[79]

Plausibility	
Efficacy	
Safety	
Cost	
Risk/benefit balance	

---

[77]Onakpoya et al. (2011).

[78]Pittler et al. (2005).

[79]Eichner et al. (2016).

11.26 Traditional Chinese Medicine

(related modalities: acupressure, acupuncture, biopuncture, gua sha, Chinese herbal medicine, Kampo, macrobiotic diet, pulse diagnosis, qigong, shiatsu, tai chi, tongue diagnosis, tui na)

Traditional Chinese Medicine (TCM) is the umbrella term for modalities historically used in ancient China (Fig. 11.5)

1. TCM is a construct of Mao Zedong who lumped all historical Chinese treatments together under this umbrella and created the 'barefoot doctor' to practice TCM nationwide—not because he believed in TCM, but because China was desperately short of real doctors and needed at least a semblance of healthcare.
2. TCM includes many therapeutic and some diagnostic modalities most of which are discussed in separate chapters of this book.
3. TCM has become hugely popular in the West; it is estimated that, in the US, some 10,000 TCM-practitioners serve more than one million patients each year. As such, TCM is financially and ideologically a very important export item for China.
4. Even though, the modalities differ in many respects, they are claimed to have in common that they are based on assumptions which originate from Taoist philosophy:

Fig. 11.5 Traditional Chinese Medicine, very much supported by Mao and his successors. *Source* US National Library of Medicine

- The human body is a miniature version of the universe.
- Harmony between the two opposing forces, yin and yang, means health.
- Disease is caused by an imbalance between these forces.
- Five elements—fire, earth, wood, metal, and water—symbolize all phenomena, including the stages of human life, and explain the functioning of the body and how it changes during disease.
- The vital energy, qi or chi, flows through the body in meridians, is essential for maintaining health.

5. These assumptions are from a pre-scientific era and are not in keeping with the known facts about physiology, anatomy etc. In other words, they are not plausible.
6. The effectiveness and safety of TCM cannot be evaluated globally, but each modality must be assessed on its own specific merits.
7. Advances in TCM can, according to one team of sympathetic authors, be characterised into three phases: "Phase I (1950s–1970s) was fundamental for developing TCM higher education, research and hospital networks in China; Phase II (1980s–2000s) was critical for developing legal, economic and scientific foundations and international networks for TCM; and Phase III (2011 onwards) is concentrating on consolidating the scientific basis and clinical practice of TCM through interdisciplinary, interregional and intersectoral collaborations."[80] One prominent critic of TCM, however, rightly cautioned: "TCM is a pre-scientific superstitious view of biology and illness, similar to the humoral theory of Galen, or the notions of any pre-scientific culture. It is strange and unscientific to treat TCM as anything else. Any individual diagnostic or treatment method within TCM should be evaluated according to standard principles of science and science-based medicine, and not given special treatment."[81]

Plausibility	👎
Efficacy	👎
Safety	👎
Cost	👎
Risk/benefit balance	👎

---

[80]Xu et al. (2013).

[81]https://sciencebasedmedicine.org/what-is-traditional-chinese-medicine/.

11.27 Unani

(related modalities: Ayurvedic medicine, herbal medicine, massage)

Unani (or Yunani) is an Islamic healing philosophy that combines elements of ancient Greek medicine with those of Ayurvedic medicine. In the course of the current boom in alternative medicine, Unani has become popular also in the West.[82]

1. Unani means "Greek" in Arabic. Ancient Greek medicine was based on the erroneous concept of four elements: earth, fire, water, air, corresponding to four humours: Phlegm (balgham), Blood (dam), Yellow bile (safra) and Black bile (sauda).
2. Unani is popular in the Middle East, India, Pakistan and their neighbouring countries.
3. It is based mainly on Ibn Sina's The Canon of Medicine from the 11th century. Ibn Sina (or Avicenna) is regarded as one of the most significant physicians, astronomers, thinkers and writers of the Islamic Golden Age.
4. According to proponents of Unani, "the health of the human body is maintained by the harmonious arrangement of al-umoor al-tabiyah, the seven basic physiological principles of the Unani doctrine. These principles include (1) arkan, or elements, (2) mizaj, or temperament, (3) akhlat, or bodily humours, (4) aaza, or organs and systems, (5) arwah, or vital spirit, (6) quwa, or faculties or powers, and (7) afaal, or functions. Interacting with each other, these seven natural components maintain the balance in the natural constitution of the human body. Each individual's constitution has a self-regulating capacity or power, called tabiyat (or mudabbira-e-badan; vis medicatrix naturae in Latin), or to keep the seven components in equilibrium."[83]
5. Unani treatments can consist of diet, massage, exercise, blood-letting, leeching, and medication.
6. There are very few rigorous clinical trials of Unani. Their results vary and depend on the modality tested. e.g.[84,85]
7. Unani remedies can include substances or products, including herbs, minerals, that are not safe for human consumption.[86] The risks may therefore be considerable.

---

[82]Poulakou-Rebelakou et al. (2015).

[83]https://www.britannica.com/science/Unani-medicine.

[84]Khanna et al. (2018).

[85]Ali et al. (2015).

[86]Gogtay et al. (2002).

Plausibility	
Efficacy	
Safety	
Cost	
Risk/benefit balance	

11.28   Yoga

(related modalities: Ayurvedic medicine, mind-body therapies)

Yoga is a system of healing that originates from ancient India. Today, it has become popular across the globe. Many different types of yoga can be differentiated.

1. Yoga has been defined in several different ways in the various Indian philosophical and religious traditions.
2. From the perspective of alternative medicine, it is a practice of gentle stretching exercises, breathing control, meditation and life-styles.
3. The aim is to strengthen prana, the vital force as understood in traditional Indian medicine. Thus, it is claimed to be helpful for most conditions affecting mankind.
4. Most people who practice yoga in the West practise 'Hatha yoga', which includes postural exercises (asanas), breath control (pranayama) and meditation (dhyana). It is claimed that these techniques bring an individual to a state of perfect health, stillness and heightened awareness.
5. Other alleged benefits of regular yoga practice include suppleness, muscular strength, feelings of well-being, reduction of sympathetic drive, pain control and longevity. Yogic breathing exercises are said to reduce muscular spasms, expand available lung capacity and thus alleviate the symptoms of asthma and other respiratory conditions.
6. There have been numerous clinical trials of various yoga techniques. They tend to suffer from poor study design and incomplete reporting. Their results are therefore no always reliable. Several systematic reviews have summarised the findings of these studies. An overview included 21 systematic reviews relating to a wide range of conditions. Nine systematic reviews arrived at positive

conclusions, but many were associated with a high risk of bias. Unanimously positive evidence emerged only for depression and cardiovascular risk reduction.[87]

7. Yoga is generally considered to be safe. However, the only large-scale survey specifically addressing the question of adverse effects found that "approximately 30% of yoga class attendees had experienced some type of adverse event. Although the majority had mild symptoms, the survey results indicated that attendees with chronic diseases were more likely to experience adverse events associated with their disease. Therefore, special attention is necessary when yoga is introduced to patients with stress-related, chronic diseases."[88] The warning by the Vatican's chief exorcist that yoga leads to 'demonic possession'[89] might not be taken too seriously by yoga fans.

Plausibility	👎
Efficacy	👍
Safety	👎
Cost	👍
Risk/benefit balance	👎

References

Ali A, Mohiuddin E, Shahabuddin Hannan A, Shah SM, Usmanghani K (2015) Clinical evaluation of unani ear drops herbotic for earache. Pak J Pharm Sci 28(6 Suppl):2243–2248

Atwood KC 4th (2003) Naturopathy: a critical appraisal. MedGenMed 5(4):39

Austin G (2013) Buteyko technique use to control asthma symptoms. Nurs Times. 109(16):16–17

Baatsch B, Zimmer S, Rodrigues Recchia D, Büssing A (2017) Complementary and alternative therapies in dentistry and characteristics of dentists who recommend them. Complement Ther Med 35:64–69

---

[87]Ernst and Lee (2010).

[88]Matsushita and Oka (2015).

[89]https://www.social-consciousness.com/2017/06/vaticans-chief-exorcist-warns-that-yoga-causes-demonic-possession.html.

Bannuru RR, Osani MC, Al-Eid F, Wang C (2018) Efficacy of curcumin and Boswellia for knee
    osteoarthritis: systematic review and meta-analysis. Semin Arthritis Rheum 48(3):416–429
Barrett B, Marchand L, Scheder J, Plane MB, Maberry R, Appelbaum D, Rakel D, Rabago D
    (2003) Themes of holism, empowerment, access, and legitimacy define complementary,
    alternative, and integrative medicine in relation to conventional biomedicine. J Altern
    Complement Med 9(6):937–947
Bar-Yoseph R, Kugelman N, Livnat G, Gur M, Hakim F, Nir V, Bentur L (2017) Halotherapy as
    asthma treatment in children: a randomized, controlled, prospective pilot study. Pediatr
    Pulmonol. 52(5):580–587
Baum M (2010) Concepts of holism in orthodox and alternative medicine. Clin Med (Lond) 10
    (1):37–40
Borchers AT, Sakai S, Henderson GL, Harkey MR, Keen CL, Stern JS, Terasawa K,
    Gershwin ME (2000) Shosaiko-to and other Kampo (Japanese herbal) medicines: a review
    of their immunomodulatory activities. J Ethnopharmacol 73(1–2):1–13
Burke FJ (2012) Ozone and caries: a review of the literature. Dent Update 39(4):271–272, 275–
    278
Carlson LE (2017) Distress management through mind-body therapies in oncology. J Natl Cancer
    Inst Monogr 2017(52)
Carmona L (2006) Ozone therapy in rheumatic diseases: a systematic review. Reumatol Clin 2
    (3):119–123
Cherniack EP, Govorushko S (2018) To bee or not to bee: the potential efficacy and safety of bee
    venom acupuncture in humans. Toxicon 154:74–78
Clavo B, Santana-Rodríguez N, Llontop P, Gutiérrez D, Suárez G, López L, Rovira G,
    Martínez-Sánchez G, González E, Jorge IJ, Perera C, Blanco J, Rodríguez-Esparragón F (2018)
    Ozone therapy as adjuvant for cancer treatment: is further research warranted? Evid Based
    Complement Altern Med 2018:7931849
Coon JT, Ernst E (2004) Andrographis paniculata in the treatment of upper respiratory tract
    infections: a systematic review of safety and efficacy. Planta Med 70(4):293–298
Cooper S, Oborne J, Newton S, Harrison V, Thompson Coon J, Lewis S, Tattersfield A (2003)
    Effect of two breathing exercises (Buteyko and pranayama) in asthma: a randomised controlled
    trial. Thorax. 58(8):674–679
Diehm C, Diehm N (2002) Kneipp hydrotherapy, sclerotherapy, crossectomy. What really helps in
    varicose veins and spider veins? MMW Fortschr Med 144(35–36):22–27
Doering TJ, Thiel J, Steuernagel B, Johannes B, Konitzer M, Niederstadt C, Schneider B,
    Fischer GC (2001) Changes of cognitive brain functions in the elderly by Kneipp therapy.
    Forsch Komplementarmed Klass Naturheilkd 8(2):80–84
Eichner S, Maguire M, Shea LA, Fete MG (2016) Banned and discouraged-use ingredients found
    in weight loss supplements. J Am Pharm Assoc 56(5):538–543
Ernst E (1996) Towards quality in complementary health care: is the German "Heilpraktiker" a
    model for complementary practitioners? Int J Qual Health Care. 8(2):187–190
Ernst E (2001) 'Neue Deutsche Heilkunde': complementary/alternative medicine in the Third
    Reich. Complement Ther Med 9(1):49–51
Ernst E (2002) Heavy metals in traditional Indian remedies. Eur J Clin Pharmacol 57(12):891–896
Ernst E (2005) The efficacy of herbal medicine–an overview. Fundam Clin Pharmacol 19(4):405–
    409
Ernst E (2007) Placebo: new insights into an old enigma. Drug Discov Today 12(9–10):413–418
Ernst E (2008) Frankincense: systematic review. BMJ 337:a2813
Ernst E (2012a) Integrated medicine. J Intern Med 271(1):25–28
Ernst E (2012b) Alternative detox. Br Med Bull 101:33–38
Ernst E (2016) Integrative medicine: more than the promotion of unproven treatments? Med J Aust
    204(5):174–174e1
Ernst E, Lee MS (2010) Focus Altern Complement Ther 15(4):274–279
Ernst E, Resch KL (1995) Concept of true and perceived placebo effects. BMJ 311(7004):551–553

Fisher C, Adams J, Frawley J, Hickman L, Sibbritt D (2018) Western herbal medicine consultations for common menstrual problems; practitioner experiences and perceptions of treatment. Phytother Res. 32(3):531–541

Fishman JR, Flatt MA, Settersten RA Jr (2015) Bioidentical hormones, menopausal women, and the lure of the "natural" in U.S. anti-aging medicine. Soc Sci Med 132:79–87

Fitzpatrick E, Holland OJ, Vanderlelie JJ (2018) Ozone therapy for the treatment of chronic wounds: a systematic review. Int Wound J 15(4):633–644

Fleming SA, Gutknecht NC (2010) Naturopathy and the primary care practice. Prim Care 37 (1):119–136

Fratellone PM, Tsimis F, Fratellone G (2016) Apitherapy products for medicinal use. J Altern Complement Med 22(12):1020–1022

Givati A (2015) Performing 'pragmatic holism': professionalisation and the holistic discourse of non-medically qualified acupuncturists and homeopaths in the United Kingdom. Health (London) 19(1):34–50

Gogtay NJ, Bhatt HA, Dalvi SS, Kshirsagar NA (2002) The use and safety of non-allopathic Indian medicines. Drug Saf 25(14):1005–1019

Guo R, Canter PH, Ernst E (2007) A systematic review of randomised clinical trials of individualised herbal medicine in any indication. Postgrad Med J 83(984):633–637

Hamre HJ, Glockmann A, Heckenbach K, Matthes H (2017) Use and safety of anthroposophic medicinal products: an analysis of 44,662 patients from the EvaMed pharmacovigilance network. Drugs Real World Outcomes 4(4):199–213

Huang X, Wang X, Shang J, Lin Y, Yang Y, Song Y, Yu S (2018) Association between dietary fiber intake and risk of ovarian cancer: a meta-analysis of observational studies. J Int Med Res 46(10):3995–4005

Huebner J, Marienfeld S, Abbenhardt C, Ulrich C, Muenstedt K, Micke O, Muecke R, Loeser C (2014) Counseling patients on cancer diets: a review of the literature and recommendations for clinical practice. Anticancer Res 34(1):39–48

Hunt KJ, Hung SK, Ernst E (2010) Botanical extracts as anti-aging preparations for the skin: a systematic review. Drugs Aging 27(12):973–985

Ikegami F, Fujii Y, Ishihara K, Satoh T (2003) Toxicological aspects of Kampo medicines in clinical use. Chem Biol Interact 145(3):235–250

Janson M (2006) Orthomolecular medicine: the therapeutic use of dietary supplements for anti-aging. Clin Interv Aging 1(3):261–265

Jones M, Harvey A, Marston L, O'Connell NE (2013) Breathing exercises for dysfunctional breathing/hyperventilation syndrome in adults. Cochrane Database Syst Rev (5):CD009041

Kattge S, Goetz K, Glassen K, Steinhäuser J (2017) Job profile of non-medical practitioners: a cross-sectional study from the health service perspective. Complement Med Res 24(5):285–289

Khan MA, Kotenko KV, Korchazhkina NB, Chervinskaya AV, Mikitchenko NA, Lyan NA (2016) The promising directions for the further development of halotherapy in pediatric medicine. Vopr Kurortol Fizioter Lech Fiz Kult. 93(6):61–66

Khanna N, Nazli T, Siddiqui KM, Kalaivani M, Rais-ur-Rahman (2018) A non-inferiority randomized controlled clinical trial comparing Unani formulation & psoralen plus ultraviolet A sol in chronic plaque psoriasis. Indian J Med Res 147(1):66–72

Locher C, Pforr C (2014) The legacy of Sebastian Kneipp: linking wellness, naturopathic, and allopathic medicine. J Altern Complement Med 20(7):521–526

Maisch P, Gschwend JE, Retz M (2018) Efficacy of a ketogenic diet in urological cancers patients: a systematic review. Urologe A 57(3):307–313

Maizes V, Rakel D, Niemiec C (2009) Integrative medicine and patient-centered care. Explore (NY) 5(5):277–289

Matsushita T, Oka T (2015) A large-scale survey of adverse events experienced in yoga classes. Biopsychosoc Med 9:9

Motoo Y, Arai I, Tsutani K (2014) Use of Kampo diagnosis in randomized controlled trials of Kampo products in Japan: a systematic review. PLoS One. 9(8):e104422

Onakpoya IJ, Wider B, Pittler MH, Ernst E (2011) Food supplements for body weight reduction: a systematic review of systematic reviews. Obesity (Silver Spring) 19(2):239–244

Ooi SL, McLean L, Pak SC (2018) Naturopathy in Australia: where are we now? Where are we heading? Complement Ther Clin Pract 33:27–35

Pasupuleti VR, Sammugam L, Ramesh N, Gan SH (2017) Honey, propolis, and royal jelly: a comprehensive review of their biological actions and health benefits. Oxid Med Cell Longev 2017:1259510

Pauling L (1968) Orthomolecular psychiatry. Science 160(3825):265–271

Pittler MH, Schmidt K, Ernst E (2005) Adverse events of herbal food supplements for body weight reduction: systematic review. Obes Rev 6(2):93–111

Posadzki P, Watson LK, Ernst E (2013a) Adverse effects of herbal medicines: an overview of systematic reviews. Clin Med (Lond) 13(1):7–12

Posadzki P, Watson L, Ernst E (2013b) Herb-drug interactions: an overview of systematic reviews. Br J Clin Pharmacol 75(3):603–618

Poulakou-Rebelakou E, Karamanou M, George A (2015) The impact of ancient Greek medicine in India: the birth of Unani medicine. Acta Med Hist Adriat 13(2):323–328

Rashleigh R, Smith SM, Roberts NJ (2014) A review of halotherapy for chronic obstructive pulmonary disease. Int J Chron Obstruct Pulmon Dis. 9:239–246

Vandamme L, Heyneman A, Hoeksema H, Verbelen J, Monstrey S (2013) Honey in modern wound care: a systematic review. Burns 39(8):1514–1525

Saks M (1997) Alternative therapies: are they holistic? Complement Ther Nurs Midwifery 3(1):4–8

Schencking M, Wilm S, Redaelli M (2013) A comparison of Kneipp hydrotherapy with conventional physiotherapy in the treatment of osteoarthritis: a pilot trial. J Integr Med 11(1):17–25

Schmidt K, Ernst E (2004) Assessing websites on complementary and alternative medicine for cancer. Ann Oncol. 15(5):733–742

Smith MJ, Logan AC (2002) Naturopathy. Med Clin North Am 86(1):173–184

Sridharan K, Mohan R, Ramaratnam S, Panneerselvam D (2011) Ayurvedic treatments for diabetes mellitus. Cochrane Database Syst Rev 12:CD008288

Wang S, Shen P, Zhou J, Lu Y (2017) Diet phytochemicals and cutaneous carcinoma chemoprevention: a review. Pharmacol Res 119:327–346

Weiss KJ (2017) Linus Pauling, Ph.D. (1901–1994): from chemical bond to civilization. Am J Psychiatry 174(6):518–519

Xu Q, Bauer R, Hendry BM, Fan TP, Zhao Z, Duez P, Simmonds MS, Witt CM, Lu A, Robinson N, Guo DA, Hylands PJ (2013) The quest for modernisation of traditional Chinese medicine. BMC Complement Altern Med 13:132

Zhang J, Wider B, Shang H, Li X, Ernst E (2012) Quality of herbal medicines: challenges and solutions. Complement Ther Med. 20(1–2):100–106

Postscript

This book offers an introduction into the issues related to alternative medicine as well as a critical evaluation of 150 specific modalities. My aim was to provide a fact-check that prevents readers from wasting their money on ineffective or even harmful treatments. I have taken great care to ensure that my text is accurate. If, however, you have spotted errors or omissions, please let me know (e.g. via my blog: edzardernst.com).

The dangers of accepting implausible concepts or mystical ideas reach far beyond healthcare. Many consumers are being misled to the point of being brain-washed. Some forms of alternative medicine can even draw them into a cult-like environment where rationality is actively undermined or suspended completely. Alternative medicine can become a quasi-religious belief system where evidence is no longer relevant. The consequences are damaging not just for the individual but, if sufficiently wide-spread, also for society. "Those who make is believe in absurdities can make us commit atrocities", warned Voltaire.

Our best protection against irrationality lies in improving our capacity of thinking critically, while keeping an open mind towards new developments; "… what is called for is an exquisite balance between two conflicting needs: the most skeptical scrutiny of all hypotheses that are served up to us and at the same time a great openness to new ideas. Obviously those two modes of thought are in some tension. But if you are able to exercise only one of these modes, whichever one it is, you're in deep trouble. If you are only skeptical, then no new ideas make it through to you. You never learn anything new. You become a crotchety old person convinced that nonsense is ruling the world. (There is, of course, much data to support you.) But every now and then, maybe once in a hundred cases, a new idea turns out

© Springer Nature Switzerland AG 2019
E. Ernst, *Alternative Medicine*,
https://doi.org/10.1007/978-3-030-12601-8

to be on the mark, valid and wonderful. If you are too much in the habit of being skeptical about everything, you are going to miss or resent it, and either way you will be standing in the way of understanding and progress. On the other hand, if you are open to the point of gullibility and have not an ounce of skeptical sense in you, then you cannot distinguish the useful as from the worthless ones."[1]

I hope my book has helped a few readers to sharpen their critical mind and to protect them from exploitation and harm. If so, the effort has been worthwhile.

---

[1] https://www.goodreads.com/quotes/558528-it-seems-tome-what-is-called-for-is-an

Glossary

Abstract As used in medicine (and in this book), abstract is a summary of a scientific article or paper.

Acupuncture Point An acupuncture point or acupoint is a specific site on our body surface where acupuncturists place their needles. These points are located along the assumed energy pathways called meridians.

Adjustment Adjustment is the term chiropractors often use for spinal manipulations.

Adjuvant Therapy An adjuvant or complementary therapy is a treatment administered in addition to other interventions.

Adverse Effects Adverse effects are unwanted side-effects of medical or surgical interventions.

Bias Bias is a systematic deviation from the truth. In research bias has the power to produce results that are wrong or misleading. In studies of alternative medicine, bias often generates false positive results. The most important types of bias in this context are 'publication bias' and 'selection bias'. The former describes the tendency that positive results get published, while negative findings remain unpublished, a phenomenon that will inevitable generate a false-positive overall picture, for instance, when conducting systematic reviews. Selection bias is an inherent limitation of clinical trials where the allocation of patients to two treatments, for instance, homeopathy and a conventional drug, is by choice of the patient or the physician. The consequence can be that those patients expecting benefit from homeopathy chose homeopathy and those who don't choose the conventional drug. In turn, these expectations would influence the outcome. Such selection bias is best eliminated through randomised allocation to treatment groups.

Blinding Blinding is a term used in controlled clinical trials to describe the fact that trial participants and/or researchers are masked as to the allocation of patients into the experimental or control group. A single-blind study is usually one where the researchers are blinded while in a double-blind study the patients are blinded as well.

Chakras Chakras are energy or focal points that are assumed to exist in our bodies by practitioners of Ayurvedic and other Asian forms of treatment.

Case Report A case report is an outline of all the details of one single patient's history signs, symptoms, diagnosis, treatment, outcome and prognosis. Such reports can be valuable in alerting us to certain aspects or possibilities of clinical practice. However, they can never constitute proof of effectiveness or establish a cause and effect relationships between the treatment and the outcome.

Case Series A case series is a document describing several case reports. The cases normally have some important aspect in common. For instance they could be relating to patients who all had the same symptoms or who all received the same treatment.

Cherry-Picking Cherry-picking is the term often used for using evidence selectively according to the direction of the result. Thus some advocates of alternative medicine select the positive trials of their therapy in an attempt to convince others of its value of. Cherry-picking is a hallmark of pseudoscience. The correct way to present evidence is on the basis of all the available and reliable data.

Chronic Condition A chronic condition is a disease or symptom that has lasted for several usually three or more, months.

Conditioning Conditioning (or 'classical' or Pavlovian' conditioning) is a subconscious learning process where a certain reaction to a potent stimulus comes to be elicited in response to a previously neutral stimulus. This is achieved by repeatedly pairing the neutral stimulus with the potent stimulus.

Contra-Indication Contra-indication is a condition that prevents or limits the use of a given therapy.

Control-Group Control group is the name of the group of patients in a controlled clinical trial who receive a treatment often a placebo, to which the experimental therapy is being compared.

Controlled Clinical Trial Controlled clinical trials is a study where patients are divided into two or more groups receiving different interventions the effects of which are being compared.

Correlation Correlation is a relation between (usually two) phenomena or variables which occur in a way not expected based on chance alone.

Clinical Trial The effectiveness or efficacy of treatments are best verified in clinical trials. These are experiments where a group of patients is divided into typically two subgroups. One subgroup receives the experimental therapy while the other subgroup, the control group, receives a different treatment. At the end of the treatment period, the outcomes for each group are documented and compared. Depending on the exact research question, the control group might receive a placebo, no therapy at all, or another therapy.

Cochrane Collaboration, Cochrane Reviews The Cochrane Collaboration is a worldwide organisation of researchers who agree that systematic reviews are important for making the best possible therapeutic decisions. Their aim is to help others by publishing systematic reviews of the highest quality and keeping them up-to-date. Cochrane reviews tend to be transparent and minimise bias. They are freely available on the Internet for anyone who wants to read them.

Compassion Compassion is the feeling that often arises when one is confronted with another person's suffering and one feels motivated to relieve that suffering. Alternative practitioners are often very compassionate clinicians and this fact significantly contributes to the benefit many patients experience after consulting them.

Conflicts of Interest A conflict of interest arises when a person or organization is involved in multiple interests one of which could possibly corrupt their motivation or objectivity. In health care, we often focus on financial conflicts of interest, but other conflicts, such as strong beliefs, can be just as powerful. In alternative medicine, it is foremost the latter that is relevant.

Cost-Effectiveness Analysis Cost-effectiveness analysis is an economic evaluation where the relative costs and outcomes of two or more treatments for the same condition are compared. Such assessments are important for deciding which treatments should and which shouldn't be funded from the public purse for instance. Treatments that are not effective cannot be cost-effective. There is not a single disease or condition for which alternative medicine is demonstrably more cost-effective than the appropriate conventional treatment.

Critical Analysis Critical analysis is a process for making decisions based on (often confusing) evidence. According to the 'National Council for Excellence in Critical Thinking' it is the intellectually disciplined process of actively and skilfully conceptualizing applying, analysing, synthesizing, and/or evaluating information gathered from, or generated by, observation, experience, reflection, reasoning, or communication, as a guide to belief and action.

Cure/Curative Treatment A curative treatment is a therapy that cures the disease as opposed to one that merely alleviates the symptoms, i.e. a symptomatic treatment.

Dogma A dogma is a notion put forward as authoritative without adequate grounds. Dogmas hardly ever change or evolve while evidence does both.

Empathy Empathy is the awareness of the feelings and emotions of other people. It is a key element of 'emotional intelligence' which connects oneself with others because it is how we as individuals understand what others are experiencing as if we were feeling it ourselves. Empathy goes beyond 'sympathy' which might be characterised as 'feeling for' someone, while empathy might be described as 'feeling with' that person through the use of imagination.

Energy In physics energy is the capacity to perform work and is measured in units of Joules. Energy exists in several forms such as heat, kinetic or mechanical energy, light, potential energy, electrical energy. In alternative medicine, the term is applied loosely to a patient's vitality or to the life force as postulated by proponents of the long-obsolete philosophy of vitalism.

Epidemiological Study An epidemiological study is a study of entire populations. In alternative medicine they can be useful for a range of questions. For instance, epidemiological studies can suggest that eating a certain diet is associated with certain health benefits or certain risks.

Evidence Evidence is the body of facts that leads to a given conclusion. Because the outcomes of a treatment depends on a multitude of factors the evidence for or against its effectiveness is best based not on experience but on clinical trials and systematic reviews of clinical trials.

Evidence-Based Medicine Evidence-based medicine often abbreviated as EBM, is defined as the integration of best research evidence with clinical expertise and patient values. It thus rests on three pillars: external evidence, ideally from systematic reviews, the clinician's experience, and the patient's preferences.

Expectation The prospect of any treatment will almost inevitably generate expectations both in the patient and in the clinician. Such expectations can significantly influence the clinical outcome. Expectations are part of the placebo response to medical interventions. They occur inadvertently in most clinical settings. Some characteristics of alternative medicine are likely to maximise the expectations of patients. This can contribute to the benefit experienced by patients and is thus a welcome effect in most clinical settings. By contrast, in clinical research, when one usually aims at determining the effect of a therapy per se, expectations would distort the results. In rigorous clinical trials, investigators therefore often try to minimise the impact of expectations by blinding patients and/or clinicians to knowing whether the experimental or the control treatment is being administered to any given patient.

Fallacy A fallacy is a popular argument that appears to be logical but in fact, is erroneous. In alternative medicine, several fallacies are used to support its usefulness or promote its use. For instance, many proponents claim that it has stood the test of time suggesting that this proves its effectiveness. Another classical fallacy is the notion that alternative medicine is supported by highly intelligent or famous people and therefore must be good.

Individualised Treatment An individualised treatment is a therapy that is tailored not primarily to the diagnostic category but to the personal characteristics of a patient. Alternative practitioners often pride themselves of individualising their treatments.

Lay-Practitioner A Lay practitioner is a clinician who has not been to and graduated from medical school.

Life Force Life force or vital force or vital energy are the terms used for the metaphysical concept of a power that allegedly animates all organisms. A disturbed life force is according to many proponents of alternative medicine, the reason why humans fall ill. Such concepts existed in many cultures and contexts: chi in China, prana in India, pneuma in ancient Greece, animal magnetism in Messmer's hypnotherapy, the inert in chiropractic etc. These ideas originate from the concept of vitalism and are now obsolete.

Medline Medline is the world largest electronic database of medical articles. It currently holds over 300,000 articles on alternative medicine.

Meta-Analysis A Meta-analysis is a systematic review where the results of the included studies have been pooled to generate a new overall result.

Meridian Meridians are the assumed pathways in which according to the concepts of traditional acupuncture, the life energy chi flows. Despite of much research, the existence of meridians has never been verified.

Natural History of Disease The natural history of a disease describes the progress of a medical condition when left untreated. Some diseases e.g. cancer, tend to worsen over time, if left untreated. Many other conditions get better without any treatment at all. If such conditions are treated, it is easy to confuse the natural history with an effect of the treatment applied. The best way to differentiate the two is to conduct a controlled clinical trial.

Non-specific Effects Any therapeutic response has two main components: specific effects of the therapy per se and non-specific (or context) effects. The latter describe all phenomena which can determine the clinical outcome but are not due to the treatment. The best-known non-specific effect is the placebo effect.

Observational Study An observational study is a non-experimental investigation usually without a control group. In a typical observational study patients receiving routine care are monitored as to the treatments administered and the outcomes observed. Such studies have the advantage of being close to a real-life situation it is thus relatively easy to recruit large numbers of patient. Observational studies can unquestionably provide valuable information but they are not an adequate method for establishing cause and effect between the therapy and the outcome.

Outcome Measure Outcome measure often also called endpoint, is the parameter employed in clinical studies for quantifying their result. The optimal outcome measure depends on the nature of the study and might include subjective endpoints such as pain or quality of life and/or objective variables such as blood pressure or body weight.

Paradigm A paradigm is a distinct set of concepts or thought patterns including theories, research methods, postulates, and standards.

Palliative Care Palliative or supportive care is the treatment of patients aimed not at curing the disease but at improving their quality of life.

Panacea Panacea (or cure all) is a therapy that allegedly is effective for every condition symptom or disease. Many alternative therapies are being promoted as a panacea. Yet, a therapy that can cure all diseases does not exist.

Pilot Study A pilot study is an investigation that is preliminary and typically aimed at determining whether a given protocol is feasible for testing a hypothesis or at identifying what can be improved before conducting a definitive trial.

Potency/Potentisation Potency is according to homeopathic thinking, the 'power' of a remedy based on the degree to which it has been potentised, i.e. diluted and succussed (agitated). Low potency remedies are not highly diluted whereas high potency remedies are. Low potency remedies contain detectable concentrations of the starting material, whereas high potency remedies contain no detectable amount of the starting material.

Pseudoscience Pseudoscience is anything that tries to imitate science but does not fulfil its standards nor abide by its rules. Critics have long insisted that much of alternative medicine fulfils the criteria for pseudoscience.

Quality of Life This term describes the state of well-being of a person. Quality of life can be measured by various means (e.g. validated questionnaires such as the 'SF36') and can be used to monitor the success of alternative treatments. It can also be employed as an outcome measure in clinical trials.

p-Value The p-value is a term used in statistical analyses to determine the probability that an observed outcome is due to chance. Conventionally the p-value is set at 5% which mans that a result is considered statistically significant if p is smaller than 0.05.

Quack/Quackery A quack is an ignorant misinformed, or dishonest practitioner of medicine. Quackery is the practice of a quack.

Randomisation Randomisation is a method used in some controlled clinical trials; it means dividing the total group of participants in typically two subgroups purely by chance e.g. throwing dice. The effect is that the two subgroups are comparable in all known and even all unknown characteristics.

Randomised Clinical Trial A randomised clinical trial (RCT) is a controlled clinical trial where patients are allocated to experimental or control groups by randomisation.

Regression Towards the Mean Regression towards the mean is the phenomenon describing that over time, extreme values tend to move towards less extreme values. Patients normally consult clinicians when they are in somewhat extreme situations (e.g. when they have much pain). Because of the regression towards the mean, they are likely to feel better the next time they see their clinician. This change is regardless of the effects of any treatment they may have had. Thus, regression towards the mean is one of several phenomena that can make an ineffective therapy appear to be effective.

Sample Size Sample size is the term used to describe the size of the group of individuals entered into a research study.

Sceptic/Skeptic Sceptic is a person who habitually questions notions which most other people view as established.

Science Science is the identification description, observation, experimental investigation, and theoretical explanation of phenomena. See also pseudoscience.

Significance Statistical significance describes the likelihood by which a given research result is due to chance. Often it is expressed by providing a 'p-value' i.e. a number of probability. The commonly used p-value of 0.05 indicating statistical significance means that chances are 5 in 100 that the result in question is due to chance.

Clinical significance or relevance are terms often used to describe the likelihood by which a clinical result is important in a clinical context. For instance, a study might show that a homeopathic treatment has lowered systolic blood pressure by 3 mmHg this could well be statistically significant but few experts would call it clinically significant.

Specific Effect Specific effects are those effects of a therapy that are directly caused by the intervention and not by other phenomena such as the placebo effect or the natural history of the disease.

Subluxation Subluxation as used in chiropractic, is an abnormality in the relative position of vertebrae which chiropractors claim to be able to adjust.

Symptomatic Treatment A symptomatic treatment is a treatment that alleviates symptoms without treating the cause of a condition.

Symptom Score A symptom score is a tool used in clinical research where several symptoms are rated and subsequently an overall score is created by pooling all symptoms.

Systematic Review A systematic review is a project where the totality of the available evidence related to a well-defined research question is summarised and critically analysed to provide the most reliable answer possible. Systematic reviews are thus valuable in guiding evidence-based therapeutic decisions. They minimize the bias inherent in each single study and the save others to do the hard work of analysing the often-substantial amount of clinical trials in order to find the answer to a pertinent clinical question.

Therapeutic Claims Therapeutic claims are statements of therapeutic effectiveness for specific diseases or conditions e.g. therapy x is effective in treating disease y.

Therapeutic Relationship The term describes the relationship between a patient and his or her clinician. In alternative medicine therapeutic relationships tend to be particularly intense, not least due to the length of time consultations often take.

Vital Force See life force.

Vitalism Vitalism is the now obsolete metaphysical concept that life depends on a force distinct from chemical, physical or other principles. It is a concept found in many different cultures and healing traditions, e.g. chi in China, pneuma in ancient Greece, and prana in India. The common denominator is the assumption that a metaphysical energy animates all living systems.

Yin and Yang Yin and yang are to two opposing vital energies as postulated in Traditional Chinese Medicine.